# Innovate India

AF516867

# Innovate India

## *A Road Map for Atmanirbhar Bharat*

Praveen Tiwari

BLOOMSBURY
NEW DELHI • LONDON • OXFORD • NEW YORK • SYDNEY

BLOOMSBURY INDIA
Bloomsbury Publishing India Pvt. Ltd
Second Floor, LSC Building No. 4, DDA Complex,
Pocket C – 6 & 7, Vasant Kunj,
New Delhi 110070

BLOOMSBURY, BLOOMSBURY INDIA and the Diana logo are trademarks of Bloomsbury Publishing Plc

First published in India 2021
This edition published 2021

Copyright © Praveen Tiwari, 2021

Praveen Tiwari has asserted his right under the Indian Copyright Act to be identified as the author of this work

All rights reserved. No part of this publication may be reproduced or transmitted in any form or by any means, electronic or mechanical, including photocopying, recording or any information storage or retrieval system, without the prior permission in writing from the publishers

The book is solely the responsibility of the author and the publisher has had no role in creation of the content and does not have responsibility for anything defamatory or libellous or objectionable

Bloomsbury Publishing Plc does not have any control over, or responsibility for, any third-party websites referred to or in this book. All internets addresses given in this book were correct at the time of going to press. The author and publisher regret any inconvenience caused if addresses have changed or sites have ceased to exist, but can accept no responsibility for any such changes

ISBN: PB: 978-93-90513-15-4; e-Book: 978-93-90513-23-9
2 4 6 8 10 9 7 5 3 1

Typeset by Fortune Graphics, Naraina, New Delhi
Printed and bound in India by Thomson Press India Ltd.

MIX
Paper from responsible sources
FSC® C010615

To find out more about our authors and books, visit www.bloomsbury.com and sign up for our newsletters

This book is dedicated to the start-up revolution and the vision of Prime Minister Narendra Modi. The book also belongs to every youngster who aspires to become an entrepreneur. Our effort is also dedicated to all those role models in the business sphere, who have redefined entrepreneurship in India.

# CONTENTS

# ACKNOWLEDGEMENTS

This book primarily addresses the questions of young entrepreneurs. We pay our sincere gratitude to the start-ups and youngsters who shared their curiosities on different occasions. My team is extremely thankful to all such start-ups that helped us understand their needs and requirements as future businessleaders.

I feel penning your personal experience makes no book meaningful. Expert opinion counts a lot in the field as complex as start-ups and business in India. Many role models of the industry have shared valuable tips regarding entrepreneurship. We are grateful to all experts, thinkers and educationists, who have contributed to this book.

Heartiest thanks to the The Capital Post, Zee Business, DD National and DD Urdu, which became an inspiration for this book. Interactions with numerous well-known business experts and start-ups for special shows like *Innovate India*, *Kamyaab Hindustan*, *Naujawan Hindustan* and *Startup ki Baat* became the foundation of this book.

We are especially indebted to Dr Shailesh Kharkwal, K.P. Singh, Anshul Sharma, Aakanksha Pandey, Mohammed Salim, Anurag Darshan, Vikas from Vstart and Ritesh Malik from Innov8, who helped us at the various stages of this book production.

Our special thanks to Garima Singh and her team for the research work behind this book. The talent of the award-winning designers Ruchit Yadav and Amit Gaur deserves a special mention for the beautiful cover and design of the book.

Our sincere thanks to Deepak Sharma who translated this book and Hilsa Mishra for editing the book. This book would not have been possible without senior journalist Radheshyam Rai and senior IAS officer Deepak Singh, who were a constant motivation. This book is based on the research that results from the hard work of many people.

Special thanks to Startup India, Invest India, Making India and Government e-Market Place for their constant motivation and help.

We have been working on this book for the last three years. However, our efforts gained momentum during the past year. We would like to extend our heartfelt gratitude to all those whose names could not find a mention here, and we hope that these collective efforts bear enormous fruit for the start-ups and innovators in India.

# SPECIAL THANKS

Our hearty thanks to Mahesh Gupta of Kent RO who helped us in making this book possible. We would like to thank Dr Vinod Tibrewala, chancellor at J.J.T. University, for giving us his kind support. We would also like to mention that this book would have not been possible without the support of Garima Singh and her team at The Capital Post. A special thanks for the kind guidance of senior journalist Mr Upendra Rai and senior industrial psychologist and academician Dr Ritu Sharma.

# PREFACE

## *The Beginning Is Always Today*

India has never been short of talent. We were never deprived of possibilities in the field of science and technology. Still, we bemoaned the outcomes of our ignorance. It felt that we suffered from all possible problems. The times have changed now as we move towards a more prosperous future. The start-up revolution has initiated a new era. It is a new beginning for a country marching on the path to progress.

Not long ago, words like 'start-up' or 'innovation' were almost alien to most Indians. Though a glorious legacy of entrepreneurship adorns our history, business was seldom the first choice of career for most young Indians. This was more true for those who lacked a trading background. Start-ups were only the forte of Silicon Valley and developed nations. India has encouraged innovation since ages, but we lack the technological advancement when compared to the first-world countries. Achievements of the Western world form the basis of most of our scientific progress. Still, the world has always acknowledged our prowess in innovation and the sheer size of our market.

However, we couldn't capitalise well on both these advantages. The dreams of our youth had offshore lands as their settings. We had accepted 'brain drain' as fait accompli. In contrast, the vast unorganised market was befitting only of the poor, in our eyes. The power of outlook can change the entire picture even if all other circumstances remain the same. The success of 'Clean India Mission' was dismissed as a political gimmick by the opponents. They believed that nothing could change the situation on the ground. However, small steps taken to fulfil the mission have turned into a big leap.

I have visited states like Uttar Pradesh, Madhya Pradesh, Rajasthan and West Bengal to cover elections. I could see great awareness and enthusiasm among the rural and urban masses for cleanliness. The same spirit was palpable among the youth who used to be cynical about the lack of employment opportunities. Programmes like *Skill India* and *Innovate India* have given them a new ray of hope. This is still the beginning, and there is still a long way to go. Yet, we can see a clear roadmap ahead.

I have seen over 300 start-ups, understood their challenges and functioning. Interviews with dozens of people associated with programmes like Startup India, Invest India, Make in India and Government e-Market Place were a great learning experience. Having spent a good part of my career in political journalism and anchoring, I had very little to do with the world of start-ups. That was until I started working for *Innovate India* in 2016. My association with this Zee Business show was a great opportunity to understand a budding generation of young Indian entrepreneurs.

I also had the chance to work with mentors and specialists of the Federation of Indian Chambers of Commerce and Industry (FICCI) and Department of Science and Technology (DST) among others. I filmed shows with over 60 innovators during this stint. The stories I witnessed and the spirit that I imbibed was exhilarating. I started to research this subject deeper. Taking time out of my journalism and writing, I studied Industrial and Organisational Psychology. I had been addressing youngsters as a motivator for some time. My initial books dealt with subjects related to spiritual motivation. However, this subject was not only different from the traditional subjects but also had a technological side to it.

I met several other experts and proprietors of start-ups while writing the 'Innovate India' column for The Capital Post. The journey continued as I worked for Doordarshan shows *Startup ki Baat*, *Naujawan Hindustan* and *Kamyaab Hindustan* which aired on various DD channels. I could see the reflection of the India of my dreams in this subject, a country that Swami Vivekananda had imagined.

India has the world's largest youth population, and it is this power of the youth that is India's biggest asset. We have several challenges but also billions of minds to deal with them. PM Modi has shown great insight into this statement. Start-ups are born out of the womb of innovation. The key to innovation lies in finding a solution to some existing problem. Since we have challenges aplenty, there are opportunities unbound for start-ups. Unlike traditional business models, start-ups defy monopolies. Only those who understand the complexities of legal, political and tax system can manage businesses in this model. Attracting investments, managing market competition and making a place among the existing players have been insurmountable tasks for most of the aspiring entrepreneurs. But the growing start-up revolution has disrupted the existing norms. It has promoted social entrepreneurship like never before.

Buoyed by programmes like the 'Startup India', start-ups are making money while walking hand in hand with the government in this journey to meet many of our social challenges.

Foreign writers have authored most of the literature related to start-ups, therefore, it lacks Indian context. This book fills the gap. Global success stories entice many young entrepreneurs. They are not aware of many such examples closer to home. I have incorporated some such examples in this book. From a Singapore-based scientist of Indian-origin to a next-door middle-class youth, these are the stories of Indian dreams turning into reality. The book captures a journey that began with the registration of Startup India and reached a level where it is attracting a massive foreign trade. It also shares with you the experiences of an MBBS doctor who left a secured life to make his Startup India a grand success.

The book explains the key learnings from these examples. It also apprises readers of some start-ups that have established new milestones in social entrepreneurship and worked to organise

India's huge unorganised sector. From empowering villagers through sanitary pads to providing them with cheap electricity, from offering solutions to water crisis to securing data through block-chain technology, there's a lot to learn from these sagas. The book also gives details of the opportunities in some of India's biggest sectors like agriculture and textiles.

The world of start-ups present endless opportunities because here you can give shape to any potent idea. It is probably for the first time that the prime minister of this country is directly communicating with start-ups. I have been a part of some such video conferences between the PM and the start-ups. The book offers a glimpse into various government initiatives in this sector and how the relevant departments are functioning.

Corruption has harmed India's business environment over the years. Efforts like Government e-Market Place are helping change this scenario by allowing start-ups to work directly with the government. It has also reduced the scope of corruption in the government tender process. The government is now working to increase the purchase limit through this platform. The time is not far when all the purchases will happen through digital platforms. A right assessment of capability and recognition from platforms is ensuring the participation of start-ups in the government's schemes. This book also gives an idea of the numerous possibilities for start-ups in the government sector.

The book has valuable insights from reputed market experts, investment gurus, civil servants, Padma Shree awardees and industrial psychologists. They emphasise the need for staying ready for any circumstance alongside professional training. The world of business has many pitfalls and a lack of proper guidance can make you vulnerable to them. Sometimes, getting carried away by initial success can also prove detrimental for young entrepreneurs. The book delves into the psychological aspects of a successful entrepreneur. It answers many of your questions regarding the start-up ecosystem. You can also take away some good start-up ideas from the book. It also enumerates potential mistakes that you should avoid while formulating a strategy for any new business venture.

Books are great teachers, even for professionally untrained. Reading international bestsellers on start-ups may not connect you with the Indian ground realities in this context. However, you must keep in mind the core lessons of some books. To save you from reading these voluminous reads, this book presents the summary of five such masterpieces.

The book also highlights how doing business was always a part of core Indian ethos. It gives details of some ancient trades and tribes involved in them. It was not possible to include all the case studies I have come across during the past three years. I will keep working to highlight the good work of many Indian start-ups. I hope the book will share my journey of *Innovate India* with you and will pave the way for your success.

– Praveen Tiwari

# 1
# LET'S START

***The start-up and innovation ecosystem is developing in India. Prime Minister Modi has made his vision clear through initiatives like Startup India, Make in India and Skill Development. Let's start; this should be the mantra of your life. This little phrase can make wonders in whatever you want to do; be it planning, meeting new people, constituting a team or learn new things. So let's start. Think less and do more.***

**'Once we decide we have to do something we can go miles ahead.'**

These words reflect PM Modi's style of functioning. His only focus is on work despite all the opposition. Rather than being worried about the outcomes, he concentrates more on how to accomplish a job. You are bound to reach somewhere if you make a beginning. Nothing better, if you know where you want to go. Clarity of goal and a concrete plan ensures success.

**'If you can't fly then run, if you can't run then walk, if you can't walk then crawl, but whatever you do you have to keep moving forward.'**

– Martin Luther King Jr

These words fill you with energy. Despondency is poison for youth. Either indolence or lack of purpose is its genesis. India has the world's largest young population. It will be a burden if the young generation has no direction. However, the same power of youth can also fulfil the dreams of both the Narendras, the one we know as Swami Vivekananda and the other, who is at the helm of the country's affairs. The country's youth only require a proper guidance in the right direction. This book will discuss the leadership qualities of both the personalities in the coming chapters.

**'The best way to not feel hopeless is to get up and do something. Don't wait for good things to happen to you. If you go out and make some good things happen, you will fill the world with hope, you will fill yourself with hope.'**

Stop thinking and do something if you want to overcome despair. You have new vistas for career options. A favourable atmosphere is being built to help you realise your goals. Innovate India is one such attempt. The path is long and much remains to be done, so let's do it! As PM Modi says, no journey is impossible once we have a strong resolve.

There will be doubts and opponents. Yet, the most successful strategy is to do what you always wanted to do. What are you waiting for?

The core of our spiritual philosophy lies in *Karmanye Vadhikaraste Ma Phaleshu Kadachana* (You have a right to perform your prescribed duty, but it does not entitle you to the fruits of action).

We need to plan beyond doubts and aspirations to set up a new business or any start-up. Planning is an art and one must learn from the past precedents for a successful execution.

Think about who you want to idolise. Learn from the struggles of the recent achievers. The stories of those who are at the top of the success ladder should inspire your dreams. However, it may not be possible to emulate them in taking the first step towards your venture. You will not find every solution in the success stories of stalwarts like Steve Jobs, Mark Zuckerberg or Bill Gates. Their saga should motivate you. But you will need a role-model much closer to the ground for learning.

The tricks of the trade change as fast as the circumstances in today's world. Therefore, your ideas cannot be rigid.

Keep investing in your biggest asset, which is you. Keep reading good books and be ever ready to learn new skills. I have seen many grand dreams crumbling in the face of trifles. One factor is common among all successful stories; their protagonists were experts in their core skills, but they also learnt other aspects like marketing, sales and branding. It is not just about product innovation. New ideas should also fuel other business aspects. This is what many successful businesses are doing. We will talk about innovating the innovation in this book.

This book will inspire you for your start-up. It will also teach you the art of successful planning. There are seldom any permanent failure in business. You will establish a profitable venture if you are doing the right things.

There can broadly be five reasons for any failed enterprise:

1. Lack of planning
2. Wrong market assessment
3. Not having the right team on-board
4. Not having enough self-confidence
5. Lack of purpose in establishing the business

Lack of planning means not having a proper roadmap. Working hard on the right plan is necessary before implementing any business idea. It is just like the film-makers preparing a storyboard before shooting a movie. They have to learn it at the cost of their success then. Every failure makes you wiser. However, there are other ways to attain wisdom.

We need to understand this aspect. Even after practising almost all other tasks in life, small or big, we are ready to count on hearsay and the experience of others instead of attaining practical knowledge ourselves. What will happen if you run against seasoned athletes without ever practising running? You will fail and can also faint on the track. The same applies to the race of life. This book will teach you the art of effective planning and unveil the secrets of innovation in start-ups. We hope it will give you the confidence to start your enterprise.

There are many possibilities for the youth in new India. But most young citizens are unaware of them. Following PM Modi's vision can lead to a complete eradication of unemployment from the country. The inability to do so would worsen the crime situation in the country, denying India her rightful place in the world community. Therefore, these possibilities must reach every young Indian. This book will explain the nuances of start-ups and innovations and will help you develop an innovative mind. The power to think is the most precious gift to humankind.

This power to think is behind every leap of development that humans have witnessed. A vision of success precedes name, fame and money. This book seeks to illuminate young minds with the same vision. No task is impossible if you can learn how to think and plan.

My TV programme *Innovate India*, and later, a column by the same name, was a great opportunity to meet hundreds of people from the world of start-ups and innovations and to understand their expectations. I saw how these people were overcoming the challenges and working on some superb ideas. During my stint with another TV programme *Naujawan Bharat* (Young India) aired on Doordarshan, I came to witness the intense curiosity the young lot has towards career opportunities. It was also a chance to see the endless possibilities in less conventional sectors like garments and shoemaking. I have shared these experiences in the book.

There is no dearth of literature on start-ups and innovations the world over. However, very few of them touch upon the Indian context. India does not lack start-up success stories, but what we need is more innovation. Most of our start-ups are based on borrowed ideas from abroad. We seem to be worried less about how we are succeeding. All we bother about is how many people are making the most of the opportunities. There is still a lot of scope for small start-ups and innovations to generate jobs. We just need to apply our mind to this direction. Along with the largest youth population in the world, we are also a country with the largest number of unemployed people. We should ensure that the country's youth is not reduced to a mere crowd. There is a need to improve our ranking on the innovation index. India is still far behind in this respect and does not figure even in the top 50 countries. Whereas, a country as small as Singapore ranks eighth as per the Global Innovation Index (GII) 2019.

The young innovators and fresh start-ups can help the country meet several challenges. This book narrates many such stories. PM Modi has sounded a new bugle for water management in the form of *Jalshakti* (water power). Anil Madhav Dave, the environmentalist who later also became a union minister, had tried to integrate the same concept with start-ups, a few years ago. He had advocated learning lessons from Singapore in this respect and had taken steps in this direction. But these efforts ended with his unfortunate demise.

PM Modi has given a golden opportunity to the country's youth for participation through his *Janshakti4Jalshakti* (people's power for water power) campaign. Such challenges fuel social entrepreneurship. Anil Madhav Dave was an environmentalist par excellence. He was also a worshipper of the Narmada River. The start-up he had tackled for the country's water crisis has an interesting story behind it. This book begins with the saga of an Indian youth who helped Singapore become a 'water power' against all odds. The same endeavour became Dave's inspiration for his efforts to conserve water and energy.

This is keeping in view the need to focus on practical examples. You should note success stories like Amazon, Apple, Microsoft, PayPal, etc. However, you will understand the challenges associated with start-ups and innovations by learning from the people who are using their education, innovation and expertise in the Indian context. You are most likely interested in starting your venture if you have taken hold of this book. You can also become a precedent by implementing the tips given in this book. So let's start!

# 2
# WE GROW BECAUSE WE STRUGGLE

## *Case Study: H2O Mantra*

PM Modi had announced *Janshakti4Jalshakti* (people's power for water power) as one of his priorities at the outset of his second term. Like the cleanliness campaign, he seeks to turn water conservation into a mass drive. This is an important step and requires the same attention as the cleanliness mission. Therefore, it presents many opportunities for start-ups. Any successful entrepreneur must identify challenges around him or her. Many possibilities of a successful start-up emanate out of working out solutions for these challenges. An innovative mind can turn adversities and challenges into opportunities. India has an abundance of these qualities. Therefore, there are possibilities for greater innovations.

Never did we have such a robust discourse around start-ups and innovations. The business climate was mostly restricted to the conventional methods of earning money. We are still copying developed countries in the name of innovations.

India was never short of fertile minds. What she lacked was an initiative like 'Startup India' to channelise her potential. The new India gives youth a chance to not only realise their dreams but also provides opportunities of employment for the others. Dr Shailesh Kharkwal's achievements present one such story. A Singapore-based water scientist of Indian origin, Shailesh epitomises PM Modi's vision of the youth's participation in enhancing India's *Jalshakti* (water power). His start-up 'H2O Mantra' finds mention as a role model for youth in many of the government's departments related to innovation like Startup India/Government e-Marketing Platform. While luminaries like Mark Zuckerberg, Bill Gates and Steve Jobs are a source of motivation for youngsters across the world; you can learn real lessons from innovators who have found their way by tackling local circumstances and challenges. The government must also promote such start-ups to inspire young people. India has no dearth of youngsters who have not only established themselves but also shown the way to the budding entrepreneurs.

## AN INDIAN INNOVATIVE MIND IN SINGAPORE

Dr Shailesh started his journey from a nondescript town of Tanakpur. After completing his M.Tech from IIT Kharagpur, he reached the National University of Singapore and gifted that country many of his valuable innovations. He is now using his expertise for India. Shailesh believes PM Modi's vision is opening new doors of opportunities in India. This vision has inspired him to innovate for water conservation in India as part of the *Jalshakti* campaign. Shailesh is well aware of the Indian milieu for practical education, challenges in the business sector and the gap in the Indian public sector. His story holds valuable lessons for start-ups and innovations in India.

The Startup India has opened the fray for youngsters who would not otherwise dare to take on the established business empires. The conventional wisdom dictated the essence of capital before setting up any venture suggesting thereby, that only the rich could grow in trade. You can learn five things from Shailesh's case study in this respect:

1. Keep your motive clear.
2. Prepare fully and make a clear road map.
3. Begin with a small yet effective team.
4. Be ready for setbacks.
5. Upgrade innovations as per requirement.

## Keep Your Motive Clear

PM Modi's schemes like Startup India, Government e-Marketing Platform, Skill India and Make in India has facilitated social entrepreneurship among the youth. The government aims at creatingn new employment opportunities. But Shailesh's story also highlights some of the other benefits of start-ups in India. Any start-up is much more than a mere business venture if it also serves the country. Shailesh is leading a successful life in Singapore. He gives consultancy services in water management all over the world. Shailesh believes that the future of any start-up is sealed the moment its purpose becomes clear.

The spirit of social entrepreneurship gives you a greater purpose. The sole aim of earning money money can never fetch big results. People associate themselves with higher and clearer vision. This makes your initial journey easier and save you from challenges like:

- Not finding enough work
- Not finding capable associates and employees
- Lack of funding
- Losing money in branding and marketing

Shailesh has the technology and the expertise which most Indian start-ups lack. Being a scientist, he can improvise as well. This makes him a trusted partner for clients, especially the governments, thereby ruling out the first contingency of not finding enough work.

Earning money is the primary motive of any business. Yet, a clear and higher purpose begets money. Associating people with such vision will give new dimensions to your venture.

Delivering on big government contracts will require funding. Only robust future possibilities attract investors. Finding them was never a problem for Shailesh as his start-up was a long horse. A clear purpose and social entrepreneurship will attract the media and government machinery. Shailesh remains a go-to person for the Indian media on issues related to water conservation. His start-up finds a place in the official Twitter handles and Facebook pages of Startup India and GeM. What could be a better way of reaching out to customers, that too, without spending money!

## Prepare Yourself and Make a Clear Road Map

Shailesh started H2O Mantra after PM Modi announced Startup India. He was a scientist and having learnt most of his skills in Singapore, he did not understand the intricacies involved in doing business in India. Yet, he believed in the prime minister's vision and expectations from fresh blood. He pored the Startup India scheme and began preparing a road map. He found capable support in Professor Hu Jiangyong, the director of Water Research Department at the National University of Singapore. Shailesh's case shows the challenges one faces while setting up an innovative start-up in India.

The start-up culture of Singapore is not the same as India. The city state is globally acclaimed for its innovative culture and an atmosphere conducive to start-ups. It ranks at the eighth position in the Innovation Index, whereas this sector is still in its nascent stages in India. Coming from such a country and that too from a scientific background, Shailesh's challenges were no less. He sought help from many Indian experts.

According to Shailesh, his biggest strength is his penchant for research. He delved deep into the prospects of setting up a start-up in India. This included studying entrepreneurial prospects in India and the state facilities for start-ups. This made him register with the Government e-Marketing (GeM) platform. Thereby began his working association with the various government departments.

Lack of preparation spells doom for many start-ups. Mere dreaming and reading other people's success stories may not suffice. You should work on your road map. Consult experts if required. Product innovation and expertise in one particular field will not be enough. Learn all the aspects of a related trade. Shailesh's story proves that it does not require a formal qualification but understanding the nuances, thorough research, and a lot of study.

## Begin with a Small Yet Effective Team

Dr Shailesh started with a small team. He needed to reach out to the people who could implement his plans. Shailesh says red-tapism is the biggest impediment in doing business in India. PM Modi must intensify efforts to simplify the government procedures. The officials are well educated but they complicate the system. Working in India under the current circumstances requires knowledge of how the Indian system works. You must lookout for people who can help.

A start-up can never take-off if its core team members are only onboard for salaries or shares. Popularising an innovation at low cost with a small team is the defining aspect of any start-up. An innovative idea makes a mark in the market in no time. There is a problem only if it is not properly presented. H2O Mantra began with a small team, but they selected each member of the team on merit. Soon, the team needed expansion. Shailesh says that one can hire people at the outset itself. However, a compact core group can run a start-up more efficiently during the initial phases.

A small team means hiring only on need basis. Roping in people with diverse skill set adds strength to any start-up. Your success counts on your colleagues. Do as much work as you can in the beginning. Things like office, reception, branding and staff may not be available at the first step. Follow this tip even if you have liquidity. Innovation and its outreach to the market is the essence of a start-up.

You will hear most youngsters talking about venturing beyond a regular job. Yet, they fall into the trap of wielding power as a boss while starting their own business and end up hiring more people than required. Check this urge if you want to play the long innings. Start-ups are supposed to provide employment. However, it can happen only after your enterprise is established.

**Be Ready for Setbacks**

The story of H2O Mantra seems to be taken straight out of a movie script. It is appealing because of Shailesh's determination in the face of adversities. He was inspired by the noted environmentalist and former Union Minister Anil Madhav Dave. He was the first person to motivate Shailesh to bring his technology to India. Shailesh fitted his system at Dave's ashram at his own expense. Dave was so impressed that he allocated his entire quota of Members of Parliament Local Area Development Scheme (MPLAD) fund to establish a similar project on the banks of the Narmada River. It was a substantial project and a great opening for Shailesh's start-up in India. Preparations began in full swing. Dave's stamp of approval became a sort of certificate for Shailesh's idea.

Shailesh was working at his laboratory in Singapore when he received the unfortunate news. Dave had passed away. It was a loss for the government and the country. It rattled H2O Mantra. Shailesh says that he was worried more about the country that had lost such a visionary leader. Dave was a quick decision-maker with a deep knowledge of the environment and technology. It was indeed an irreparable loss.

H2O Mantra's bagging of a big project had attracted investors. But Dave's demise dissuaded them. They suspected that the start-up may never get such a substantial contract again.

Shailesh was disappointed but not disheartened. He returned to India and started contacting officials that Dave had lined up through letters. It was a tiring process as most of the officials were hard to convince. However, some exceptions gave Shailesh a chance to set-up a few systems. Shailesh believes one should never stop working, no matter how hard the circumstances are. Keep walking and you will find the way.

## Upgrade Innovations as per Requirement

Dr Shailesh's start-up was offering an alternative to the RO water purifying technology. Mud, bacteria and viruses, besides other pollutants, had infested Narmada River's water and Shailesh was innovating to clean it through a non-RO technology. This is what Dave liked the most. Most prevalent water purification technologies waste up to 70 per cent water. The treated water lack minerals. They wanted to find a solution to this problem. The company was trying to bring its patented technology to India with the aim to make the country's rivers free from pollution. The Singapore government has adopted this innovation and the company hopes that the Indian government will show the same sagacity.

You can steer your boat through the storm if you know the basics of your job. Shailesh gave precedence to social entrepreneurship. People liked his technology. However, poor power supply was posing some problems. He redesigned the solar-powered systems and established the first such plant for a women's self-help group at a small town in Madhya Pradesh. These women started supplying mineral water to the local market. They named it *Nimad Neer*. Soon, the company introduced the same technology in several cities across seven states. The focus everywhere was about economising water and energy along with the supply of safe and mineral-rich water.

Sound research and preparation led to H2O Mantra's registration with GeM (Government e-Marketing Platform). The start-up team showed this technology to officials in several districts. PM Modi's vision aided a nascent start-up. New and small companies used to struggle for finding buyers. Preconditions like three years of mandatory turnover nipped their growth in the bud. However, facilities like GeM provided an opportunity to H2O Mantra to compete with big manufacturers. This example also teaches how updating innovation and the company's profile is important. Shailesh is himself an IIT alumnus and he has now entered several research and development (R&D) contracts with IITs and institutes like CSIR. His research will always keep him in a different league of start-ups.

Dr Shailesh and his start-up teach many other lessons. He came out of his affection for books and focused more on research. He is an avid reader, but the motive is to keep him updated and upgraded. For him, the courage to face every situation and the strength to keep working, spells success.

While launching the Startup India scheme, PM Modi had stated that the country may have a million problems but she also has more than a billion brains to solve them. We don't need these many brains. Even a hundred entrepreneurs like Shailesh can change the face of the innovation ecosystem in India. We have the labour force in plenty but only limited innovative minds. They are not born but groomed. The chapters ahead will focus on some case studies showing how innovative minds thrive in the Indian scenario.

## THINGS TO REMEMBER

- Link your start-up to common people's problems. In other words, develop social entrepreneurship.
- Product innovation is not enough. You also need marketing, branding, legal knowledge and an understanding of the government system.
- Begin with a small yet effective team. Don't try to become a boss on the first day. Learn to be an efficient employee first.
- Keep updating your innovation. Don't remain stuck in old ideas.
- It is natural to go through rough patches at any stage. This is a part of the game that you should be prepared for.

# 3

# EXPERIENCE IS THE TEACHER OF TRUE EDUCATION

## *Case Study: Arogya Medical and Opera Cinema*

My journey with *Innovate India* gave me a chance to see many interesting start-ups and innovators. Few impressed me like K.P. Singh. We usually expect only the alumni of institutions like IITs and IIMs or those with professional degrees to make their way to success. K.P. Singh is an exception as he does not give much weightage to school and college education. He does not discount academic knowledge but believes that the curriculum books lack the practical knowledge required for a successful entrepreneurship. In his view, we need a balance between both kinds of knowledge. There is no greater school than life and it prefers students with a passion to learn. Success or failure is immaterial in learning. In every failure lies the seed of success as it helps us to understand our path better.

K.P. Singh was never a brilliant student. He failed many a time during his science graduation studies. However, life was educating him in business. His case study will show you how one must strive to learn from the market instead of simply running behind professional courses. According to him, putting efforts into making the mind more innovative is the most valuable investment. He takes part in informative seminars and workshops. He is invited by many prestigious institutions like IITs to guide students.

K.P. Singh began with selling oil at a petrol pump during his school days. Today, he owns a major business group. He has established brands like Arogya Medical, Shouraditya Advertising,

Opera Cinema and Kup n Puff as innovations in a tough market. According to K.P. Singh, the market offers equal opportunities to everyone. However, there are so many players in the market that it becomes difficult for the new entrants to make a mark for themselves. Innovation is the only weapon to secure a place for your venture. To him, innovation is about presenting existing products in a new and better way to the consumers.

K.P. Singh is among the world's most authentic experts in the trade of medicines, with no formal medical education. He has attained this distinction through self-study, by meeting experts and spending time with the other successful operators in this market. He says that information is for all to attain. The secret lies in how you utilise it.

Though he started his career with a job at a petrol pump, his heart was always in setting up his own business. From selling oil to taking annual maintenance contract (AMC) for truck repairing, he never stopped working on new ideas. Small ideas lead to a grand vision. This belief led to his Shouraditya Advertising. However, his biggest calling was Arogya Medical.

In today's time, traders all across the country line up to associate with his Arogya Medical chain. K.P. Singh's story is special because he never had any lineage with pedigree institutions. He learnt the hard way through small steps. His style of functioning can be summed up in six points:

1. Don't be afraid to enter a saturated market.
2. Knowledge is more important than a degree.
3. Dream not of getting a job, but giving it.
4. Get people with similar thinking onboard. Upgrade yourself with other people's innovations.
5. Strive to be a social entrepreneur, more than just being a businessman.
6. Learn to turn *jugaad* (MacGyer) into a serious effort.

## Don't Be Afraid to Enter a Saturated Market

The conventional business logic evades the overcrowded markets. Innovation is not about introducing a new product. It can also find new ways to do an existing trade. K.P. Singh's is a glowing example of how to break the monopoly of big players. What innovations can one think of for medicine shops? You will find it difficult to become a successful businessman if you can only think of a question and not come up with an answer.

K.P. Singh's mind could come up with an answer. Many successful traders of this field were quick to dismiss his idea. The same lot turned against him as Singh grew in popularity and market share.

K.P. Singh sensed early the lack of awareness for generic medicines. PM Modi also talks about encouraging them. Singh believes that a successful business is the one that makes life of a common man easier. He collaborated with the local administration of many cities to start Arogya shops. The aim was to provide cheap medicines to people. Soon, these outlets became popular with discounts as high as 75 per cent. People prefered Arogya shops over their competitors. It came as a relief to those who were already marred by skyrocketing drug prices. But how was such a heavy discount possible? Singh explains that every pharmaceutical company has a generic medicine division. These medicines are cheaper as compared to their branded counterparts, though their composition and effects are the same. Furthermore, marketing ensures that customers only have a knowledge about expensive and branded medicines. Most of the chemists sell only these drugs for a higher profit.

K.P. Singh researched for two years to find a solution to this anomaly. He met several proprietors of pharmaceutical companies, enhanced his understanding of the market and entered the market once he was convinced of his plans. His idea did not go down well with the competitors. Singh had to face stiff opposition, even conspiracies. However, market principles prevailed and soon there were hoardings declaring discounts outside other chemist shops. True innovation has the power to set the market trend.

An innovative mind never ceases at one milestone. Singh also did not stop. He established a new set up—Opera Cinema with another young entrepreneur Shivendra Pratap Singh. This was also a saturated market. Singh was providing a cheaper alternative to expensive multiplexes. Most of these multiplexes are restricted to big cities and provide a costly experience. Opera Cinema brought the multiplexes to smaller towns and made them cheaper for the common person.

Blending advertising with technology is the key to Opera Cinema's success. It is giving the multiplex experience in tier-2 and tier-3 cities for as low a price as ₹19; this includes cold drinks and popcorn. Singh says that people found it difficult to believe in his vision at the beginning. However, Opera Cinema not only turned it into reality but it is also expanding. Few could have imagined multiplex business as a patented start-up innovation. Such learnings will always stay if attained through small initiatives.

K.P. Singh has not only patented Opera Cinema, but he is also taking it to other countries. He has showed that a business operation can also be a patent-worthy innovation.

## Knowledge Is More Important than a Degree

A research carried out in the US in 2016 showed that one out of every three billionaires across the world did not have graduate degrees. Stalwarts like Bill Gates, Steve Jobs, Mark Zuckerberg, Michael Dell, Walt Disney, Dhirubhai Ambani and Azim Premji were college dropouts. Many successful start-ups in today's era are the products of minds who weren't brilliant in academics. India has its share of such entrepreneurs. Kailash Katkar of Quickheal technologies, Deepak Ravindran of SMS Gyan and Lookup, Ritesh Aggarwal of OYO Rooms, Kunal Shah of Freecharge gained by Snapdeal, Bhavin Thurakhia of Directi are some such examples.

All these people preferred self-learning over formal degrees. Yet, they are at the top of the success ladder.

Normally, we see students from IITs and IIMs doing innovations. But one reputed IIT institute introduced Singh's innovations to its pupils. K.P. Singh believes that academics are meaningful only if it develops the capability to generate ideas. He is a commerce graduate who hasn't kept his average academic record a secret. Singh feels that many students lose their potential under pressure to score high marks. They can excel if they learn to work on innovative ideas alongside academics. Singh points out the lack of specialised education based on individual talent.

Most of the world's ideal dropouts had shown an interest in business innovations at an early stage. Learning a trade takes as much hard work and time as attaining a degree. Most people spend their lives chasing jobs before realising that they should be their own masters. It is like beginning from scratch like some 18-year-old dropout. Such a youngster still has a better chance of success. Degrees and jobs may not come handy at a later stage. Learn to do business before doing it. It is not everybody's cup of tea. It takes as much of an effort as learning music, dance or any sport.

## Dream Not of Getting a Job but Giving It

While launching the Startup India scheme, PM Modi had exhorted the youth to become empowered to give jobs rather than seeking it. He had suggested some fields like education, health and handicrafts to the young generation. The PM also mentioned cyber security as one of the areas of innovation.

PM Modi had also emphasised that the power of thoughts can never be underestimated. He further stated that focusing on solutions is always more important than focusing on problems and obstructions. Finding solutions to the big unemployment problem can also lead to a start-up. This case study is an example of finding brilliant minds for employment. Most employers would like to keep workers for a lifetime.

Singh motivates them to start their venture. The difference lies in understanding that while one must focus on earning, he/she should also be aware of the harms or difficulties of business. Such considerations come to mind only under performance pressure. Singh believes that motivating the workers for their own business enhances their efficiency.

## Get People with Similar Thinking Onboard. Upgrade Yourself with Other People's Innovations

Even the simple trade of tea selling can be done. K.P. Singh entered a saturated market with the strategy of earning 1 per cent margin from 1 lakh people instead of aiming at a 10 per cent profit from a 100 buyers. This was his Kup n Puff idea. Along with another young entrepreneur, he tasted success in this attempt. Remember that taking along ambitious people with a positive mindset will double your strength.

Kup n Puff is working with tea stalls in many cities. Singh visited several tea estates and tried to understand the business model of many successful tea shopkeepers. According to Singh, there is no chain of small and cheap tea stalls in the country unlike fast foods. Those chains present focus more on ambience than on taste. Through this venture, Singh could harness a huge market of quality tea. Kup n Puff is creating employment for many young people.

K.P. Singh not only provided a platform to talents like Ankit but also collaborated with H2O Mantra. He started an awareness campaign about drinking water at his outlets. He is still enlightening people against RO technology and working on developing his taste of tea.

## Strive to Be a Social Entrepreneur More than Just Being a Businessperson

The French word 'entrepreneur' is in vogue. The management technology experts have identified two essential ingredients as its integral parts: innovation and courage to take risks as well as bear risks. K.P. Singh linked his business to people's problems and solutions. Medicines are an essential item and are out of reach for many people. The punchline *dawa ab dard nahi degi* (medicines will no longer give pain) aptly defines the character of Arogya pharmacy outlets. Many people wonder why social entrepreneurship is part of the curriculum in a course like MBA. PM Modi's emphasis on social entrepreneurship must have answered their curiosity.

Modi's policies have also given hope to those who wish to make a career out of social service. It remains to be seen how the country's youth will find profitable innovations for social good. Social entrepreneurship increases the reach of your product. More the beneficiaries, more the profit; even at a lesser margin. For example, you can earn more money at 5 per cent margin from a 100 medical stores than earning from 1 store at 30 per cent margin. The number of customers defines profitability. K.P. Singh's start-ups work on the same principle.

## Learn to Turn *Jugaad* (MacGyer) into a Serious Effort

The *jugaad* phenomenon is identified with our country. It is symptomatic of the many negative realities of our society. Yet, it signifies the capability of our citizens to innovate at low cost. Accepting such innovations motivate our youth and give them the courage to turn *jugaad* into a viable career option. While announcing Startup India, PM Modi had promised low-cost patents for such innovations. To what extent this promise is fulfiled remains to be seen, but the assertion is encouraging.

This case study proves *jugaad* can make even big projects possible. K.P. Singh fitted air conditioners into iron containers after convincing the local authorities about his initiative. This saved him from hefty investments in medical shops. In his view, looking eye to eye in the face of any problem solves it. Most Indians are already familiar with *jugaad*. We only need to give it a big scale.

Food, clothes and shelter are necessities. But K.P. Singh understood the importance of another basic need—medicines. Costly medicines are no less painful than diseases. This reality was at the root of Arogya Medical. Singh collaborated with the Red Cross Society for this initiative. He was not a qualified medical practitioner or a pharmacist. But he consulted many financial experts. Singh believed in his idea and had done his homework in making a clear road map. This inspired his initial associates. Singh realised how commissions and profiteering were exploiting needy customers. He reduced the percentage of his profit and offered a discount of up to 75 per cent. His start-up is growing fast and is attracting investments from abroad.

## THINGS TO REMEMBER

- Don't be afraid of established players. Your uniqueness can become your strength.
- Invest in yourself. Keep adding to your knowledge. Learn all the aspects of your business. A sharp mind is an entrepreneur's real property.
- Find solutions to challenges faced by the common people. Focus more on making their lives easier than earning money. Prosperity will come on its own.
- Don't get carried away with initial successes. Keep innovating. You are now a part of the same market that you have broken.
- Bring together people with a similar vision. Be informed about other's innovations. Try to bring them onboard.
- Look to earn a small profit from a large consumer base than earning big from a small number of buyers. Increase the volume of clients.

# 4

# HELPING OTHERS IS YOUR MOST VALUABLE OFFERING

## *Case Study: Innov8*

Start-ups are working in many fields. They are also creating opportunities by helping the government. The start-up ecosystem has evolved to a point where many start-ups are now helping other set-ups stand on their feet—be it helping them with accounts, HR, business development or providing them with digital platforms. Most of these start-ups are run by people who did not have any business background and lacked any knowledge apart from their innovation and idea. Many start ups have emerged by offering them solutions. Innov8 Coworking is one such example.

Dr Ritesh Malik left his practice at Delhi's Sir Gangaram Hospital to start his business. He began by investing in start-ups through Guerilla Ventures and then established one of his own by solving a major problem faced by many start-ups. Finding and managing office space is one of the initial challenges for a new venture. It is difficult to deal with property dealers, make agreements, install furniture and look for support staff. Many youngsters start either from their homes or makeshift places. However, the lack of professional ambience affects productivity. Getting a corporate space without such hassles between ₹8,000 to ₹10,000 can be helpful in such a scenario.

This is what Dr Ritesh offered through Innov8 Coworking. It gave new start-ups a professional working space and also helped them witness how other start-ups function. The idea was an instant hit. Now he is handling 21 such working centres. Paytm's Vijay Shekhar Sharma and Oyo Room's Ritesh Agarwal have seen great opportunities in this idea.

A lawn on the roof of Regal Cinema offers a great view of the Connaught Place circle. Many start-ups witness this view every day as it also serves as their office. Dr Ritesh Malik has provided them with the opportunity to work from there. I had a chat with him at the same location for Doordarshan's programme *Kamyaab Hindustan*. His experiences have many lessons for budding entrepreneurs:

1. The family's safety net is an impediment.
2. Research on benefitting people.
3. Invest profit in the right way.
4. A business sense, not just bookish knowledge is important.
5. Turn around a bad situation.
6. A business degree is not mandatory.
7. Sell idea instead of asking for money.
8. Link with as many people as you can.
9. Only fools run away from competition.
10. Associate with people with a similar vision.

### The Family's Safety Net Is an Impediment

The South Asian cultural ethos is such that most parents behave like Kangaroo parents. They want to keep their children safe in their pouches. The feeling emanates out of a strong family bond and signifies their love and care. However, it can also come in the way of children's growth. This is the reason family businesses flourish in our part of the world. We find grandsons doing things the same way as their grandfathers did.

I belong to a family of doctors. I wanted to study economics but my family members insisted that I pursue a similar career path. They were hesitant to set me off to a stream they knew little about. My grandmother even threatened a hunger strike if I didn't relent.

## Research on Benefitting People

My family has 37 doctors. I was another addition to the list. They admitted me to a government medical college at Tamil Nadu's Theni village. This was the only way to fulfil my grandmother's wish. It was a great revelation. I realised for the first time that real India is not restricted just to major cities and it lives in villages like Theni. The region was notorious for the sandalwood smuggler and bandit Veerappan. The electricity supply was sparse. Around 7 lakh villages in India have a daily access to power supply for only one hour. I soon realised at Theni that while being a doctor can benefit a 100 patients, technology can enable me to work for millions of people.

Having a natural inclination for research, I worked with the Sophisticated Analytical Instrument Facility (SAIF) at the IIT Madras. Here, I worked with my co-founder and technology expert Abhishek Kumar on augmented reality. We also worked towards digitalised newspapers, something which is a common practice now. However, it wasn't easy in the beginning. We also worked for the campaigning of a political party. Our innovation allowed people to listen to the speeches of leaders by scanning their photographs. We know the same innovation today as *The Times of India's* 'Alive' feature. We were the ones who started digitalising newspapers and billboards.

## Invest Profit in the Right Way

We expanded our operation as money poured in. My co-founder looked after the technical aspects while I took care of the business side. A good start-up cannot work without a good team. We were lucky to have earned money at the beginning itself.

I belong to a traditional Punjabi family. My grandmother suggested to me to buy gold, my grandfather wanted me to invest in real estate, whereas my father thought that mutual funds will be the best way to invest this newly earned money. However, I said that I will only invest in start-ups. This led to the Guerilla Ventures. As the name suggested, we wanted to be a small but effective team like the ones led by Shivaji or Che Guevara. I researched a lot and found it appalling that an economy of India's size was nothing more than a back-office solution provider. We work on the products of others while there are only a few takers for our products.

## A Business Sense, Not Just Bookish Knowledge Is Important

India has not been successful in selling either her products or technology. Even our technological giants like the TCS or Infosys work for foreign products. When will we become a product-based economy? When will our companies make their products in other countries? It is not because our entrepreneurs lack innovative minds. Indians govern some of the world's leading companies. Around 40 per cent of the staff in companies like Apple, Google and Microsoft are of Indian origin. We have a genetic gold mine but lack the right mindset. This results from the colonial subjugation for centuries. Our disjointed education system is another problem. It is still running on the old pattern and is based on rote learning.

We have been taught about Babur since our childhood. However, nowhere do we find a mention of how he established his kingdom soon after coming to India. A lack of practical knowledge makes things difficult for our youth.

Start investing in the right companies if you lack expertise. Begin with smaller companies that show promise and zeal to work. We did the same through Guerilla Ventures. Change and failure are like the stepping stones of success for any start-up. They are your biggest teachers. We soon realised that the start-ups have little opportunity to learn from each other as they were not working together.

## Turn around a Bad Situation

Indians fear Mondays. It is not only because of the work pressure but also because of the work environment. We tried to change this. The state of Delhi offices isn't inspiring. However, it is worse in cities like Kanpur where work spaces are often dingy. It is difficult to expect productivity in such spaces. We focused on the following four things to change the office spaces:

- Location
- Community
- Design
- Technology

I had some money and took the rest from my father. We started our work in Delhi and selected Delhi's heart, Connaught Place, for our operations. A right location was imperative for us. Connaught Place is connected to 90 per cent of Delhi through metro at a traveling distance of 21 minutes. The location of Connaught Place for office was a dream for most start-ups. We gave them a workspace will all the facilities. We made some initial mistakes but could sell the entire space within the first month. It was encouraging.

### A Business Degree Is Not Mandatory

I did not have a formal MBA and did not understand concepts like customer validation. All I knew was that customers need to be offered a new product at a viable price. The Connaught Place is one of the most expensive places for real estate, and therefore out of reach for most start-ups. Getting a seat for ₹8,000–₹10,000 per month makes it easier for start-ups. They also found a more conducive atmosphere where they could learn from the other start-ups.

Innov8's lock-in period was much easier than the legal documentation with the property owners. A company requires only a month's notice to exit Innov8's workspace. A premium quality office space was a dream fulfiled for most start-ups. Finding furniture, support staff, setting up canteens, etc., used to take up a lot of time. The companies could now use this time productively. This was the reason our clients acknowledged our start-up. A good product is never hard to sell. Ours was aimed at promoting the ease of doing business. It was, hitherto, a new concept in India.

## Sell Idea Instead of Asking for Money

We expanded our operations to Chandigarh. The Y Combinator financed us followed by Paytm's Vijay Shekhar. This enabled us to start a new working centre with a capacity of 500 employees in Bengaluru.

Most start-ups face questions on funding. My advice is to sell your ideas to investors instead of asking for money from them. You must understand their psychology. They have the money but they are looking for ideas. They are keen to put their money on any idea which they think can give them a benefit. I believe investors are a reticent lot. They look at hundreds of reasons for not funding you. It is your job to convince them otherwise. Look for other investors if they are not willing.

## Link with as Many People as You Can

I would advise you to link with as many people as you can. Investment is never big or small. Any amount of money should be welcomed. I never judged my investors while taking their help. Some gave as little as ₹60,000 while there were also those who invested as big as ₹10 crore. Even a small investor would tell his circle about your start-up, and thus act as your unofficial brand ambassador. Paytm's Vijay Shekhar was a great help for me. We have grown to 21 centres with 15,000 seats. Today, we are the country's largest co-working place.

We have our campuses at Pune, Mumbai, Chennai, Gurugram, Noida and Hyderabad. It will take some time to create talent hubs in small cities. Talent from smaller centres usually move to bigger cities. Therefore, our focus is on major urban centres. My horizon grew when I moved from a village in Tamil Nadu to Delhi. This is also the reason that Kanpur's talent either moves to Delhi or fly straight to San Francisco.

## Only Fools Run Away from Competition

Those who run away from competition, I consider them to be fools. Competition is necessary to move ahead. You find it at all places. It is important to learn from other people. Our institution has a dedicated department for understanding competition. Knowing what competitors are doing is very important for any start-up. Competition draws your attention to better innovation and it is necessary to keep pace. Innov8 is special because it embraces competition. Nothing is wrong in emulating your competitors' good practices. Even imitating is not bad in today's market. Accepting defeat before fighting is the worst fate.

This was Dr Ritesh Malik explaining his vision. Let us try to understand the 10th point from the perspective of his team. His co-founder helped Ritesh in technological aspects. He invested the money to make it ideal for other start-ups. Similar vision does not mean same education or skills. The team should share your vision but it should have people with varied skills. Ritesh was good at identifying people for his team and is reaping dividends.

## Associate with People with a Similar Vision

For Innov8's Operational Chief Ankush Grover, a new idea or innovation is the seed. It will grow into a tree if the following questions are answered:

- Will the idea work in the market?
- How useful is it?
- Is your innovation viable?

Ankur says that every start-up should know its economy. It should also know how to invest the profit. Company's Chief Design Officer (CDO) Sheel Dwivedi claims that his designs are aimed at enthusing vigour and freshness in a start-ups' ideation.

According to him, working space is no less than homes for start-ups. Gaurav Gulati, the chief operating officer (COO) of the company believes that there's a different vibe when many start-ups are working under one roof. It not only facilitates exchange of ideas but also financial associations. Branch Head Aishwarya Garg enumerates the following principles for start-ups:

- Don't spend more than you earn.
- Work as a team.
- Learn from mistakes.
- Develop a fresh perspective.
- Look for partners and not merely investors.

## THINGS TO REMEMBER

- Believe in your dreams. Try what you want to do. Formal training is immaterial.
- Make problem-solving your second nature. Utilise things around you in a better way.
- It is not necessary that your family will love your dreams as much as they love you.
- Present positive results to win the trust of your near ones.
- Associate with the right people and take expert advice. One expert could be more useful than a 100 books.
- Learn to invest the initial profit in the right manner.
- Do something which has never been done before and offer it to the market at the cheapest rate.
- There is no shortage of investors. You should know why they would reject your proposal.
- Demonstrate your product to the investor and then seek money.
- Don't be afraid of change. Adapt to it.

# 5

# MISTAKES ARE GREAT TEACHINGS IN DISGUISE

## *Case Study: Fluper*

The shape and style of doing business has changed over the years. It no longer requires a big office or a team. Sometimes, it is just one mobile application that can get you going. Facebook, WhatsApp, YouTube, Google; they all started at a very low scale. Today, the market is flooded with hundreds of apps catering to our various needs. The mobile app business has become saturated to some extent. Yet, there are still innovations making their mark among customers. There is a great scope to introduce apps based on regional languages in India. Many foreign companies are also working to make a foray into the vernacular market. The reason behind this is the increase in the use of smartphones and cheap data.

The competition will ensure that innovations keep improving services at lower rates. Internet data will keep getting cheaper; it may even become free. Many start-ups and application companies, from the Silicon Valley to Bengaluru, are now working to provide better features without the internet. Jio took the market by storm by providing cheap data. Its entry proved to be a serious challenge for its competitors. This proves how innovation can be disruptive. It should be future-oriented, ahead of what the crowd thinks. But to do this you will have to understand the crowd first. This is the reason why most successful start-ups emanate from smaller experiments. They evolve from past mistakes.

The innovations are continuing in the mobile app market. It's not that taxi apps are not being made after Ola or there are no more food or hotel apps after Zomato and OYO. So many chat apps have made a niche for themselves even after Whatsapp.

This shows that there are always new possibilities in the market. App-designing companies help start-ups realise these possibilities.

Twenty-six-years old Anshul Sharma is our third case study. His story has many valuable lessons. He has also developed an app for the Indian government's Clean India Mission. Anshul never had to face poverty. However, his parents could never believe that he would establish such a successful business at this age. Anshul started his journey at 20 and had to face early setbacks. Most of the young people are impatient at this age and this can, sometimes, break their spirit.

Anshul was no exception. He was working to set up his business without an idea about how he will reach the customers. Anshul says that he even contemplated suicide. This can happen to any youngster who thinks more about outcomes than his or her efforts. App designing requires a large team and Anshul did not have a big investment. He started his company 'Fluper' with two people. The name was derived from 'Fluid Performance'.

Anshul's story has three lessons:

1. Criticism from near-and-dear ones is normal. They worry about you without knowing the details of what you do.
2. Don't be impatient. You cannot succeed merely by thinking. Skills and an understanding of the market are also necessary.
3. The term business, whether small or big, by definition, means earning money. Failing in this aspect will discourage you and increase pressure from the people around you.

Every start-up should focus on the third point. It's good to be your boss. People love to flaunt visiting cards with CEO written against their name. All this is useless unless you can make money. Anshul was also not sure where to get the customers from. According to him, one can easily find people with technical skills in app-designing market. You need to have an equally strong sales team.

## IMPORTANCE OF A SMALL YET STRONG TEAM

Anshul understood marketing and app development. But he could not have handled both the aspects alone. He found help in Akanksha Pandey and Vinay Kumar. The trio took the journey forward together. Akanksha knew sales well while Vinay was good with the technical aspects of web development. It started with web development and soon, the business moved towards app development. From one or two projects, clients soon began lining up for Fluper. Today, it is the topmost app development company in the UAE. The company has expanded to the UK, Canada, USA and the African countries. The company which was finding hard to earn money is now bringing money to India's coffers. What started as a three-member-team is now a family of 300 employees. Most of them are below 30 years of age.

It is easy to win small projects with a small team. Expanding the team is a challenge. You will need more people as the business grows. The same thing happened to Fluper. The core three-member-team lacked in handling HR and accounts. Richa, Anshul's sister, came to their rescue. She was working with another banking organisation. She brought a sound understanding of HR and accounts with her. Anshul recounts how Richa's addition to the team helped the company pave its way into several international markets.

## FIVE LESSONS FROM MY SUCCESSFUL START-UP

1. Like most of us, Anshul is also afraid of committing mistakes. Yet, his brief life journey has taught him a valuable lesson—mistakes are the greatest teachers. Anshul feels that he could have utilised his energy, time and urge to succeed in a far better way, if only he were to do some things. We need to understand that there are only two ways of learning.
2. We are fortunate enough to find a guru. We train and get experience before thinking of starting our own business.

3. We start our work. Learn from others, commit mistakes and learn from them. It is better to take lessons from others' follies.
4. Most of us would like the first way. The best way is to have both. Try to start your own business soon after completing a professional course. But don't rush merely by imitating others.
5. You need a deep understanding of all aspects of your preferred vocation. It is not only about the product but also HR, sales, marketing and accounts. You can hire professionals. Still, if you don't have a basic know-how of all these fields, you are on the harder way of learning from your own mistakes. One thing is common in all successful companies I have come across; they have never ceased to move forward. Recognising and rectifying your mistakes is the only right way forward.

Therefore, mistakes were an essential part of the process for Anshul. He has turned his flaws into a stepping stone. He enumerates five main shortcomings which taught him the most:

1. To do business under father's secure umbrella
2. Lack of experience
3. Lack of connections
4. Lack of consistency
5. To prepare plans without a team

### To Do Business under Father's Secure Umbrella

Most start-ups begin with plenty of dreams and energy. Their proprietors are jittery. They are often under the tutelage of their family or seniors who may not appreciate their work. This adds to the pressure of performance in the initial phases. Anshul began from the office of his father who has a good knowledge of law and business. But he had no expertise in app development. Anshul considers it as a shortcoming because it is not necessary to have the same viewpoint as your father.

Parents care and give security. But this safety can turn into shackles for the mind. Most radical business ideas face an opposition—beginning from the family. It is because parents have never tried the idea, and thus find it hard to believe that you can do it. Anshul's father is still a guide to him. But he does not feel that parental pressure. Anshul is now self-assured. He knows if he has come this far, he can find a way ahead. He could gain this confidence only after stepping out of his father's safety net.

**Lack of Experience**

One needs their family's protection only for the lack of experience. Anshul had planned his business during college days. He had no trading experience. Remember that dreaming is not enough, you need necessary experience and skills. In retrospection, Anshul would have liked to start only after spending some more time learning aspects like sales, marketing and HR.

Strategise to minimise the setbacks during initial phases. It is a time when you are not only low on confidence but your dear ones also doubt your success. Hurrying to enter a trade could make you even more eager for success. Experience means knowing all facets of your business. These include:

- Road map/paper plan
- Branding and promotion
- Sales and marketing
- Accounts and HR
- Legal knowledge

You are prone to setbacks without working on these aspects, no matter how great is your idea. It is like making a machine without fixing the nuts and bolts. You stand to gain from the others' mistakes. It is not always necessary to improve at the cost of your loss.

## Lack of Contacts

In the world of start-ups, you will often hear the term 'meet up'. This implies meeting people associated with other ventures.

Seminars and programmes related to your field are among such opportunities. It is necessary to attend such events and exchange ideas. You can distribute relevant literature for this purpose. This can only happen if you have contacts. This is easy if you are ready to step out of the digital world into the real world. While the internet is important to promote your venture; getting to know other individuals and their ideas is also necessary.

Anshul considers lack of contacts as his biggest initial lacuna. We can achieve no monumental feat going solo. It always takes a team to realise one person's vision.

Anshul recounts how he tried to handle marketing, sales and digital platforms on his own, instead of adding on experts to his team. While a basic understanding of these aspects is mandatory, one cannot match the skills of an expert. Most start-ups are unaware of enough expertise in the market for solving their problems.

Contacts come in handy while finding work. Promotions and advertisements cannot always match rapport at a personal level. Connecting with people related to your field makes business easier. You earn a name for yourself after completing a few projects. Anshul also learnt this truth but the hard way. The first project came his way only through an acquaintance. This made him realise the importance of meeting new people from relevant fields and developing a rapport with them.

## Lack of Consistency

I feel that instability is the biggest impediment in the success of any new vocation. We live in a world where people are doing wonderful things. The problem lies in comparing ourselves with them. Unsolicited counsels or half-baked new business proposals often deviate us from our true goal. Anshul draws a parallel between business and scientific formulas.

Deviating from formulae can alter results. You must remain steadfast on your plans. Changing strategy at every pretext of a new idea could be fickleness of mind. Anshul also had no dearth of unsolicited advice. It was because he wasn't clear about his strategy. In hindsight, Anshul thinks a clearer road map would have saved him from many deviations.

Focus is the key to success. One must never lose it. Be it family pressure or a string of failures. You must make a clear plan and adhere to it in earnest. Remember, well-begun is half-done. Begin with a solid plan and persevere to fulfil it.

## To Prepare Plans without a Team

According to Anshul, a right team is mandatory for the effective implementation of plans. Even a clear vision, roadmap and expertise will lead nowhere without a capable team. He gave precedence to production only to realise later that a management team was the first requirement. You must take people with similar vision on board. A successful venture would require people who not only understand your dream but also share it. Building a team is not just providing jobs and gathering people around you. Anshul fell prey to similar mistakes in the beginning.

You must begin with a small but effective team. It must comprise people with different skill sets. Anshul learnt that while it is easier to hire app developers or production resources, making up a core team of team leaders in sales, marketing and accounts needed careful thought. It does not mean favouring people who like you. Their talent and dedication should be the deciding factors.

Anshul's journey was not devoid of mistakes. The important thing is that he turned them into a stepping stone by learning his lessons. He started with a team of three members. Today, he leads a team of 300 professionals. Though he belongs to a technical background, sales are his real strength. He emphasises the importance of listening to others.

He says, 'I was trained in computers, but my real talent was sales. One of my seniors understood this and advised me to work on my salesmanship. I took his words seriously. This is how the Fluper began.'

'I believe sales is at the core of any business. Any innovation is futile unless you know how to sell it,' Anshul adds.

Anshul was an early beginner and embarked on his journey of entrepreneurship with a job. He feels working for others can teach many valuable lessons. The company he worked for had no vision for growth, it had stagnated at a certain point and its promoters were not only overburdening employees but also wasting energy. Anshul used his first job as an opportunity to develop new skills. This is one of the reasons not even a single employee has resigned from Fluper till date. Anshul has inculcated a work culture which encourages each employee to take ownership of the company's fate.

## POINTS TO REMEMBER

- Be an addict of innovation. It should be your habit, not a necessity.
- Keep trying to find solutions to people's problems. Keep your eyes open to such situations around you. You can develop an innovative mind only if you develop an attitude of problem-solving.
- Your work must be financially as well as emotionally satisfying.
- Visualise where you want your start-up to be after 10–20 years.
- Don't be discouraged if your dear ones aren't helpful. Either they don't understand your idea or they worry too much for you.
- Realise that success comes with time. You will see the signs right from the outset. Earning profit, howsoever meager, is important. Do not just keep losing money all the time.

# 6

# START-UP ERA: ORGANISING THE UNORGANISED

Every challenge is an opportunity. A start-up is also an opportunity to meet the challenge of finding solutions to different problems. The problems are aplenty for the unorganised employment sector in India. Organising this sector can reap many benefits for the country. We will discuss the unorganised farm and textile sectors in the coming chapters. In this chapter, the focus will be on endless possibilities for start-ups in other unorganised sectors. The start-up culture is picking up pace in India. We can expect a massive transformation in the start-up ecosystem of the country in the next five years. The unorganised sector that still forms the bulk of India's trade, has immense possibilities for new start-ups. Today, many new ideas don't move forward as they hit against the realities in terms of lack of resources and infrastructure.

Here lies a big possibility in organising India's massive unorganised sector. The cab aggregator apps are one such example. You can emulate similar models in other unorganised sectors. Let us first try to understand what the unorganised sector is and its state in the Indian economy.

## WHAT IS THE UNORGANISED SECTOR?

The National Commission for Enterprises in Unorganised Sector (NCEUS) has defined the unorganised sector based on circumstances and the levels of livelihood. As per this definition, it includes any venture comprising all unincorporated private enterprises owned by individuals or households sold.

We will consider the goods and services operated on a proprietary or partnership to be a part of the unorganised sector.

These are businesses run by one or two people. Your milkman, car cleaner, domestic help, etc., they all fall under this definition. You will find a large part of our population employed in this informal sector.

Looking at the local markets and small artisans, I often feel how organising this sector could turn it into such a big market. Many agencies and newspapers have published reports on the subject. However, they also know that it is difficult to estimate the real size of this market.

The unorganised sector is not bound by laws governing the organised sector and we base its functioning pattern on convenience. It has the following salient features:

- You can enter the unorganised market.
- It is governed at a small level.
- The ownership is local.
- The governing laws are not defined.
- It involves hard labour.
- The work is done by old technologies.
- The prices are flexible.
- The packaging of products is less sophisticated.
- The brand name is absent.
- There are no efficient storage and distribution networks.
- Access to government schemes and grants is hard.
- Laws do not govern the hire-and-fire of employees.
- There are many possibilities of development of skills and manufacturing.
- There is no provision of leaves or holidays for employees as per the law of the land.
- Employees have no safety against the illegal treatment at the hands of employers.

It is difficult to assess the real size of India's unorganised sector. Although it has a lot of potential in big and small cities, organising it can turn it into an inexhaustible source of opportunities for all kinds of start-ups.

## PROVIDING HOME MAINTENANCE SERVICES

Managing household chores can be troublesome in this era of nuclear families. Simple tasks like plumbing, electric repairs, cooking or paying our bills can become difficult to manage. Many would spend some reasonable amount to take care of these tasks. It is not only buying convenience but precious time. Making lives easier should be at the core of any start-up idea.

There are many funded and well publicised apps in this field. However, I will cite the example of a smaller venture working at a smaller level but bringing service providers to the customers who are willing to pay.

### *Case Study: Home Sukh*

While contributing to the column 'Innovate India', I met Vishal Saxena, the proprietor of the start-up called Home Sukh. He had himself experienced the difficulty of completing homely chores. It takes a lot of energy to find the right service providers. This led to the conception of Home Sukh. It was an initiative to provide solutions to all kinds of home maintenance at an affordable price. Even a region like Ghaziabad or Delhi-NCR is a substantial market. Just imagine the number of families in a society and the sheer number of services they require every month. Likewise, think of the number of plumbers, electricians, cooks, sanitation workers and kitchen experts catering to their needs. Vishal acted not only as a bridge between these two segments but also added value to the services.

In terms of value addition, Vishal ensured that the customers got services on time, identities of the service providers were shared and there was clarity on charges. However, his start-up did not stop at that. Below are some of his other innovations which can apply to the unorganised sector:

- Special training programmes for workers from different segments

- Issuing Identity cards to workers and linking their Aadhar ID cards with the app
- Providing services through a centralised control system like a call centre
- Setting fixed rates for services
- Taking responsibility for non-fulfilment of services
- Ensuring availability of workers on time
- Ensuring the use of high-quality material
- Using dress code or providing uniform to workers
- Improving services based on feedback from customers

There can be other value additions a start-up can use while organising services of the unorganised sector. Home Sukh is expanding and now entering sectors like construction and interior designing. The venture shows how the unorganised sector can be a fertile ground for any start-up. All it needs is innovation to turn services or manufacturing into minimum viable products. Think about expansion after you have attained success in one area. Many apps are doing the same business as Home Sukh.

This does not mean you should start imitating them. Coming up with an app means little until you develop an understanding of the market. Prepare a database. As I have written before, there is no definitive research or surveys on the size of India's unorganised sector. Entering the market and developing contacts are the only means of understanding it.

Vishal's company is operating only in Delhi-NCR, Gurgaon and Faridabad. It has set high standards of quality for services and materials and this makes the company stand out. The company can handle much larger operations through apps. But Vishal gives priority to accountability towards his customers. He believes in taking full responsibility for any ommissions.

This is a significant thought because making an app without accounting for quality will not take your start-up anywhere. Such small ventures can contribute to a larger ecosystem. Many seminars and programmes under the Startup India mission helped in connecting small start-ups serving the same sector. These are opportunities for entrepreneurs to enjoy each other's experiences. Such attempts will strengthen India's start-up sector.

Big chances for start-ups lie in solutions to smaller problems. All it needs is a keen eye to identify those problems and think of solutions. These solutions can be scaled-up after understanding the market and with the help of technology. Many apps helping with domestic chores are a befitting example. According to Nandan Nilekani, the founder of Infosys and the architect of Aadhar Card, such platforms have the potential to set the price. These start-ups remove many inefficiencies, and thus increase productivity. Therefore, such businesses can benefit the Indian economy. They will also help in organising India's huge unorganised trade sector.

Following are some changes that start-ups are already bringing to the unorganised sector:

- Ensuring dignity of labour
- Rating the performance and ensuring quality through digital platforms
- Making payments easy and transparent
- Standardising the entire process and services
- Enhancing productivity and skills

Besides, such start-ups also ensure that workers don't have to work for unpaid extra hours and the migrant labour does not face exploitation. By following the mandatory procedures of identifying workers and their police verification, these start-ups are also enthusing trust among its customers. It is difficult to quantify, but we can safely state that so far we have not even explored a minuscule part of the unorganised sector.

## ENHANCING THE PRODUCTIVITY AND SKILLS OF WORKERS

India has plenty of employment opportunities and working hands. What it lacks is skilled labour. Most people enter the unorganised sector as it is their only option of livelihood. They have no luxury to think about the quality of their output.

For example, there could be a varying skill differential between your tailor or electrician. But there is no corresponding variance in remuneration. The unorganised sector does not offer money as per competence. It also has little avenues for skill development. Many labourers end up spending their entire lives doing the same work in the same manner. The modern era start-ups can help in increasing production capacity and improving skill levels. This is for their benefit. India's quality of labour will improve if employees of these start-ups get better opportunities for skill development.

One should go ahead with skill development even if it seems difficult to them. This is because it will mean more opportunities for providing solutions. Modern entrepreneurs know that the secret of successful start-ups lies in providing solutions to the existing challenges. The start-up culture is driving the country's youth in this direction. It has generated a healthy competition which is inspiring better ideas.

Start-ups are finding new solutions to existing challenges and this is leading the country towards new heights. India's economy cannot grow without improving labour productivity. The start-ups are expected to increase variables in the unorganised sector like the white-collar job market. This comprises proportional co-relation between skills and earnings. The most important aspect is the rise of new ideas in this field. We can turn the biggest lacunae in the unorganised sector into its biggest strengths.

The unorganised sector lacks formal skill training. This can prove to be a strength as it drives labourers to learn from each other. Their colleagues train them. Start-ups can set an example even by improving the standard of living of a small section of unorganised sector labour by imparting them with better skills. This is already being done by many start-ups.

## SOME UNORGANISED SECTORS WHERE START-UPS CAN REVEL

Farming and garment sector use the biggest unorganised labour force. This creates immense possibilities for start-ups in these fields. Following unorganised sectors also present similar opportunities to start-ups:

- Labelling and packaging industry
- Building and construction industry (daily wage labourers, masons, etc.)
- Leather industry (Labourers working in tanneries)
- Migrant labourers, domestic labourers, contract labourers, etc.
- Workers involved in the fishery
- Fruits and vegetable vendors
- Newspaper vendors
- Daily wage drivers, auto drivers
- Handicraft workers
- Silk manufacturing workers
- Carpenter, potters

It is not possible to mention all categories of unorganised sector. You will need to observe to identify them. These are the services essential to our daily lives and we pay in cash for them. This sector is ripe for start-ups. Many apps are already aggregating auto-rickshaws, car drivers, fruits and vegetable vendors and domestic helps. Several new start-ups are emerging to tap the unorganised sector and the young entrepreneurs adopt an already tested formulae. While this approach cannot be wrong, it is not likely to lead to disruptive innovation. Only those start-ups will set the trend which will explore new areas.

I visited the Footwear Design and Development Institute (FDDI) in Noida while shooting for one of my TV programmes. I witnessed the immense scope of business in the leather industry. The institute is collaborating with international organisations. Many students from smaller cities are coming here to learn aspects like retail and designing. It is only one among many such institutes in the country imparting professional training to aspiring entrepreneurs. Start-ups are yet to tap the full potential of this sector. While such institutes are preparing a large number of professionals every year, there is a large number of workers already employed in the leather industry. These people are yet to develop skills and are still earning their livelihood through traditional know-how.

Connecting this trained youth to the unorganised leather industry can give rise to a new ecosystem. Here comes the role of start-ups. This is just one example of start-ups in the unorganised sector.

## *Case Study: SIGNO—Working for Blue/Grey-collar Employment*

Most people in India earn their livelihood only through blue-collar jobs. One must first understand the meaning of blue-collar jobs. 'Blue-collar' jobs are typically classified as involving manual labour and compensation by an hourly wage. Some sectors that fall into this category include construction, manufacturing, maintenance, transportation (drivers and supporting staff) and mining. Blue-collared workers are characterised as the members of the working class (investopedia.com).

Likewise, blue-collar jobs are considered 'working-class' jobs The term originated in the 1920s when blue-collar workers—those in mining and construction—wore darker colour clothes (e.g., jeans, overalls, etc.) to hide dirt.

Blue-collar workers are in contrast to white-collar employees that include men (and increasingly women) who held salaried positions and performed non-manual labour in an office setting; and invariably wore clean, pressed white shirts, which they could afford to launder frequently.

Originally, a blue-collar job did not require the worker to have much education or even expertise in the slated job field, again in contrast to a white-collar position, which demanded at least a high-school diploma and, in later decades, some college. Today, however, the term 'blue-collar' has evolved, and it's common to find workers in this role who are formally educated, skilled and highly paid.

As an emerging market and a developing economy, India is trying its best to cover all the aspects it needs so as to emerge as a more developed state. Talking about the economy, the one field that goes hand in hand with it is the variety of jobs available in this blue-collar segment. While the country is trying hard to balance between coping with the great fall of the economy and providing employment opportunities for its citizens, it has still not quite hit the mark. That is when SIGNO comes into the picture.

The founders of SIGNO launched an AI-based vernacular voice call 'Bot' in October 2019 to lessen the burden of the people looking for jobs, while at the same time acting as a match-making medium, providing results within 60 seconds.

The SIGNO AI-based voice call Bot founders, Gagan Chaturvedi (IIMA), Mukesh Deogune (IIT-BHU), Shailesh Kaul (B-Tech) and Piyush Chaturvedi (IIMA) are all industry specialists who, with the strength of their core team members, namely Abhaya, Vineet and Brajesh, are experts who possess the knowledge of precisely what they are aiming for and providing thereof. Being the prime movers behind the concept, SIGNO's rapid growth in business is all thanks to their hard work and management.

SIGNO aims at simplifying the process of sourcing, recruiting with digital Know Your Customer (KYC) procedure which is a 100 times faster than the normal process and is supported by more than 8 vernacular languages. It has recently acquired 20 clients including Yolo Bus, Blue Dart, DHL, BLR, Rimjhim Ispat Ltd and many more. SIGNO has set forth a great vision and purpose to solve the Indian blue-collar industry's core problems towards building a robust and mutually beneficial business.

Within less than three months of its establishment, SIGNO has achieved an annualised revenue exceeding ₹4 crore while also having met its break-even point. Currently, the company has its presence across six metro cities and has on boarded 20,000 blue-collar job seekers with an ongoing target of 1 million blue-collar workers within the next few months.

By effectuating more than 30,000 automated call conducts within a month and more than 10,000 jobs with full e-KYC, SIGNO's founder Mukesh Deogune (IIT-BHU), and his team Siva Naik (IIT-Guwahati) and Mohit Sachan (ex co-founder EezyNaukari, IIFT Delhi) have proceeded to set up Software as a Service (SaaS), a client dashboard tool which helps in blue-collar conducting the whole sourcing procedure effectively and smoothly. The SaaS built-up enables its users to strengthen their strategy for sourcing, thus containing the following features: complete digital/video KYC, share offer letter from the portal directly, mobile number tracking of candidates based on their SIM locations, application tracking system (ATS), assign supervisor calling and an AI-driven resume builder.

Keeping in mind that there was no such dedicated and committed platform for business owners to find a trustworthy and reliable blue-collar service, SIGNO came up with a process to overcome those obstacles, thus granting the wish of an industrialist or dealer to hire blue-collar workers from anywhere they want.

Before the onset of the disastrous pandemic, SIGNO registered around 5,000 candidates in 8 months, with the technology being in a minimum viable product (MVP) stage. And now, when India is going through the harsh consequences of a global pandemic, SIGNO is still going strong with 25,000 candidates' registration in less than 4 months, and its technology at the production stage since vernacular voice Bot handles all the interview.

With reference to SIGNO's future strategy and aspirations, the software will emerge as a skilled and reliable blue-collar service for the business owners accompanied with fast sourcing and classification. And for the blue-collar job seekers, it will guide and assign them jobs keeping in mind their preferences and skills. And all that within 60 seconds!

At its prime time, SIGNO has its full attention on medium- and large-scale industries looking for blue-collar applicants such as bikers, drivers, construction workers, mining labourers and so on.

In this challenging situation where the country and its citizens are facing impediments one after another, SIGNO aims to reduce at least one problem causing factor, that is, providing work to the manual labour amidst the toughest of times. The AI Bot carries a tacit message: 'Dream big and leave it to SIGNO to take people towards their goal.'

If you know the art of finding opportunities in a disaster, then there will be limitless scope for you in India. The success story of SIGNO clearly shows how one can create business opportunities, while at the same time adding value to the lives of the workers in distress.

## THINGS TO REMEMBER

- Understand the unorganised sector before entering it.
- Building an app is not enough. Learn ground realities.
- Spend on skill development and productivity.
- Aim at improving the unorganised sector.
- Make an ecosystem by connecting skilled youth with unskilled labour.
- Go for disruptive innovation. Find unexplored fields.
- Start from small areas. Build your minimum viable product first.
- Scale up your start-up after successful MVP.
- Use existing database and develop your own.
- Do extensive research before entering the market. Study prospective competitors. Discuss with other experts.
- Visit institutes working for skill development in the unorganised sector. Here, you will learn valuable things about aspiring youth and the concerned sector.

# 7

# AGRI START-UPS: DIGGING THE GOLDMINE

Agriculture remains the backbone of India's economy. However, it is also the largest unorganised sector of our economy. The farming sector presents as many opportunities as it has challenges. I came across many start-ups capitalising on these opportunities while working for my shows *Innovate India* and *Kamyaab Hindustan*. These are small initiatives but are enough to illustrate the scale of possibilities in our agriculture sector. I also met many specialists who were mentoring these companies. We are all aware of India's farming distress. However, many innovative minds are finding solutions. I developed a good rapport with Alay Barah, one of the finest agriculture start-up experts in the country. It is imperative to present his insights on the subject. He has contributed specially to this book and we will come back to it in a while. Let us first begin with the challenges and opportunities in the agriculture sector.

## THE CHALLENGES

The farmers are the drivers of the country's economic progress. The agriculture sector remains the biggest source of employment in the country. The government seems committed to prioritising agricultural growth, increasing the farmers' income and rural development. Yet, the plight of India's farmers is an undeniable fact. The government has not only announced several great and concrete schemes for farmers but also implemented them with zeal.

The Pradhan Mantri Fasal Bima Yojana, Soil health card, Pradhan Mantri Krishi Sinchayee Yojana, National Agriculture

Market (eNam) and Paramparagat Krishi Vikas Yojana are among the many schemes launched by this government for the farmers' welfare. But many shortcomings in the implementation process have kept the farmers mired in the same set of unfortunate circumstances. It is not wrong to say that the entire system needs an overhauling. It is where the role of start-ups become vital.

The government is focusing more on increasing the income than production. This has resulted in the effective implementation of some concrete policies. The gaping holes in the implementation process present an opportunity for the start-ups to come up with solutions. These are some major challenges that our farmers are facing and then see which ones are being worked upon:

1. Farmers are not getting the right price for their produce.
2. There is a lack of irrigation resources.
3. There is not much information on the soil quality and the use of fertilisers.
4. Farmers are still not familiar with the modern methods of agriculture.
5. There is a lack of storage and processing facilities.
6. There is an increasing dependence on chemical fertilisers.
7. Farmers are still untouched by the digital revolution.
8. There is not much transparency in monetary matters.
9. The compensation does not reach the beneficiary account.
10. The right beneficiaries not getting the benefit of the government schemes.

Several reports and surveys have documented the farmers' issues. A closer look at them reveals further challenges. For example, the well-being and health of farmers is also an issue. We are trying to look at the situation from the point of view of a start-up. Exploring the possibilities in a challenging field is the first step towards the success of any start-up. We have seen earlier how such a vast unorganised sector is still an unchartered territory for the start-up sector. Agriculture is the biggest component of this sector. It has many layers of functioning.

From increasing productivity to making markets more accessible and ensuring the right price, the possibilities are aplenty. My friend Alay has tried to explain the point with the help of graphics. Let us first look at some start-ups before elaborating more on this. A brief account of these start-ups will clarify what I mean by looking for opportunities in challenges faced by the farming sector.

## *Case Study: CropIn*

I met the founder of CropIn, Kunal Prasad, while shooting for the *Innovate India* programme. He says there are many challenges in the agriculture sector but also a great scope for technology in this field. Prasad feels that data and analytics can improve farming. According to him, technologies like remote sensing are the future of India's agriculture. His app is working to increase productivity and reduce losses. Still, the question that remains is who will use technologies like CropIn. Few farmers are familiar with the use of apps for agricultural purposes. Another question is about the affordability of these technologies.

Besides the Indian government, various agencies like the World Bank are working in this direction. They have also allocated a fund for this purpose. Any entrepreneur should understand his or her market first. Many organisations are working for farmers or with them. CropIn targeted them as potential customers. It could attract investors. The company is now expanding to Africa. It is improving as its database gets bigger. CropIn claims to have reduced the loss to 12 per cent. The start-up also says it has increased productivity by 18 per cent.

I hope to write, one day, another book explaining the agriculture sector merits. The scope of this book is restricted to developing an attitude to search for opportunities amongst challenges. This example would have illustrated how it is possible to find success in the agriculture sector.

Let us now discuss another innovation called E-Deweeder, a start-up developed by my friend Dr Nitin Saluja. It will show how even a task as basic as weeding out can also be an opportunity for start-ups.

## *Case Study: E-Deweeder*

Dr Nitin Saluja has been associated with Chitkara University. He focused on a major problem inflicting almost every farmer. Dr Saluja belongs to a farmer's family, and therefore understands how vital it is to weed out unwanted plants from the crop. The conventional method is to use chemicals. However, it has side-effects on the crop and the soil. Nitin's solution was to design a machine capable of rooting out weeds without harming the crops. It uses radiofrequency waves for this purpose. This machine is not only cheaper but also non-polluting. Dr Saluja claims that this innovation can enhance productivity by up to 30 per cent.

Weeds can damage crops by 60–70 per cent, if not addressed properly. This is the reason farmers resort to a heavy use of chemicals in their fields. Unlike CropIn, Dr Saluja's innovation can reach the farmers. Apart from the farmers, the investors providing pieces of equipment to farmers and the government are also customers in this business model. Any innovation has the potential to disrupt the market. You only need an open mind to think of one. We all learn from our surroundings. It always pays to be solution-centric. Dr Saluja got this idea while studying Hyperthermia treatment for cancer. He could see that weeds are also like cancer to any crop, and thus can also be treated using radiation.

While I am only writing about case studies that I have witnessed first-hand, there are hundreds of others setting new examples. Shashank Kumar, the founder of the DeHaat App, is one such case.

## *Case Study: DeHaat App*

The talented IIT Delhi graduate, Shashank, used his intellectual skills and recognised soon that the farmers are those in social strata who have less access to smartphones and other technological advancements. So unlike many other organisations working for farmers, he has developed a system which transcends the dire need of technology, and hence came up with an idea of developing a network of trained micro-entrepreneurs working at the ground level so they can help the peasants in person and work in and out for them.

DeHaat focuses on three major agri services—agri input, crop advisory and market linkage of farm produce. Farmers can place the order related to any of their agri need through DeHaat helpline (1800 270 1420), through the mobile application DeHaat or they can go to their closest DeHaat physical centres. The demand from farmers is transferred to the respective DeHaat micro-entrepreneurs (coordinators) and fulfiled on the same day. Each DeHaat micro-entrepreneur caters to 600–800 farmers in a radius of 5 km. These micro-entrepreneurs also use 'DeHaat for Business' application to enrol farmers, to aggregate various demand, to visit a farm, to capture crop-based query and to aggregate the farm produce.

## SOME IMPORTANT THINGS TO KNOW

- When and where to sell your product
- What pesticides and weedicides should you use? New and apt agricultural practices
- What is the current cost of your produce?
- What would constitute a market for your product?
- How would you arrange the initial capital for your start-up?

I have discussed these case studies only in brief. It is not possible to document individual success journeys on some pages. The only purpose is to appraise the readers about the opportunities. It is to make a point that the backbone of India's economy is still full of potential. Here's what Alay Barah has to say on the subject:

[Note: *Alay Barah helped me in understanding the agri start-ups in India. He is the executive director of ICCo. ICCo is one of the few organisations in the country which has been playing a consistent role in promoting and handholding such enterprises. Until recently, ICCo was a member and key partner to FICCI-led Millennium Alliance, where we supported in identifying and scaling innovative solutions to address the development challenges. We work with our global investment partners Truvalu and Capital for Development (C4D) to bring in international expertise and also support in creating a strong ecosystem right from screening, incubating and taking them to the next level. One thing we are very particular about is an enterprise's ability to reinvent itself and a deep desire to make a social impact; keeping creativity and values intact. I'm putting the exact scenario of agriculture in my friend Alay's words. He has also been there with me in various television programmes as an expert.*]

## THE BIG PICTURE

In the last three decades, India has made a sound progress on the agricultural front. Much of the credit for this success should go to the several million small farming families that form the backbone of Indian agriculture and economy. The agriculture sector accounts for 17–18 per cent of India's Gross Domestic Product (GDP) employing over 50 per cent population of India.

Agriculture is one of the high-risk sectors in the country owing to several factors such as weather, market fluctuations and topographic conditions. Farmers also face scarcity of debts, inadequate storage facility, unorganised marketing produce and poor seed quality issues among others. This leads to the farmers struggling with dwindling incomes and a vicious cycle of debts.

To address some of the above-listed challenges and meet its ambitious plan of doubling the farmers' income by 2022, India will require breakthrough advancements in agriculture technology.

A major part will depend on the magic of partnerships and putting a segment of technologies and enablers to foster innovation and technology to increase productivity, efficiency and growth. The progress of the start-up industry has been slow in the past. Enterprises were taking out time to come up with viable business models, convincing investors and were trying to be more evidence-based. But the winds of change are here.

These start-ups are all set to bring in a revolution by playing a pivotal role in providing real-time solutions to the farmers. If we look at the spectrum, the opportunities for start-ups are endless—ranging from fixing the insufficient supply chain, bringing in more transparency and technology to ensure smooth and just trading, better market linkage to earn a better income and improving quality, smart farming in agricultural business and digitisation of payments. The current and past regimes have taken effective measure to curb some of these issues. But a long and arduous journey lies ahead.

## CURRENT STATE OF AFFAIRS

There are more than 400 start-ups in India ranging from agri-inputs, post-harvest, better access to inputs for farmers or market linkage, food processing, organic farming, dairy, fishery, animal husbandry, supply chain management, farm machines, etc. According to a Nasscom report, the start-up funding till June 2019 was $248 million as compared to $73 million in 2018.

A big role is being played by the Government of India through policies such as Startup India, Skill India, Atal Innovation Mission, New-Gen Innovation and Entrepreneurship Development Centres among others. This is coupled with accelerators, incubators and mentors identified for agri-tech start-up ecosystem working in tandem to provide the best technical support and reduce the gestation period of agri start-ups.

Take the example of Easy Krishi, a Bengaluru-based agri start-up focusing on bridging the agri-information gap. They started with 5,000 farmers in 5 locations. Today, it connects them to 35,000 farmers in 37 locations. They also generated funds worth ₹80 lakh post-ICCo's incubation support.

Take another example of one of our enterprise, Green Biotech, co-founded by Geetashori Yumnam and Asem Sundari. The Imphal-based start-up deals in bio-pesticides, bio-fertilisers, bio-agricultural inputs, medicines and feed for poultry, animal husbandry and aquaculture. With ICCo's support, the production capacity is 4 MT as compared to 1.5 MT earlier and total reach to farmers is 10,000 as compared to 3,500 earlier. The team is 20+ strong and the turnover is ₹1 crore. Green Biotech is also a fine example of how organisations and other stakeholders could look at feminisation of agriculture sector with an increasing number of women in multiple roles such as cultivators, entrepreneurs and influencers. There is empirical evidence that women have a decisive role in ensuring food security and preserving local agro-biodiversity.

## WHAT LIES AHEAD?

The start-up community is playing and will play a key role in defining India's $5 trillion dreams, aligning with post-2030 development agenda, supporting in the doubling of farmers' income by the 2022 mandate. Therefore, all stakeholders have to come together to make things work.

The government should have more engagement in terms of dialogue, knowledge sharing, exposure trips and dedicated programmes by NITI Aayog to give agri start-ups a platform and also attract foreign investors.

We are also seeing an interesting trend of angel investors coming in to infuse money into start-ups. We must strengthen this phenomenon as it will play a central role in driving the start-up ecosystem.

Agri start-ups should also continue its focus on driving innovation, data collaboration, working towards getting easy working capital and providing digital infrastructure to enable real-time access to farmers across the country.

Alay Barah's thoughts give an insight into the larger perspective of opportunities. You need to understand the associated challenges and find their solutions. India has the world's second-largest agricultural land and 60 per cent of its population depends on this land for livelihood. This data is yet another reminder of the scale of possibilities we are discussing.

The following can be the fields of these possibilities for agri start-ups:

1. Agriculture infrastructure like irrigation, storage and cold storage is a vast field of possibilities.
2. Various government schemes and programmes like the Paramparagat Krishi Vikas Yojana, the Pradhan Mantri Krishi Sinchai Yojana and MP Model Village Scheme, etc. The start-ups can explore possibilities in the implementation of these schemes. It is not as hard as you believe. Almost all start-ups I have known have tried to understand and contribute to the government's initiatives.
3. Agriculture remains one of the safest sectors for investment despite its challenges. No government can afford to ignore this sector. You cannot compromise with a sector that feeds your people.
4. Apart from the farmers' hard work, supply chain and a supporting ecosystem are also important for commercial success. Only the right business model can do justice to the hard labour of farmers. The start-ups can help to develop such an ecosystem.

Soil scanning, real-time data and image analytics have great opportunities for innovators. The satellite imagery can predict produce at the time of sowing. This can enable the farmers to know the dynamics of demand and supply better. They can save the effort of needless and extra sowing and manage the supply side better.

Food processing is yet another related field full of potential. It relates to developing agriculture produce to packaged edible material. Food processing makes up around 32 per cent of the entire food business in the country. It ranks fifth in terms of production, consumption, export and projected growth. This sector has grown by 11 per cent in the country during the last decade. The trend is likely to continue. This growth is accompanied by a spurt in the demand for better storage facilities. The lack of such facilities is already resulting in precious loss of food items to the country. Many innovators are looking to change this scenario. I came across many such start-ups during the *Innovate India* programme. The S4S and Parvata Foods are worth mentioning here. Below is a brief account of these examples.

## *Case Study: Science for Society (S4S)—Food Processing Start-up*

Vaibhav Tidke leaves no stones unturned in putting food processing agro-industries on storm. He qualifies as a star innovator and now a successful entrepreneur with his start-up. Sunny Driers. Tidke, with Shital Somani Kasat and Nidhi Kumari, as poised co-founders, laid the founding stones of S4S, Science for Society. S4S Technologies is a food preservation start-up that invents new food processing machines. They sell these machines to the farmers or use these machines at their facility to produce the best quality processed food. Having its initial presence in Mumbai and suburbs, now the start-up is emerging as a PAN India revolution.

Tidke, as a child, often used to visit Tuesday bazaars in Ambajogai, a small city of Maharashtra. There he could recognise the sudden price fluctuations of fruits and veggies in a very short spell, say a day. The fruit which costed him ₹30/kg in the morning was available at a reduced price of ₹10/kg. This abrupt fluctuation left him with a jolting question in his mind, 'What is compelling the farmers to bear this loss?'

'I saw, during a particular season of harvesting, fruits and vegetables were cheap. There was a lot of supply and much less demand. The farmer didn't have a way of preserving the fruit and vegetables,' said Vaibhav.

Coming from a family which earned its bread and butter from farming, he could relate to this disturbing plight of the farmers. The question kept on haunting him until he got convinced of his emerging idea of sustainable storage.

## 'Sunny' Driers!

Tidke's innovation of his solar conductive driers fed his immense desire to do something for the farmers and that it may be successful and serve the purpose.

'The dryer is a box with a clear plastic top. Farmers place produce on a black, heat-absorbent surface, and the sun does the rest. About 95 per cent of the water in the items is evaporated off, leaving dehydrated produce ready for storage.'

## Dry Chains—A Boom

Drying fruits and vegetables and storing them for future uses has been prevalent since the dawn of civilisation. But what is the new crunch in it?

Solar Energy + Machine Age = Sunny Driers

Although cold storage is a popular practice these days, but with the usage of huge fridges and enormous amount of electricity, it is costly, and it is not new to us! The dry food storage, on the contrary, through solar-powered driers, can meet the revolutionary upsurge in agro-industries, which is strived hard for by the cold storage industries since eras.

The room for thinking and innovation doesn't end here. S4S, after the resilient drier, came up with a more consumer penetrating vocation in DesiVdesi. From instant mixes like instant khichdi to sliced fruit chunks and non-fried spinach and chiku chips, nutritious products are a big attraction of this side venture.

## INDIAN PROSPECTS

India is one of the hungriest countries in the world, yet it wastes a huge amount of food. Production of vegetables and fruit totals about 220 million tons a year. About 30 per cent of that never reaches the table.

The main reason for this waste is a lack of storage infrastructure at the time of harvest. Without electricity or electric freezers, farmers have to sell everything, which means it's not sold at all. 'You wash and cut down the fruit and vegetables and load it in the drier. By evening, most of them are dry, and you take it and pack it,' said Vaibhav. The product keeps its colour and texture, just loses its volume. Farmers rehydrate the items by adding water again, and they can also use the dryer for fish or meat.

In Tidke's words, start-ups should look for:

- Experience in every opportunity, that's the real investment.
- Scale-up the possibility of business as investors consider investing in you with this possibility only.
- Passionate employees are a must for any start-up.

I had mentioned the north-east based Parvata Foods while discussing the possibility of start-ups in the Kashmir valley. Organic farming is in vogue today. However, many areas including those of Kashmir and the north-eastern states have known organic farming for ages. Yet, the farmers of these regions struggle to get a good return for their hard work. Their produce cannot reach all parts of the country and the world. Parvata Foods is trying to bring about a change.

Both of its founders, Siddhi Karnani and Anurag Agarwal are IIM graduates. They had visited Sikkim during their research.

I had asked them how they came across this idea during my conversation as part of the *Innovate India* programme. I tried to understand their venture even further and found it to be an apt example for finding opportunities amongst challenges.

## *Case Study: Parvata Foods—Breaking the Stereotype Is the Key to Success*

Anurag and Siddhi found Sikkim to be the only organic state in India during their early academic visit to the place. But despite this, they found that there was no market for these high-quality organic products. The entire organic crops and fruits from Sikkim were exported to Siliguri, West Bengal, where they were being mixed with other products and sold as a homogenous product. So the organic identity was lost; they were produced as organic but sold as conventional.

### Keeping the Lost Identity

This visit led them to develop a socio-commercial venture as a successful business. Parvata Foods came into the picture, where besides creating a chain of markets for the organic produce and retaining its lost identity, this start-up innovated an exclusive three-stage dehydration technology for spices. They also motivated the farmers to work with them in this scientific drying process.

It is only when you take challenges, that you ensure learning and then, success. A genuine question that pops up now is why have they chosen such difficult areas to work in when they could have penetrated any other market to enjoy a pinnacle position in their career? Proving the above-quoted saying, the suave organisation worked with a clear vision to undertake the challenges and work only in those estates. Therefore, Parvata Foods after Sikkim, enjoys its presence only in the tribal belt of Odisha and the toughest-mountainous terrains in Meghalaya. Apart from these places, now start-ups can also find possibilities in the Kashmir valley, which was not possible due to Section 370. Now the time has changed and youngsters from Kashmir and from all around the country can find opportunities in difficulties.

Anurag and Siddhi say that they have become the first player to build an integrated value chain of organic produce from Sikkim. Spanning the entire value chain from sourcing, processing, packaging, marketing and distributing of organic spices like turmeric and ginger, large cardamoms, and exotic fruits and vegetables, they are committed to bringing high quality, adulteration free, organic and natural agriculture products to the consumers.

### Innovation Is the Key to Success

There is no technology in India for storing fresh ginger on a commercial scale. The said technology is available in China, Australia and the Netherlands for now. China harvests ginger for 2 months and supplies to the world market for 10 months. Thus realising this astonishing fact, team Parvata set to pioneer commercial ginger storage for the first time in India. They are doing a tie-up with foreign universities and companies to bring fresh ginger storage technology. They are taking trials in Modified Atmosphere (MAP) bags for storage of fresh ginger at their plant.

Another issue observed by the organisation was that burning woods in *bhattis* was the only known method for drying large cardamom. However, it damaged its colour and flavour. This resulted in products being rejected by the customers in Europe and the US and also harms Sikkim's reputation as an organic state. Registering this very fact, Parvata Foods has also started scientific drying of cardamom in their processing unit.

### An Eventual U-Turn

Your personal experiences have a lot of potentials to lead you to an exceptional journey of excellence; but only when you are ready to learn and grasp from those happenings.

Suggesting the budding innovators to absorb the above ideology, Anurag goes back in time remembering the day when his father was into major health hassles because of a severe lack of medicines. Since then, the entrepreneur developed an innate desire to make food as an alternative to medicines. Thus, he believes he got triggered for such innovation from nothing but his life episodes. And besides all the other ventures, he then revolutionised the usage of turmeric and ginger, a forgotten medicinal product into a retail brand of spices known as Parvata Spices.

Many start-ups like Parvata and Science for Society are exploring endless possibilities for themselves. The growth of start-ups in agricultural sectors like food processing and storage illustrate the vision of the Startup India initiative. We all need to contribute to this vision for a better future. The onus is on innovators to find solutions to the country's challenges. They also need to understand the business aspects of entrepreneurship.

All successful start-ups and innovators not only find solutions but they also do so in a new field. The mindset of innovators is changing towards risk-taking. Taking risk also means opening up to more chances. We all hear or read about first movers, but only a few muster the courage to become one. One needs such an attitude to establish an agri start-up. You may find opposition in your nearest circles, but you must trust your idea. It is bound to click if it is making lives better.

## THINGS TO REMEMBER

- Study farmer-related government schemes.
- Apprise yourself with the latest research material (government and non-governmental) concerning the agriculture sector.
- Try to develop a database of farmers.
- Study various techniques being used by farmers across the world.
- Develop your understanding of traditional farming.

- You cannot understand farming without farmers. Either become one or rope them in.
- Understand not only agricultural production but also storage, commercial transaction, irrigation and use of non-conventional energy.
- Try to become the first mover. Venture into unchartered territories.
- Learn from start-ups like 'Sunny' Driers and Parvata Foods which have simplified existing technologies.
- Many organisations are helping start-ups incubate. Learn about them and avail their benefits.

# 8

# GARMENT START-UPS: STITCH IN TIME, SAVES NINE

We have to propel our garment sector to new heights in the start-up era. India will reap rich benefits if start-ups realise their possibilities. The country's garment sector has slowed down in recent years. There was a time when India was among the main suppliers of garments, importing to western countries. However, the last three years have been tough for this export sector. This is not because of a lack of demand in the international market but because of the tough competition from our neighbour, Bangladesh.

Bangladesh's garment sector rides on free trade agreements and cheap labour. A competitive incurring cost has helped the country seize a big share in the apparel market. While India's exports are falling, Bangladesh has doubled it.

The garment sector is a major contributor to India's economy with a 13 per cent share in the country's total exports. It also provides a direct or indirect livelihood to 105 million people. The garment trade is growing and hoping to capitalise on its potential. Indian government is also encouraging India's entrepreneurs to enter this market. Many groups listed under GeM are working in the garment sector. The Womaniya initiative has won special accolades. It has promoted handicrafts like embroidery.

## *Case Study: ATDC—Start-up Era, a Golden Opportunity for Apparel Industry*

The start-up era is the best time for the garment sector to thrive. There is a lot of scope for budding entrepreneurs in this field.

Introducing more professional courses which teach skills related to garment trade can brighten up these possibilities further. We have some good institutions in the field. But the young generation still needs to be sensitised. The garment business is among India's largest unorganised trade sectors, second only to agriculture. Yet, vocational education in these sectors is not popular. Bangladesh is making strides in garment trade despite a lack of professional courses in this field. The cheap labour has attracted importers to Bangladesh. The apparel industry is taking roots in common households and one can find skilled labour in almost every street.

This is not about eulogising Bangladesh, but understanding the potential of the garment sector. A robust international demand means opportunities for our entrepreneurs. Clothing is a necessity for humans. We may have reached the moon, yet the struggle for such basic requirement remains. Keeping this in view, institutes like Apparel Training and Designing Centre (ATDC) are collaborating with the Ministry of Textiles to link the textile segment to our economy by rebranding it as apparel industry. I saw this industry from close quarters during my programme. This is only one of the many examples from across the country. We talked to experts to understand the level of enthusiasm among the youth for the textile industry and related Indian market. This is the reason that ATDC is now offering courses like B.Voc in fashion and retail programmes.

## WHAT DO THE INDUSTRY EXPERTS SAY?

### Expert's View: Dr Darlie Koshy

Dr Darlie Koshy, the director general and chief executive officer of ATDC, Gurgaon, is one of the foremost authorities on the subject. He gave a glimpse of the immense scope in the textile industry. Dr Koshy narrates how ATDC has so far trained 2.17 lakh youths through its 200 centres spread across 25 states. It was under the Integrated Skill Development Programme undertaken by the Ministry of Textiles in 2010. Dr Koshy estimates the global garment and textile industry at around a $100 billion. The number of entrepreneurs associated with the trade has now risen to 19.1 million.

The National Design Fashion Incubation was established at NIFT and NID almost 25 years ago, recounts Dr Koshy, who has himself worked as NID director. This helped incubate over 200 designers. According to Dr Koshy, the apparel and fashion business can attain new heights if the government comes forward to help establish fashion parks and fashion incubation centres. This will mean greater employment opportunities for the country's youth. Dr Koshy recommends the linking of the ever-changing fashion trends in brands like Mango, H&M and Zara to the IT sector.

India has an economy of $2.5 trillion. In comparison, China has an economy of the size of $14 trillion. Its textile exports are estimated at around $179 billion. Dr Koshy claims that Vietnam's textile industry can produce 40,000 garments every hour. It can annually produce 349 million dresses. There is a little wonder then that one out of every three dresses adorn by the US citizens is manufactured in this country. India's IT sector can help our garment business catch-up to such competition by contributing to the fashion merchandising, digital merchandising and digital pattern making. As of now, the IT sector has only 12–15 per cent collaboration with this trade. There is great scope for digitalising the design, pattern making and production in the garment business.

Dr Koshy believes that the government initiatives like Make in India and Startup India can increase work efficiency and production capability of India's textile sector. Many youngsters think it is a traditional and low-income business. We have the challenge to break these stereotypes and encourage young entrepreneurs to enter this trade. According to Dr Koshy, around 10 per cent of India's total of 1.60 lakh retail market is related to the sale of garments. Indians are still enamoured by big brands like Mango, H&M, Zara, Nike and Puma. The Union Ministry of Youth Affairs and Sports, The Institute of National Imports and ATDC have come together to frame a new training curriculum for the new generation in the form of B.Voc. Though a vocational course, it is at par with the mainstream degrees. The three-year B.Voc course has 2,000 hours for skill development and 1,000 hours for other related subjects.

## THE TEXTILE INDUSTRY NEEDS ITS DUE RESPECT

Dr Koshy has done some extensive research on the international textile market. He blames our social mindset for the unrealised potential of India in this field. Dr Koshy points out how the word 'tailor' is still associated with menial job, while the designation 'fashion designer' carries more weight. We need to redefine our boundaries which start-ups are now doing as has been mentioned earlier in the chapter related to unorganised sector. The new-found prestige in the corporate sector is drawing fresh talent to such areas though much remains to be done to give them more incentives. I talked to many ATDC students and tried to understand their vision for the future.

Ankush and Avinoor are two such students who come from the family background of textile and stitching business. They have found B.Voc helpful as it not only trains them in fashion designing but also in pattern making and fashion merchandising. The ATDC curriculum also equips them with the skills necessary to sustain their ventures in the era of e-retailers like Amazon and Flipkart. Other students echo the same sentiment. Like Ankush and Avinoor, many of them belonged to families in the same business. It is encouraging to see the present generation linking their ancestral trade to innovations. I had seen the same in Noida's Footwear Design and Development Institute (FDDI). The leather industry is also growing and the demand in the international market is ever-increasing. We need initiatives in this area.

## THE POSSIBILITIES IN THE LEATHER BUSINESS

Anurag Sharma is running a start-up based on leather goods. Though with no experience in this trade, he believes in the unbound potential of this sector. Anurag points out at the existing labour force and factories in the leather business. He wants to act as a conduit between them and the new markets. This would also give more options to his buyers. Many of us want customised leather products. Anurag's start-up gives them a chance to design products for themselves.

This is a good innovation and points towards a new market. This also shows new possibilities for start-ups in the designing field. They can become a bridge between the producers and end consumers by selling customised products like Anurag. This is not as unique in the garment business as people have been getting their clothes stitched. The readymade apparels are a new phenomenon. Anurag's example illustrates that expertise is not a precondition to enter a field if you know how to do business. It also shows that the leather and the garment trade gives equal opportunities to everybody. Dr Koshy, an alumnus of prestigious institutes like IIT and IIM, is a glaring example as he has made a name for himself in the apparel business.

## COURSES TO MAKE A CAREER IN THE GARMENT BUSINESS

I discussed the options available for training in the apparel sector with Apparel Training & Design Centre (ATDC) Principal Shalini Sharma. Explaining that this sector is no more restricted to just stitching clothes, she says it is now about fashion designing and retail. The need of the hour is to design as per the buyers' demand. The trainees are equipped with marketing skills as they are also sensitised towards the needs of the international market. Anurag's innovation in the leather sector is in demand in the garment business also and professional courses are mindful of this reality.

The University Grants Commission (UGC) started B.Voc in 2015. The aspirants can opt for this course after Class XII. The course includes printing, apparel and fashion designing. ATDC's Gurpreet Kaur says B.Voc was started not as a degree course, but as an attempt to develop the students' skills. The course has now entered its fifth year and two batches have already passed out. The ATDC provides free training to 6,000 students from poor backgrounds every year. It also takes care of their other expenses and provides stipend during the course.

ATDC's Chief General Manager Gopal Bhasin claims that the institute tries to give these students all the facilities that they are not likely to get in their villages and towns. It also provides them with hostel facilities and a four-week on-the-job training in factories. This strengthens their employment prospects.

The skill development plan can prove to be a milestone. Rupali Shukla has been associated with the Deen Dayal Upadhyay Rural Skill Development Scheme (DDU-GKY). She says that the scheme has helped to connect the students from all parts of the country. They train the ATDC teachers in helping the rural students adapt to the urban milieu and introduce them to the curriculum. They also impart values like discipline and make them career conscious. Its curriculum is at par with any other private fashion designing institute and focuses on the industry requirements.

Many institutes are emulating ATDC's work across the country. They can help promote skill development programmes. You can also benefit from them and start your venture. Good labour force and a big market is already present. A good start-up can organise this huge unorganised sector.

India already has an elaborate cotton production chain. The country has every resource required to become the world's largest garment exporter and start-ups can play a leading role in this endeavor.

## SMALL-SCALE BUSINESS IDEAS IN THE GARMENT SECTOR

The garment sector is full of possibilities. Many doors open once a start-up shows interest in this field. The scope of this trade is not restricted to designing and stitching clothes. We have the manufacturing infrastructure and the market. The main task is to attract the customers. Anurag gets his leather bags made in one of his friends' factories. But he gets them designed by his buyers. They can implement the same idea in the garment sector. The online platform has brought the market near to you. Yet, India's garment sector lags. Many start-ups do not require big showrooms. They are focusing more on building a customer base. You can think of a start-up to help other start-ups with little investment. You can establish your small manufacturing unit. Some options available in this sector are discussed below.

### Building a Small-Scale Garment Manufacturing Unit

- You will need a sewing machine, a cloth-cutting machine, an ironing machine and garment finishing equipment. Make a list of the machines you will require, research how much they will cost you and enquire with suppliers.
- You will need to establish an infrastructure for the factory, lighting, water, material handling equipment, furnishing, etc.
- You will also need land or space for setting up your unit. Keep in mind factors like time, manufacturing processes, floor, office spaces, showroom, pantry and godowns while completing the space.
- You will need skilled labour force and service providers.

- Look for the sources of raw materials. The raw material includes clothes, trims and associated equipment.
- Prepare a commercial strategy and build a customer base.
- Plan how you will meet the investment needs. You can apply for business loans.

### The Garment Wholesale Business

Know about some garment manufacturing centres to source wholesale garments. Attain dealership for some products and brands. You can decide on the quantity of goods to order once buyers visit your place.

### Establish Your Laundry

You need a washing machine, hydro-extractor and a tumble dryer for a washing plant. Washing machines come in varying capacities. You will get orders of different weights and volumes based on the capacity of your plant.

### Customised Products

You can repeat Anurag's innovation in the garment sector by offering garments customised by the buyers themselves. The customised print business takes orders from customers or a group of customers who design on their own. You deliver the products at their doorsteps.

## THINGS TO REMEMBER

- The textile trade is India's second-biggest unorganised sector after agriculture. It presents a lot of opportunities to start-ups.
- India and Indian start-ups have a lot of potential in the international markets.
- India already has enough base for this sector to excel.

- Technology and innovations will make new start-ups stand out in this sector.
- It is not necessary to be an expert in apparel-making.
- Knowledge of fundamental business skills is sufficient.
- It is very important for start-ups in this sector to build a customer base.
- Start from a small scale and grow. You can find big possibilities even in small investments.
- India already has labour force, factories and raw materials.
- Start-ups only need to find markets.
- Contact people or organisations working in this field. Their research and data can help you.
- A small sector has a much better chance of succeeding in the garment sector than any other.

# 9

# SOCIAL ENTREPRENEURSHIP: WE RISE BY LIFTING OTHERS

The French word entrepreneur is now a part of the common parlance. The concept has also branched into social entrepreneurship. PM Modi used this term several times while launching the Startup India programme. He chose this phrase over words like trade. This would have answered many students' doubts over why courses like MBA have a special emphasis on teaching social entrepreneurship.

All major business schools teach social entrepreneurship because new vistas for business open only when you think of making lives better.

Noticing problems around you and thinking of innovative ideas to solve them are at the core of any start-up's success. Management gurus count on two vital factors for the success of any start-up: innovation and the capability to take risks.

Both attributes should be coupled with a motivation to contribute to society. This chapter has many case studies that are a shining example of finding opportunities in the face of challenges. PM Modi's appeal for social entrepreneurship would have encouraged those youngsters who want to make a career out of social service. We have many examples where people have found success even in social welfare.

NGOs and similar organisations also work for social welfare. However, it is now transforming from philanthropy to entrepreneurial ventures.

The best thing is the government turning into a prospective client in ventures related to social entrepreneurship. The government's help assures new start-ups of remaining afloat if it has come up with an innovation for the society.

I met many young social entrepreneurs during my journey of *Innovate India*. I am presenting some stories here. You may find their ideas difficult but the aim is not to motivate you to imitate them. The point is to develop a thought process that develops an innovative approach.

## *Case Study: Samman Foundation—An IIM Graduate 'Rickshawala'*

As the editor of the *Live India* magazine, I had published a special edition of the young achievers of India. The story of a 'rickshawala' particularly impressed me in this series. You don't come across IIM-graduate rickshawalas too often. Irfan Alam is a successful social entrepreneur. He is a great example of finding opportunities in difficult circumstances. He could have opted for a job after completing his MBA. But Irfan wrote a new destiny for himself.

Linking industries to social causes is a big question. We often accuse young entrepreneurs of being too career oriented and not contributing enough to the society. Irfan Alam is an exception. It is also a success story for thousands of people associated with him. Irfan's Samman Foundation has organised many rickshaw pullers into one business entity and helped them raise their living standards. All this while he improved services for the passengers.

Irfan recalled that while riding a rickshaw once, he asked for water from the puller. He expressed an inability to help as rickshaw pullers don't earn enough to keep water bottles with them. This prompted Irfan to sell eight water bottles to five rickshawalas. It fetched him a profit of ₹16. He kept ₹8 for himself and distributed the rest among the rickshaw pullers. Irfan completed his MBA from IIM Ahmedabad in 2006 and started developing the same idea during his internship.

Irfan started the Samman Foundation with a 100 rickshaw pullers. He took a loan of ₹25 lakh from a bank in Patna for this purpose. Irfan found out that one rickshawala can barely pull not over 125 kg weight and that 95 per cent of them hire their rickshaws. He not only focused on better design of rickshaws but also provided basic amenities like water, newspapers and first-aid to their customers. This enabled them to charge better money.

This innovation was an instant hit and half of the profit goes to the foundation. They distribute the rest among the rickshaw pullers. Irfan's face glows while narrating his success story. It shows the level of satisfaction, as if you are dreaming not only for yourself but also for others.

Irfan has received dozens of awards including the World Bank's Innovation Award. Even the former US President Barack Obama praised his efforts in his meeting with Irfan. This young man's story is taught at universities like Harvard and Oxford.

Irfan is an example to all those who migrate to other places in pursuit of greener pastures. It shows how one can make it big even in smaller cities of India.

Recounting the former US Ambassador, Timothy Rome, embarking on one of his foundation's rickshaw along with her parents, Irfan acknowledges that recognition gives you the courage to pursue your path. No task is big or small, it only has to be innovative.

## *Case Study: Boond—A Start-up in the Renewable Energy Sector*

The future of this planet depends on the success of the renewable energy sector. All countries leading global innovations are focusing on clean energy. Yet, a lot remains desired for start-ups in this sector. Boond is one exception in India. Of all the start ups that I came to know, only a few were working in the power segment. Founded by Rustam Sengupta, Boond was among those start-ups that I grilled the most. The reason was the lack of innovations in the renewable energy sector. However, Rustam was up for answering all my questions.

This venture promotes alternative energy in Rajasthan, Uttar Pradesh, Delhi-NCR and other North Indian states. Boond is providing power, clean water, pest control and cleanliness to the poor people in India's hinterland since 2010. It has turned villagers into entrepreneurs for products like solar lamps, solar home systems, water filters and cooking stoves. The start-up has developed a distribution channel.

Boond is a perfect example of social entrepreneurship. Rustam says, 'We are not only providing clean energy but also trying to find a solution to many social issues. It is only if we try to reach the far-flung regions and this is what we are doing. Our focus is to provide appropriate solar energy solutions to a spectrum of communities and regions.'

Rustam has studied at some of the finest Indian and foreign education institutions. He knows the latest research in solar energy field well. Being an electrical engineer, he understands the importance of innovation in this field. Boond has a mission to take electricity to the villages marred by frequent power cuts. Rustam claims the situation is improving. Yet, initiatives like Boond will be required in the years to come. Rustam is also well-versed with the power of data analysis. His start-up has a mission to give equal opportunities to the rural population and bring it at par with the global urban middle class.

A village in Uttar Pradesh's Unnao district has families of 25 poor farmers. They earn less than ₹5,000 per month. These families use pre-paid cards to pay for their electricity. The pre-paid cards work like pre-paid SIM cards and offer a solution to the poor families incapable of paying for solar energy.

Boond has established some solar power stations on its own. These stations provide a certain amount of power every month to such poor households through inverters. They charge the power at a nominal rate to maintain affordability. Boond innovation is to build a solar power grid that can supply electricity to poor people at a very low cost.

This electricity comes from the apico grid system. A grid system of 1-kilowatt capacity has been established near the village. Each of the 25 households has a regulator or a meter. The consumers can choose pre-paid or post-paid services. They can regulate the power supply as per the requirement.

The start-up had built 11 such apico grids in May 2014. These grids are now lighting up the lives of 275 families in Rajasthan and Uttar Pradesh. Such systems reduce villagers' dependence on kerosene and provide them with clean and cheap energy. Boond gives the option of a fixed payment system to consumers. They also get the facility of charging their portable solar batteries at central charging stations. A customer pays ₹50–₹100 on an average for the service.

Rustam reminds of the 200 million Indians who are still striving for access to electricity. This challenge is also an opportunity for the market. We still have villages where kerosene lamps are the only source of light during nights. The government's efforts will reach them someday. Meanwhile, initiatives like Boond are chipping in. It is a win-win proposition for all the stakeholders. I found this solar power start-up as a great example of social entrepreneurship and commercial success.

## *Case Study: Nirog Street—Linking Masses to Ayurveda*

Nirog Street has done a commendable work in Delhi and Gurgaon for Ayurveda. This start-up is working to organise the unorganised Ayurveda sector. We witnessed the possibilities of making profit in providing cheap medicines to patients. Nirog Street is not only taking the scientific aspects of Ayurveda to the masses but also giving credence to the medical practitioners of this field. I met Nirog Street's founder Ram N. Kumar during Doordarshan's show. Hundreds of Ayurveda brands along with medical practitioners are today associated with this start-up.

Nirog Street's target customers are Ayurveda doctors. It is a huge lot still deprived of a work culture based on modern technology, diagnostic facilities and extensive research. This creates a trust deficit between these doctors and their prospective patients. Bridging this gap will not only promote our indigenous medical system but also give cheap and safe treatment to billions of people. Nirog Street saw this opportunity and now it has Ayurveda doctors from all across the country lined up.

The Ayurveda sector has also been explored in a big way by Baba Ramdev's Patanjali. Research-based medical treatment will enhance this stream's credibility in the medical world. Nirog Street has shown social entrepreneurship by coming good on this task. The company is collaborating with the Council of Scientific and Industrial Research (CSIR) and Indian Institute of Integrative Medicine (IIIM) to research the medicinal qualities of Marijuana. It is now focusing on diabetes and pain management. Developing nutritional supplements using rich Himalayan herbal resources is also its priority.

Kumar understood the importance of Ayurveda while fighting a disease himself. After Ayurvedic methods cured him, Kumar wondered why Ayurveda is not reaching every household. He concluded that there is a lack of trust among the patients for Ayurveda doctors. The lack of modernisation in Ayurveda stream is one reason. Most of the Ayurveda practitioners still rely on conventional methods to carry out any new research.

Kumar began meeting more and more Ayurveda practitioners. His company hired many experts in this field. We have already discussed the need to organise the unorganised sectors of the economy. Ayurveda is a huge unorganised sector. It has both effective medicines and capable doctors. However, these doctors don't get good medicines. Patients lack the knowledge about diseases that Ayurveda can cure. Kumar developed an app and connected Ayurveda doctors from all across the country.

Nirog Street is also working on Alzheimer and liver diseases. Kumar emphasises on the importance of a continuous research in Ayurveda. This is what his start-up is doing. They share the conclusions of these researches with Ayurveda doctors through the company's app. Nirog Street aims to make Ayurveda a priority treatment for patients. It can cure most of the diseases at a much cheaper rate and with no side effects. Modern research will only make it more effective.

A majority of Indians dwell in villages. Rural India still lacks doctors and we all know how crowded the government health facilities are. This crowd can be reduced to a great extent if patients get Ayurveda treatment at home for common ailments. We will need to raise public awareness towards Ayurveda. The practitioners also need to be better trained. Nirog Street is also working on training programmes for Ayurveda doctors.

Kumar wants to form a global trust for the Ayurveda practitioners and medicines. He aims to promote evidence-based Ayurveda treatment by collaborating with agencies like CSIR and IIIM. The western medicine system has by-and-large monopolised the medical, technological and innovative space. Ayurveda is one of the most ancient systems of medicines and free from any side effects. Yet, it awaits its rightful place in the world's health infrastructure.

India has over 500,000 registered Ayurveda doctors. Over 21,000 students graduate in this stream every year.

Developing Ayurveda in India qualitatively at this scale is a challenge. People are so used to allopathic medicines that they find it hard to believe in a safer alternative. Nirog Street is working to instil this confidence. Ayurvedic medicine is a $3 billion market in India. We estimate it to grow to $15 billion in the next decade. As Ram Kumar puts it, 'The best thing is that Ayurveda is "Make in India" product for the world. Every aspect depends on the domestic supply chain.' Start-ups can create employment opportunities and help several other businesses by promoting Ayurveda.

## *Case Study: MozziQuit—A Cheap and Effective Innovation to Tackle Mosquito Menace*

Can mosquitoes also pose a danger to the society? Do we need innovations to tackle them? Can saving humans from mosquitoes also present new opportunities for start-ups? According to the World Health Organization (WHO) report, about ₹1.25 lakh crore will be required to wipe out this menace till 2030.

Orwin Noronha's start-up, MozziQuit, is working in this field. Dealing with mosquitoes has turned into a big industry over the years. We have invented many new methods to save humans from them. This market witnesses a spike every year during dengue, viral fever and malaria seasons. Orwin's start-up is based on an effective technique to kill female mosquitoes. We will come to this technique in a while but let us first discuss Orwin's vision behind this venture. We have seen how social entrepreneurship is full of business possibilities while solving some of the society's gravest problems.

Mosquitoes are a serious problem to the masses in the developing world. People have latched on to any innovation in dealing with them. From coils, mats, sprays, liquids and creams, the demand for this category of products is ever-increasing. In India, several traditional techniques like mosquito nets and burning Neem leaves to keep mosquitoes away are still prevalent in society.

Yet, neither modern nor traditional techniques offer a foolproof solution to this problem. Also, some modern products have side effects. Orwin's company has seen an opportunity in this shortcoming. I met him during an episode of *Innovate India*. His start-up was widely praised by the investors and mentors in the show. MozziQuit could bag some investment after the show. Although MozziQuit is focusing on animal breeders, it has a lot of potential for expansion.

MozziQuit's product is a net that attracts female mosquitoes in large numbers and kills them. There is no chemical used in the process. This innovative technology protects animals at less than 10 paise/day. Orwin has presented evidence to prove an increase in the milk yield after the use of his product and shown that animals are more healthy if protected by MozziQuit. Orwin has patented this trap technology. All innovators should be sincere in getting their technology patented.

The MozziQuit device works on a temperature generator technique. This machine attracts female mosquitoes at a specific temperature and a fan installed in it traps them. Orwin was inspired to come up with this machine after his mother was infected with Filariasis. She contacted the disease while working in a cow shed. Orwin's device costs only ₹1,800 and it is mostly used in cattle sheds. Considering the size of India's cattle breeders, even a small margin can fetch a good profit in such products.

Orwin's example underlines the fact that an idea or an innovation is any start-up's biggest asset. Therefore, it is important to get a patent and certification. Media publicity can help you gain credibility, but it also requires relevant certification. Orwin also showed his technology in many big institutions to gain this credibility.

Many of these government and non-government institutes issued evaluation reports which authenticated the positive results like an increase in the milk yield and weight gain in the cattle. Such approval helps win the customer's trust in your products. The Bengaluru-based National Institute of Malaria Research presented an evaluation report on MozziQuit to the Indian Council of Medical Research. The report stated that the device can kill all kinds of mosquitoes. Furthermore, it is 2.5 times more efficient than similar US technologies. This validation is proof enough that certification is helpful for any start-up. The story has two other morals; the possibilities can be huge even in small things like mosquitoes. Second, patents and certifications from prestigious bodies matter.

## *Case Study: Aakar Foundation—Women's Right to Sanitary Pads*

A lot remains desired in providing basic health facilities to women. One of the most common health problems they face is related to menstruation. In a conservative society like India, the subject remains a taboo. Even the urban middle-class women are shy of discussing this topic in open. As a result, menstruation-related diseases are not revealed until they become serious. A little awareness can control many of these diseases at an early stage or prevent them altogether.

There is a great need for Indian women to open up on this subject. Their diffidence on menstruation-related discussions has turned into a social malice. This is the reason the lack of sanitary pads for menstruating women remains an unaddressed issue. Although the government has tried to tackle this issue, there is a great opportunity for start-ups as well.

After meeting many entrepreneurs in this field, I deduced that it does not require a huge investment and many young innovators are foraying in this segment. The reticence of the Indian women on this topic remains their biggest challenge.

The Aakar Foundation is trying to break the stereotypes on menstruation among rural women. The Foundation's Deepika Rana, Global Lead-Program and Outreach at The Pad Project, discussed the challenges involved in this task with me. These are:

- Establishing a dialogue with rural women
- Manufacturing a 100 per cent compostable sanitary pad
- Building mini-manufacturing units in villages to manufacture these pads

According to Deepika, the biggest task is to break the taboo around the subject. Most women prefer suffering than discussing their pain in the open. This attitude remains our society's shame. This was one reason that Deepika's venture was constituted as a foundation and not as any other start-up. As Irfan aimed to provide dignity of labour to rickshawalas, similarly, Aakar

Foundation sought to break the myth around menstruation. It rallied women across many villages to run awareness campaigns. However, this was just one aspect. Aakar Foundation also worked to manufacture a compostable sanitary pad. It established small manufacturing units in villages. These units not only created new employment opportunities but also provided cheap and safe sanitary pads to women.

The good thing is that such initiatives get generous government support. Many ministries have funds allocated to help such ventures. These funds are often left unused for the lack of innovations. The incumbent government is encouraging start-ups to increase their social contribution. Since women health remains one of its priorities, any start-up entering this field can get government's good support. I met Aakar Foundation's Deepika Rana during a programme organised by FICCI and Department of Science and Technology (DST). She evoked confidence in many investors.

Any attempt at solving social challenges can run a long race, and thus presents good investment opportunities. Production of hygienic and accessible sanitary pads for poor women comes in the same category. I have met many other innovators who are eyeing the same segment. Aakar Foundation has won many accolades for its work. Deepika says men need to be equally sensitised on menstruation-related issues and her organisation is working in that direction.

## *Case Study: MIRA (Mobile Integrated Resources for Aurat)—A Boon for Pregnant Women*

This is another digital innovation by Hilmi and Subhi Quraishi. Besides India's hinterland, MIRA app has also found its way to the smartphone users in Uganda and Afghanistan. I met MIRA app's founder Subhi Qureshi during my journey with *Innovate India*. This app provides crucial information to pregnant women in a very interesting manner. Just like menstruation, there is a widespread ignorance on pregnancy-related issues in rural India.

The figures related to pregnancy-related deaths in the villages of India tell this story. This makes MIRA a life-saving app.

The first question I asked Subhi Qureshi was how this app will reach the poor Indian rural women. His answer is a lesson of preparedness for budding social entrepreneurs. His start-up monitors the health of pregnant women and newborn babies with the help of health care centres and volunteers.

The app informs these women about the right food, immunisation and other precautions. Lets look at its business model now. Government support is vital to most of these start-ups. ZMQ, the company behind MIRA app, began by introducing its Minimum Viable Product (MVP) to some villages and then connected it with many related government's schemes. The results showed a better implementation of the government's schemes through innovative ideas.

The Accredited Social Health Activists (ASHA) workers are the government's flag bearers in taking care of pregnant women. They are the foot soldiers in imparting information on prenatal care and post-natal measures. Yet, training these ASHA workers in every part of the country is a logistical challenge. This is where MIRA app chipped in and results were encouraging.

The ZMQ's team hit the rural ground to train women in using the app, asking questions and sending data through it. They designed the app as an audio-visual medium for illiterate women's benefit. Success does not easily come for any private venture in India's health sector. The ZMQ is teaching how to do it.

MIRA app started this journey from a village in Haryana and expanded to Odisha. Soon, it found international traction. The results achieved by this app in Haryana's Mewat attracted investors' attention. The Millennium Alliance reposed its faith in MIRA app. Later, the ZMQ received funding from many other agencies and was widely appreciated as a beacon of hope. MIRA app shows how one can make a difference to the rural lives even from a small office in one corner of Delhi. The government has funds and the will power to support such initiatives, but the lack of technology and innovation holds it back. Any start-up willing to fill this gap can avail government's support.

Many entrepreneurs expect funds at the onset of their start-up journey. It is important to remember that you will have to prove the viability of your idea first. It can only happen when you work on the ground. Be it Boond's electricity project or MIRA app, all successful entrepreneurs first prove their idea on the ground. Funds and recognition automatically follows. The secret of MIRA app's success lies in its outreach to the women in India's far-flung areas.

When I met Subhi Qureshi, I was sceptical about any smartphone app's relevance to rural women. This is what I asked him. He said that one will only get superficial answers by looking at any innovation from a usual perspective. His app could reach such women only through a well-trained ground team and some interesting stories and games. Don't forget that the app is only one of the aspects of a start-up. The team that takes it to the people is vital. The way you prepare this team is part of your innovation.

The challenges facing India's women are not restricted to pregnancy or sanitary pads. We still have running health campaigns against diseases like TB and AIDS. The organisations like the ZMQ, with their database and a team of workers, can tap the opportunities hidden in this field.

## *Case Study: DALI—Dyslexia Assessments for Languages of India*

Special-needs children have special capabilities and they could shape the world in a better way. We just have to understand their needs and make them learn new things in the right way. Dali is the first ever kit in India for an early detection of dyslexia. In our country, major issues like dyslexia and autism are not properly addressed or discussed. In fact, assessment and awareness is so poor that people sometimes start considering their child as inferior. On the contrary, such children with special abilities are far more superior in learning a particular skill. The hurdle is how to assess them and understand their abilities. Professor Nandini Chatterjee Singh and her team developed Dali at the National Brain Research Centre, Manesar. They also got support from the Department of Science and Technology, Government of India.

Remember the day-dreamer Ishaan (from the film *Tare Zameen Par*), who just can't seem to get anything right in his boarding school but the art teacher, Ram Shankar Nikumbh, helped the dyslexic student discover his true identity. However, not every child is as lucky as Ishaan.

Dali, the very first indigenous kit of India that screens and identifies kids suffering from reading disabilities, and provides remedial measures for dyslexia in your child through diligent assessment tools, has now been innovated. The tool has been standardised and validated across a large population of 4,840 children from various parts of the country.

I've done some work on these children. As a psychology enthusiast, I found these kids as creative. *Innovate India* programme allowed me to meet Professor Nandini Chatterjee Singh. She told me about the many interesting opportunities that lies in this field. She said, 'We need to change the mindsets of parents and schools that it is nothing to be hidden. It is something for which one has to come forth and take initiative. We first need to brain wire and remove that stigma, and thus this becomes a mass movement!'

## First Know Dyslexia!

Dyslexia is a learning disorder. Dyslexic children face serious difficulties in reading and writing skills, as taught in a classroom. Thus, Dyslexia is a learning disorder and is the single most important reason for school dropout. Anywhere between 5–10 per cent of school-going children across the world today have dyslexia. We believe, the incidence of dyslexia in India to be 15 per cent. According to a survey, there are 228,994,454 students enrolled in recognised schools, which brings our count of dyslexic Indian children to 35 million. We estimate that there are 35–40 million children with or at risk of dyslexia in India.

### Dali's Uniqueness

Until now, no tests or screening measures have been developed and standardised across the regional Indian languages for identifying children who might be dyslexic. To address this gap, National Brain Research Centre (NBRC) developed, validated and standardised a set of screening tools in four regional languages, to be used by school teachers to early identify children suffering from dyslexia and assessment measures to identify reading-related problems among the children. The full set of these screening tools and language assessment batteries has been compiled under the umbrella term 'Dali'.

### Dali in Making

Professor Nandini Chatterjee Singh, born and brought up in Nagpur, after completing her PhD in Physics and returning from the US started working with schools under neuro-imaging projects. There, in 2013, she came to know that many children in India are under the grip of dyslexia. And the worst part is that people associate an unwanted social stigma with the disability instead of understanding that it is just a small discomfort in one's verbal ability that can do wonders if treated in earlier stages.

### Advancements So Far

It was first released by the Hon'ble Minister for Science and Technology and Earth Sciences, Dr Harsh Vardhan on 15 October 2015. The success of Dali depends on dissemination and awareness. Professor Nandini says, 'We hope to use social innovation platforms to make Dali available. They have trained, so far, nearly 500 teachers in Delhi and neighbouring areas to use Dali in Hindi.' Up till now, 250 psychologists have been trained under the Delhi Government's project Smile to use Dali. The robust system now serves as an example for countries across the globe as they seek to duplicate this model to enable accurate dyslexia assessment for children in non-English languages.

## Future Prospects

Dali modules are available in Hindi, Marathi, Kannada and English and development in other languages is in process. By the end of the year, it will be available in Tamil and Telugu too. It has now been registered as a NERD Tool and the UNESCO also recognises it. Serving 500 teachers and around 25,000 students across India, the pioneer screening and remedial organisation is planning to expand their reach to 5,000 teachers, 1,000 psychologists and 1 lakh students at large.

Also, In July 2017, Dali was awarded the Millenium Alliance Award for Innovation by FICCI. Entitled project 'Invisible Visible' under this award, teachers and psychologists will be trained to use Dali, and remediation tools like mobile applications and tablets will be developed to help children with learning.

## Be Patient, Nurture the Passion for Perfection

Dr Nandini says, 'Doing something in the laboratory which can impact society is a success.' She believes that patience and passion are two major constituents of success.

Besides fields like waste management, social security, child education, health, water conservation and supplying safe water to households, a lot of work needs to be done in areas like traffic management, child safety and learning apps like Dali and MIRA.

## THINGS TO REMEMBER

Such examples leave us with the following things to remember:

- Don't just observe social challenges. Study them by working on the ground.
- Monitor the government's schemes. Think of the roles you can play in the fields on which the government is focusing.
- Don't be impatient in garnering funds. It will come after you have showed the solution to a problem. You need to begin with MVP to give a practical shape to your ideas.
- Patent your innovation. Go through the process of registration and certification.
- Test your innovations through prestigious institutions. Try to certify your product's quality and impact through them.
- Think about how you can contribute to providing solutions to the problems you read or see in the media. There is a possibility in every social field in India.
- From mosquitoes to sanitary pads, there is a scope for social entrepreneurship in every field. Focus on areas that have been ignored so far.
- Try to make lives better, bring dignity to them. Be it poor rickshawalas or specially-abled children.
- Collaborate with existing social organisations and experts. There is a need to bring technology to the social work being already done.
- The mere urge to make money will not take you far in social entrepreneurship. It is not only about money but also about the recognition. You are on the right path if it is coming your way.

# 10

# IN THE MIDDLE OF DIFFICULTY, LIES OPPORTUNITY

India is a fertile ground for start-ups as it faces plenty of challenges. The Startup India mission is significant because it is helping meet many of these challenges by encouraging young entrepreneurs to find innovative solutions. I had the chance to meet the team behind this mission several times and understand its functioning. I was positively surprised when the digital team of the mission introduced me to its website. The extensive level of research and hard work behind this website impressed me. A lot of work has gone into ensuring that the website has answers to all the queries.

There are incubation centres for start-ups which may need further help. The core factor for the success of any start-up is the attitude to find problems and seek their innovative solutions. Many youngsters ask me if India is not behind the world in developing a healthy start-up culture. I always say no, as nowhere else can we find as many possibilities for start-ups as in India. Here, start-ups are not just mobile apps but a medium to bring about social change. Our country is witnessing a new wave of start-ups. However, we still face substantial challenges in the social sector and the government needs the active support of start-ups in meeting them.

We have seen in the previous chapters how innovative thinking can seek opportunities even in killing mosquitoes, helping the rural pregnant women or providing cheap electricity to the poor masses. The best segment of the Startup India mission's website is the one which explains social challenges and the role of start-ups in addressing them.

Conservation of natural resources is one such challenge. We could not maximise the use of water and electricity yet. Switching to renewable sources is still a far cry. The *Janshakti4Jalshakti* initiative is addressing this gap and start-ups can play a vital role. The first case study in this book is related to the field of water conservation. We need to motivate other international water conservationist scientists like Dr Shailesh to come up with more such innovations.

You can find detailed information on social challenges and the possibilities they present on Startup India's official website. The portal is continuously updated. Pratham Varshneya introduced me and the audience of my show *Kamyaab Hindustan* to the various facets of this website. I am presenting the part of the it that talks about opportunities for start-ups. We have discussed social entrepreneurship in the previous chapters. Most case studies in this chapter also fall into the same category.

## WATER RESOURCES

- **What is the problem?** According to the reports, the average annual per capita water availability in India fell by 15 per cent between 2001–2011. It's predicted to fall another 13 per cent by 2025 and 15 per cent again by 2050. There's too much demand and not enough supply. India's burgeoning population woes, climate change and ill-managed water distribution system are the main culprits. Agriculture, which as per the estimate, accounts for 80 per cent of India's water consumption is suffering because of the unavailability of water and fickle monsoon.
- **What is the government doing?** The Indian government is taking this issue and has launched multiple initiatives and plans to not only ensure the supply of clean drinking water to everyone but also to better manage India's water supplies. The setting up of the National Water Mission and the launch of the Swajal scheme have been the two major steps taken by the government.

- **What can you do?** Some avenues that can be explored are—building check dams and catchment areas with local communities, developing micro water filtration and water recycle devices, solutions to check water wastage across the country.
- **How will your solutions help?** Innovative and implementable solutions are the need of the hour to stem this potential country-wide water crisis and make sure that India's population gets a good living.

### Concerned Ministries

The concerned ministries include the Ministry of Drinking Water and Sanitation and the Ministry of Water Resources; River Development and Ganga Rejuvenation.

Besides water, we also need to focus on solar power. Water and electricity supplies are essential for irrigation. The government is encouraging the farmers to set up solar-powered pumps. This will not only ease power shortage but also ensure better and timely supply of water to the fields.

Boond is an attempt to improve power supply in the villages. We can replicate innovations helping farmers on a larger scale. Likewise, bio-energy can also be of great use in the rural landscape. It would provide clean cooking fuel while making the people self-reliant. The kind of energy we use is directly related to the state of our environment. We know how the conventional sources of energy have lived their age. This is the reason the start-ups can make it big in clean energy.

The cheap and continuous supply of energy is vital to any country's development. Energy is the engine of development. We need to develop new and eco-friendly sources of energy. The fossil fuels will not last long. The world is heading towards an energy crisis. We need more sources of renewable energy to solve it. Solar energy is one such source, but producing electricity from waste is another door of opportunity for start-ups. It will also help in managing the huge waste from sewage, farming, industries and households. Biomass is an eco-friendly source of energy. Being cost-effective makes it apt for the rural areas. Many start-ups are trying to tap its potential.

Sandeep Joshi of the 'Expert Gyan' start-up has played a part in making Indore the country's cleanest city. His start-up has now expanded to Delhi and Gujarat. He says that there are many opportunities in solid and medical bio-waste management. Even the rising mountain of garbage in Delhi's outskirt area of Ghazipur is a start-up opportunity. The country's capital needs urgent action for managing its waste. Other cities also require new technologies in this field. The budding entrepreneurs can also look for possibilities in the Clean India campaign. This is what the Startup India team has suggested on the mission's website.

## ENERGY CRISIS

- **What is the problem?** India is the third largest energy and oil consumer in the world, after China and the US. Oil and gas occupied 35 per cent share in India's energy consumption. It is estimated that India will overtake China as the largest growth market for energy by late 2020 with the country's energy consumption growing by over 4.2 per cent per annum, the fastest among all the major economies of the world. Given these numbers and the fact that India is also the world's third largest emitter of carbon dioxide and other greenhouse gases; it requires a rapid and effective shift in India's current energy policy and generation methods to prevent a nationwide energy and environmental crisis in the long run.
- **What is the government doing?** The Indian government under Prime Minister Narendra Modi has made universal access to electricity a key part of its energy ambitions. PM Modi has announced that he would seek to add 100 gigawatts of solar power capacity along with increasing renewable-energy capacity to 175 gigawatts by 2022.

- **What can you do?** Some avenues that can be explored are innovative ideas to increase the implementation and efficiency of renewable energy devices such as solar panels, developing affordable solutions such as electric cars and home appliances that can run on renewable energy, and initiatives to increase awareness about the methods to reduce everyone's energy consumption.
- **How will your ideas help?** Solutions to reduce India's dependence on fossil fuels and coal to produce energy will not only have a positive impact on the environment but also reduce India's import bill, which might reduce inflationary pressure on the economy. India has a huge potential for renewable energy and the ability to use this potential will fuel the next phase of India's economic growth.

### Concerned Ministries

The concerned ministries include the Ministry of Coal; Ministry of Power; Ministry of Science and Technology; Ministry of New and Renewable Energy; and the Ministry of Petroleum and Natural Gas.

Apart from the alternative sources of energy, take a look at the scale of problem of food wastage and how it opens new vistas for start-ups.

## PREVENT FOOD WASTE

- **What is the problem?** Food waste or food loss comprises uneaten or discarded food. Indians waste food worth ₹88,800 crore per year, which is equivalent to ₹244 crore being wasted daily. Even after producing more food than it needs, 194 million people go hungry in India every day and as a result, India ranks a disappointing 103 among 119 countries in the Global Hunger Index. This wastage has a knock-on effect on the environment, as the efforts made to produce this food generates greenhouse gases, uses water and can lead to deforestation.

- **What is the government doing?** The Indian government is making efforts to curb the wastage of food by setting up new storage facilities, making distribution more efficient and distributing excess grains.
- **What can you do?** Some avenues that can be explored are—educating the farmers on good storage practices, providing transportation and storage facilities, redistributing leftover food from parties and events, and setting up compost plants
- **How will your ideas help?** Solutions to reduce or remove this problem will solve a multitude of problems for our country including widespread malnutrition, hunger, deforestation and groundwater depletion.

### Concerned Ministries

The concerned ministries include the Ministry of Agriculture and Farmers Welfare; and the Ministry of Food Processing Industries.

We have already discussed solid waste management. This waste is detrimental to health and the environment. Start-ups can play a crucial role in this field. Many young entrepreneurs are trying to walk on Sandeep Joshi's footsteps. However, we have not even scratched the surface yet. New innovators can turn heaps of garbage into gold mines. But you need to show your idea at a smaller scale first. The Startup India team is there to help.

## WASTE MANAGEMENT

- **What is the problem?** India generates 62 million tonnes of waste every year, of which less than 60 per cent is collected and around 15 per cent processed. And we expect India's daily waste generation to reach 377,000 tonnes by 2025. This is a major problem as unprocessed waste or waste dumped in open dumpsites is an environmental hazard and causes public health issues, environmental degradation and resultant climate change.

- **What is the government doing?** The government has launched initiatives to improve waste management in India including the Swachh Bharat Abhiyan and promoting the concept of reduce, reuse and recycle.
- **What can you do?** Some avenues that can be explored are innovative solutions that allow waste to be sorted before being dumped so it can be treated by devices which can generate products from waste such as biogas and recycling plants.
- **How will your ideas help?** Innovative ideas to overcome the problem of inefficient waste management is crucial in a growing economy such as India, because the lack of a proper waste management system is not only harmful to the economy but after a time, it becomes a roadblock in the country's development.

### Concerned Ministries

The concerned ministries include the Ministry of Drinking Water and Sanitation; and the Ministry of Environment, Forest and Climate Change.

The start-ups working on waste management, water management and renewable sources of energy are helping reduce pollution. Tackling pollution can open the following doors for start-ups.

## POLLUTION CONTROL

- **What is the problem?** Rising air pollution is a menace for India, with multiple Indian cities making it to the top 10 most polluted cities in the world list. India is also struggling with the widespread pollution of its water bodies, case in point being the Yamuna River. This is leading to a rapid increase in the number of chronic diseases across the country; the younger demographic being the ones most affected.

- **What is the government doing?** In recent years, the government has taken several steps to fight the rising pollution problem. The National Clean Air Programme has been launched in conjunction with state governments to come up with specific targets along with setting-up of a comprehensive action plan by the Ministry of Environment, Forest and Climate Change.
- **What can you do?** The avenues that can be explored are solutions easing the adoption of electric vehicles, ideas to enhance manufacturing processes and water filtration process.
- **How will your ideas help?** Solutions to tackle the problem of pollution will help combat one of the most pressing problems facing the country along with helping in the increase of the economic output and providing employment opportunities.

### Concerned Ministries

The concerned ministries include the Ministry of Environment, Forest and Climate Change; and the Ministry of Health and Family Welfare.

Indian railways are the country's lifeline that connects the country. The railway reforms are yet another opportunity for start-ups. We have seen many recent efforts. Many start-ups have made efforts at their end. I feel the bigger the problem, the greater the opportunity. The railways already have a huge infrastructure. It is all about its effective management. Following is the information shared on Startup India's website in this field.

### CLEANER RAILWAYS

- What is the problem? The Indian Railways is the fourth largest railway network in the world and carries over

23 million passengers every day. However, it is also rife with problems such as unhygienic platforms and coaches, rodent-infested pantry, and malfunctioning washrooms. This has been a major cause of concern as it makes the journey uncomfortable for the passengers and increases the chances of illness.

- **What is the government doing?** The government has started a plethora of initiatives such as providing On Board Housekeeping Service (OBHS) in 980 trains for cleaning coaches during the run of the trains; on demand 'Clean My Coach' service, where passengers can request for cleaning services through mobile apps; bed linen provided for AC passengers is washed after every single use, while blankets are cleaned every two months.
- **What can you do?** Some avenues that can be explored are web-based solutions to track hygiene standards maintained at platforms, toilets that process human waste, advanced food storage systems to keep rodents and pests in check.
- **How will your ideas help?** Devising methods, technologies, and resources to ensure a cleaner rail network in India will provide an essential solution for the millions of Indians using the railways daily.

## Concerned Ministries

The concerned ministry includes the Ministry of Railways.

We have seen how MIRA and Dali apps are working in the health and education sectors. I have met many educationists during my stint with *Innovate India*. Padma Shree Dr Bimal Roy and Dr Vinod Tibdewala laid a special emphasis on linking our education system to technology. If MIRA app can teach the rural women, then you can imagine the scale of possibilities in other education missions across the country. Therefore, this sector is also mentioned in Startup India's website.

## QUALITY EDUCATION

- **What is the problem?** Quality education and an employable workforce are very critical for a developing country such as India. However, maintaining the standard of education in more than a million schools nationwide, offering training programmes to teachers and keeping a good balance with the education system worldwide, has been a big challenge for the Indian government. This problem is visible from the fact that about 25 per cent of the Indian students in the age group of 14–18 years cannot read basic text in their language and more than half of them face challenges in performing basic arithmetic. This is a dismal state of affair as a quarter of India's population is of school/college going age.
- **What is the government doing?** The Indian government has taken several steps to address this problem. Initiatives like Sarva Shiksha Abhiyan seek to address school infrastructure, teacher quality and training, and filling vacancies; they have increased government budget allocated for quality education three-fold under the Rashtriya Uchhatar Shiksha Abhiyan; and Global Initiative for Academic Network has been launched with the aim to internationalise education and bring renowned professors from global universities to India.
- **What can you do?** Some avenues that can be explored are—social enterprises that focus on bringing more students under the formal education set-up, awarding meritorious students, developing interactive methods of teaching through the internet and mobile and bringing out programmes that explain the concepts in vernacular languages to students for a better understanding.
- **How will your ideas help?** Solutions to educate Indian students will help the most and will also play a key role in driving the economic engine of India. These solutions will play a key role in determining whether India's demographic situation will be an asset or a liability for the country.

## Concerned Ministries

The concerned ministries include the Ministry of Human Resource Development; Ministry of Science and Technology and the Ministry of Youth Affairs and Sports.

We have discussed the impact created by the Dali app. It would be useful to mention one interesting interview in this respect.

Namita Singh is an old friend who works as an HR consultant for big companies in Bengaluru. She is also a software industry expert. I would like to share what she told me about attention deficit hyperactivity disorder (ADHD) and autism. It is not what the world thinks about you, rather how you look at yourself that makes all the difference. People with learning disabilities can also make it big in the start-up sector.

Your start-up can get wonderful results by training them. This is what Namita is doing. I was very impressed by her example.

Research says these people have creative minds as they can think out of box. Namita Singh mentors many autistic adults in various companies. She has an important responsibility of interviewing such adults with ADHD or autism. We need to identify these talents to fulfil the real dream to innovate India. Namita says that these adults are not bored of repetition and that's why are far more efficient than other employees around. Some adults have behavioural issues but those are some extreme cases. Jobs for people with ADHD and autism are plentiful. These disorders are often a sign that such people possess some precious traits. They have natural talents and personality characteristics that many employers seek in potential new hires. What seems like a difficulty during the childhood of an ADHD or autistic adult, may contribute to their future success.

Most of the humanity's greatest achievements have directly resulted from the contributions by people who didn't fit the prevailing idea of what was normal. It is the people considered as different or special—people with special abilities because of their differences—who move the society forward. More and more of today's employers are recognising the truth of this statement. They need these special talents.

## Special Abilities, Innovation and Theory of Creativity

When creative ideas are proposed, they are often viewed as bizarre and useless even though these creative ideas may be both novel and valuable. Why are they rejected? This is because the creative innovator stands up to the vested interests and defies the crowd. The crowd does not maliciously or willfully reject creative notions; rather it does not realise and rarely wants to realise, that the proposed idea represents a valid and superior way of thinking. The crowd perceives opposition to status quo as annoying, offensive and these are reasons enough to ignore innovative ideas. Society and the employer should look for such creative minds, which many of the world's most famous and successful people have already discovered.

## Blessing in Disguise

ADHD may help give an individual powerful traits like creativity and imagination, greater flexibility, compassion, problem-solving abilities, talent for multitasking, greater adaptability and higher energy to fulfil tedious tasks. These abilities may be different for different people but these are some common traits which make ADHD adults more efficient than other people.

American Professor Tempel Grandin wrote about her experiences of being an autistic person. She identified that autistic adults have a creative mind. Their string visual thinking makes them extraordinary in many professional fields. Some are listed by Professor Grandin: computer programming, commercial art, photography, animal trainer, automobile mechanic, computer troubleshooter, web page design, handicrafts of different types such as wood carving, jewelry making, ceramics, etc.

## Let's Stereotype Less, and Embrace Individuality

Tempel Grandin has said that the most interesting people you'll find are the ones that don't fit into your average cardboard box. Perhaps, autistic people are also the ones who are the most creative. When we look further, there are many examples of great autistic artists, musicians, actors, poets and writers. Sometimes, this creativity seems to go hand in hand with the more traditional talents, leading to detailed drawings or the ability to play a concerto after hearing it only once. In research, and in society, we seem to have a tunnel vision when perceiving and interpreting autistic behaviour. The recent findings, together with the many examples of creative autistic people in books, films and on the web, suggest that we need to avoid getting stuck in a particular way of thinking about autism. So let's stereotype less and embrace individuality.

## How Are They More Creative?

A study published in *The Journal of Autism and Developmental Disorders* found a strong link between autism and creativity. People with more autistic traits, when asked to name as many uses as they could for a common object such as a paper clip, came up with fewer suggestions, but the suggestions they offer are more unusual than those of their neurotypical counterparts. They exhibit more divergent thinking. The finding surprises most people because they associate autism with rigid thinking, restricted interests and a literal interpretation of speech and behaviour. How could a person with these traits be creative? To get the right answer we must have a new approach to measure creativity. This is the era of innovation and we should be more innovative to find the creative minds.

## Employers' View of Autistic Employees

Some research has examined the benefits and costs of using adults with autism spectrum disorder (ASD) from the perspective of the employee, taxpayer and society. But only a few studies have considered the employer perspective. These studies examine the benefits and costs of using adults with ASD from the perspective of employers. Fifty-nine employers employing adults with ASD in an open employment were asked to complete an online survey comparing the employees with and without ASD based on job similarity. The findings suggest that employing an adult with ASD provides benefits to employers and their organisations without incurring additional costs. That's the reason why many employers in the IT field and in many creative fields are hiring adults with ADHD and autism. You get innovative thinkers among these adults. In Australia, subsidies are available for employers employing individuals with disability, for financial assistance and for payment of pro rata wages, workplace modifications and services and as a financial incentive for ongoing employment. In India, the government should take initiatives to encourage such creative minds to innovate.

## Need for Awareness in Employers

Autism is a lifelong disorder. While they pay much attention to rising autism rates in children, the number of adults on the autism spectrum is increasing and the nation is not prepared for the special challenges that come with this segment of population.

One area of desperate need is employment. According to some estimates, the unemployment rate for adults in this spectrum is very high. The problem is that many employers don't see the pros in hiring individuals who can be rigid and moody with poor communication skills. We need new approaches that let businesses tap into the potential of these people. According to many, autism advocates and the experience of progressive employers, innovative employment programmes that focus on individuals with special needs can churn out some of the most diligent, dependable and productive employees.

## Social Awareness Is Required

Some studies reveal that autistic and ADHD people have mathematical giftedness. Some people with autism shared that they have an obsession; this obsession can be about trains, programming or a TV-series. The object that they are obsessed about is also the thing they know everything about. Autistic people don't like working with other people, and they are not very social. This means they have more time to focus on what they like. But this also means that they like to have a job where they can work alone. The reason autistic people aren't social is because they can't understand other people, and are therefore bullied a lot. Social awareness is also required for encouraging these innovative and creative minds, but these gifted people are more trained to do things even better than the educated class of people. For example, an autistic person learns driving and he/she is possessed with an ingrown behaviour to follow traffic lights and other rules, no matter what the situation is. It's just one example from umpteen to ponder on the social status of these genius minds among us.

It is not only about these disorders. The country has a large pool of talented specially-abled people. Start-ups can work to help them realise their talent. This is the reason Startup India has included this idea in its list.

## MAKING INDIA A DISABLE-FRIENDLY COUNTRY

- **What is the problem?** India has around 80 million people with disability. According to the World Bank, one in every 12 households in India has a person living with a disability. This means that a significant proportion of India's population is disabled and the persistent issue is that the disabled population are an excluded section of the society. They face several problems in their daily life such as lack of accessibility to most buildings, lack of healthcare services, non-inclusive educational system, and general discrimination and stigmatisation.

- **What is the government doing?** From introducing the Rights of Persons with Disabilities Act in 2016 to address some of the concerns faced by the differently-abled persons in India to the prime minister rolling out Sugamya Bharat Abhiyan in 2015, with a motive to make it convenient for persons with disabilities to access administrative buildings and transport facilities; the Indian government has made efforts to improve on this front.
- **What can you do?** Some avenues that can be explored are design solutions that assist the disabled people in accessing buildings and transport facilities; tech solutions that help in their inclusion in workplaces and society; and general sensitisation initiatives.
- **How will your ideas help?** Solutions and initiatives to uplift the societal status of disabled people and ease their daily life, have a huge potential in India. They will not only help uplift the stigma surrounding the disabled people but also help them become productive members of society and contribute to the economic growth of the country.

## Concerned Ministries

The concerned ministries include the Ministry of Social Justice and Empowerment.

We need a lot of work in sports. We need to think beyond the Olympics and the Commonwealth Games. India has immense potential in sports. We need collective efforts to realise it. Many start-ups are now doing the same, but it is not even a beginning yet. I talked to Dr Piyush Jain on this subject. He is the man behind a significant effort in physical education in this country. We have to cater the need to build up a strong physical education development system. Sports development will be meaningless unless we develop a strong physical education system in India.

## Grassroots-Level Development

First, we need to provide resources at the rural level. In over 60 per cent of schools in the country, playgrounds and trainers are not available. If the country has to move ahead in sports at the world level, then physical education should be implemented at the primary level. At present, there is no shortage of talent across the country. But on the other hand, we do not have adequate trainers to cover these talents though there is no dearth of playing fields.

## Why Only Haryana and Not Other States?

We don't have to find any formula. We already have a good example of Haryana. Haryana government has made sports grounds till its block level. This is the reason Haryana is producing international medal winners and creating Olympians. It's not just about India, even other countries do the same; including leading sports countries like China. Our effort is to create an environment at the grassroots level in the country. Games should not be seen only through the prism of Olympics, Asian Games or medal tally of Commonwealth Games. Sports help in an all-round development of a person.

Dr Piyush points out the reasons for our country's talent not translating into medals in international sports. Start-ups can collaborate with experts like Dr Jain to enter this field. Roping in experts who have the ground experience will propel your journey towards success. I have also benefitted from interacting with start-up mentors in understanding this sector better. The young entrepreneurs should follow the following suggestions if they want to establish a start-up in sports.

## SPORTS IN COUNTRY

- **What is the problem?** World's second-most populous nation has the worst Olympic record in terms of medals per head and several smaller countries with limited talent pools to choose from, outperform India at the Olympics. India cannot produce a steady stream of world-class talent that can bring medals at the world stage. The problem is not a dearth of talent but systematic failures that are responsible for India's historic poor performance at the Olympics; the major ones being lack of proper infrastructure, paucity of funding, politicisation of sports, and the lack of emphasis given to sports culturally.

- **What is the government doing?** The government has started several initiatives to promote sports and sportspersons in India. Khelo India aims to encourage the participation of school students in sports while Target Olympic Podium Scheme assists elite sports professionals capable of bringing Olympic glory for the country.
- **What can you do?** Some avenues that can be explored are technology and scientific expertise to improve the performance of athletes, initiatives to provide talented youngsters with a platform to come in the limelight, and developing means to better meet the nutritional needs of athletes.
- **How will your ideas help?** Sports have the power of bringing a positive transformation in the society. Building a proper infrastructure of sports for children has a huge potential in a country where only a few have won medals. An impressive performance in the Olympics will lead to an increased awareness about sports in our country which will lead to the rapid growth of the sports and nutrition industry in India.

## Concerned Ministries

The concerned ministry includes the Ministry of Youth Affairs and Sports.

Another troublesome area is traffic management and here it applies to discuss my show with a senior IPS officer Meenu Chaudhary, for Doordarshan. She explained the role of technology in making Delhi's traffic safer. There is a lot that start-ups can do in this area. Most of the efficient traffic systems around the world keep direct interaction between the public and the cops at the minimum. This is possible only when monitoring is driven by technology. Start-ups can use CCTV monitoring and related technologies to enter this sector.

## TRAFFIC MANAGEMENT

- **What is the problem?** India has the second-largest road network in the world. The number of cars sold in the country is increasing day by day and so is the congestion and instances of road rage. Traffic congestion in Delhi, Mumbai, Bengaluru, and Kolkata during peak hours cost the Indian economy ₹1.47 lakh crores annually and this number is projected to increase unless relevant measures are undertaken. There is a pressing need to come up with methods and solutions to handle the increasing traffic in India, in the metros, along with improving the discipline and driving conditions prevalent.
- **What is the government doing?** The government has undertaken several initiatives such as constructing 599 highway projects across the country under the Smart Cities Programme, a National Electric Mobility Mission Plan 2020 which proposes to incentivise the adoption of green vehicles, and an AI-based traffic management system being adopted by the Delhi Police.
- **What can you do?** Some avenues that can be explored are developing tech-enabled solutions that can manage the flow of traffic, identify and track traffic violations, and understand the pain points of the current road network.
- **How will your ideas help?** Solutions and ideas to decongest roads and better manage the traffic flow has the potential to not only increase the productivity of the Indian workforce but also save significant economic and social costs for the Indian economy.

## Concerned Ministries

The concerned ministry includes the Ministry of Road Transport and Highways.

I once interviewed Deputy Commissioner of Police (DCP) Anto Alphonse. It surprised many when I asked him about start-ups and innovators. However, Alphonse was forthcoming in explaining how the Delhi police were awaiting start-ups and innovators to help them deliver better service. Echoing Joint Commissioner of Police (CP) Meenu Chaudhary's emphasis on using technology for reducing direct contact between the traffic police and the common people, DCP Alphonse also recommended better use of technology for policing. Using apps for reporting crimes was one such idea. Police are working on many such apps to get timely information about crimes.

We have already known Paras Batra's efforts for women security. This example has shown how good innovations attract investors.

Crime and women security are important issues in India and governments spend a lot of money addressing them. We need better research in this field. You have great chances of success if you can think of some great idea in this respect. Startup India team also emphasises on this.

## CRIME CONTROL

- **What is the problem?** The crime rates in India have been increasing every year. Crimes such as robberies, thefts, molestation, rape and murder have seen the most spike. The time-consuming process of the judiciary and ineffectiveness of the authorities leads to culprits escaping scot-free and people losing trust in the judiciary system of the country.
- **What is the government doing?** Government has introduced initiatives to control crime and fast-track the resolution. Setting up of fast-track courts for rape cases, installing CCTV cameras for better monitoring and harsher punishments

for violent crimes are part of the efforts made by the government.

- **What can you do?** Some avenues that can be explored are devices that can inform friends and family members in case of a threat or crime, ideas that can help in better monitoring of vulnerable areas and solutions to better track and predict probable crimes.
- **How will your ideas help?** The need of the hour is for innovative and technological solutions that focus on preventing crimes from happening. This will not only have a trickle-down effect but also will save a lot of time and effort in the resolution process. It will also help countless innocent people from becoming victims of any crime.

### Concerned Ministries

The concerned ministries include the Ministry of Law and Justice; Ministry of Home Affairs and the Ministry of Social Justice and Empowerment.

## WOMEN SAFETY

- **What is the problem?** Women safety is a big challenge in India. A report by the Thomson Reuters Foundation ranked India as the most dangerous country for women, ahead of war-torn countries like Afghanistan and Syria. In India, there are four rape cases every hour and this trend has not shown a downward trajectory in the last couple of years, making it a pressing issue.
- **What is the government doing?** The Indian government has launched several initiatives to tackle the problem of women's safety in the country and introduce a shift in the general mindset of the people. Initiatives such as One Stop Centre Scheme that provides shelter, police desk, legal, medical and counselling services to victims of violence under one roof and the hostels for working women encourage women

to join formal workforce by providing them with safe accommodations.

- **What can you do?** Some avenues that can be explored are safety measures such as wearables that can inform the authorities or the nearby people in case of an emergency, devices or applications that can identify or track the aggressors and initiatives that sensitise people towards women's safety.
- **How will your ideas help?** There is a pressing need for ideas, solutions and methods that work towards women's safety as this will not only allow the women to live without fear but also help unleash the potential that women have. Also, this will help women when faced with such challenges and help to transform the mindset of people.

### Concerned Ministries

The concerned ministries include the Ministry of Women and Child Development; Ministry of Law and Justice; and the Ministry of Home Affairs.

The agri start-ups have shown a lot of promise. Ruining of crops due to a variety of reasons is the biggest calamity afflicting farmers. A lot can be done for insuring their crops. We have already discussed the examples of DeHaat app and CropIn. The Startup India team also considers crop insurance as a big field of opportunity for the start-ups.

## CROP INSURANCE

- **What is the problem?** In a country like India, where a significant proportion of the population is engaged in agriculture; the adoption of crop insurance is important. However, this is not the case for India as despite having 52 per cent of the gross cropped area rain-fed, agricultural insurance mechanism in India is very weak. This lack of adoption of crop insurance in India and the unpredictable nature of monsoons has led to major issues such as farmer suicides.

- **What is the government doing?** The government has introduced several schemes and measures to help farmers with crop insurance; the most notable being Pradhan Mantri Fasal Bima Yojana. This scheme aims to bring more farmers under crop insurance and help them get back on their feet in case of crop failure.
- **What can you do?** Avenues that can be explored include forming self-help groups or organisations that provide crop insurance to farmers at minimal premiums, initiatives to educate farmers about the benefits of crop insurances and how to find a credible crop insurance company along with tech solutions to improve the agricultural life cycle.
- **How will your ideas help?** Solutions and ideas to bring crop insurance to more farmers will play a pivotal role in making agriculture an attractive sector once again, increasing output and productivity of farmlands and helping stem farmer suicides.

### Concerned Ministries

The concerned ministries include the Ministry of Agriculture and Farmers Welfare; Ministry of Chemicals and Fertilisers; and the Ministry of Finance. Likewise, there is great scope for start-ups in transportation.

This sector has basic infrastructure like the railways. It is all about proper utilisation. This is where start-ups can chip in. This is an unexplored field for young and serious entrepreneurs. You need to develop an attitude of seeing every problem as an opportunity.

## TRANSPORT INFRASTRUCTURE

- **What is the problem?** Even though India has the second largest road network and has the world's largest rail network in terms of passenger traffic, most of it is not well-maintained and leads to sub par utilisation of resources. Poor public transport infrastructure compounds this problem and causes traffic congestion.

- **What is the government doing?** Government has launched new schemes to improve the transport infrastructure in India. Schemes such as Bharatmala Pariyojana aims to optimise the efficiency of freight and passenger movement across the country by bridging critical infrastructure gaps and through the development of new highways.
- **What can you do?** Avenues that can be explored are solutions that make the railways and roadways more efficient and better maintained, making air travel more accessible and implementing global best practices in transport infrastructure.
- **How will your ideas help?** Solutions that improve the transport infrastructure in India at a rapid pace are critical as they will enable India's economic growth to not only continue but even increase.

### Concerned Ministries

The concerned ministries include the Ministry of Railways; Ministry of Road Transport and Highways; Ministry of Civil Aviation and the Ministry of Shipping.

You saw how Orwin's technology of saving cattle from mosquitoes found its market. It also gave international recognition to his start-up. Mosquito menace is a serious issue. They spend a lot of money to deal with it. Other start-ups can also follow suit to help the government in protecting the people from mosquitoes.

### MOSQUITO DISEASES

- **What is the problem?** Vector-borne diseases such as malaria, dengue, Zika virus, swine flu, chikungunya and Nipah are on the rise. Mosquitoes are responsible for around 725,000 human deaths every year and are found everywhere except for Antarctica. This makes them a menace and tough to control.

- **What is the government doing?** The government has undertaken a slew of initiatives to eradicate vector-borne diseases from India including fogging, providing mosquito nets and repellents free of cost, launching awareness programmes and providing vaccinations and medicines.
- **What can you do?** Some avenues that can be explored are developing smart traps, efficient mosquito repellents, biological variations that can reduce the mosquito populations in problematic areas.
- **How will your ideas help?** Vector-borne diseases are responsible for a significant number of deaths every year and have a significant impact on the healthy population of the country; also causing financial loss. We need to find innovative solutions that can tackle this and will be a major step towards reducing the incidence of diseases in India.

## Concerned Ministries

The concerned ministries include the Ministry of Health and Family Welfare; and the Ministry of Drinking Water and Sanitation.

Let's have a quick look (I must recommend you to visit startupindia.gov.in for such priceless information and details) at some of the other problems listed by Startup India as an opportunity for start-ups.

1. **Hygiene:** According to the world bank, 1 in 10 deaths in India occur due to poor sanitation. Top rivers in our country are facing a major pollution crisis. Providing affordable and sustainable sanitation solutions, environment-friendly hygiene products and setting up accessible public restrooms, could be the avenues that can be explored here.
2. **Education and Literacy:** Education in India has always been an important issue. Some avenues that can be explored

are bringing more individuals under the formal education system through the use of internet; improving the quality of education offered by providing affordable innovative education solutions; partnering with world-class universities to understand global best practices; using technology to start schools in remote areas where physical infrastructure is non-existent. Along with this, technology to assist the blind and deaf people read can make a serious change as many people stay illiterate because of some physical or mental disabilities.

3. **Financial Inclusion:** India has 190 million adults without a bank account. And almost half of the bank accounts remained inactive in 2017. Some avenues that can be explored are innovative solutions that can explain the benefits of the formal financial system to people in rural areas in vernacular languages, ideas to incentivise and help individuals get connected to public banks and government schemes.
4. **Skilled Workforce Labour Department:** Just 4.69 per cent of India's workforce is skilled, as against 52 per cent in the US, 75 per cent in Germany and 96 per cent in South Korea. Some avenues that can be explored are providing training and apprenticeship programmes for young graduates which will allow them to gain industry-relevant skills, designing web-based courses that provide people information about the fourth industrial revolution and developing innovative solutions to revamp the current school curriculum.
5. **Insufficient Public Distribution System:** The Public Distribution System (PDS) of India has been criticised for its inefficiencies and its failure to serve the poorer sections of the population. Some avenues that can be explored are innovative ideas to track the disbursal of the food items through PDS, devices to ensure that every unique individual is getting their share of food items, and solutions for a robust grievance process in case the benefits are not reaching their intended beneficiaries.

6. **Epidemic Management:** Over the next decade or two, the Indian disease control establishment will have to fight several new diseases apart from the already problematic Dengue, Chikungunya, Tuberculosis and HIV. Some avenues that can be explored are innovative and affordable solutions to detect the early onset of major diseases, setting up of small hospitals in remote areas of the country, and initiatives to increase awareness and bring more people under the current government schemes.
7. **Superstition:** Superstition is a widespread social problem in India. So much so, that India is known in the world as the land of snake charmers and black magic. Initiatives to educate and make people aware of the ills of superstitions, innovative ideas to change people's beliefs and make the reporting of crimes related to superstition easier, are just some of the avenues that can be explored.
8. **Animal Welfare:** Over 3,500 captive elephants in India live in abysmal conditions. In 2017, over 700 camels were rescued from smugglers who would sell them for illegal slaughter. Some avenues that can be explored are affordable solutions to allow tracking of animals, innovative ideas to predict and test the current state of animal along with checking for diseases and initiatives, and solutions to rescue animals that have been victims of cruelty with provision for safe areas where they can be rehabilitated.

## THINGS TO REMEMBER

- Every social problem is an opportunity for start-ups. Helping people in distress can be a profitable business.
- The government has already started many schemes. Approach them with effective solutions.
- Follow print and TV news to gain a deeper understanding of society's problems.
- Start-ups should have a universal reach, be it cops or farmers.

- Opportunities are awaiting you. The world is waiting for your big idea.
- Only preparation will decide whether or not you can come good on expectations.
- Get the help of experts. Their wisdom drawn from the groundwork will benefit you.
- Every problem has a solution. Think like a scientist and an innovator.
- Hire innovators if the business is all you can do.
- Reach out to the team of Startup India. It can take your idea or work to the relevant ministries.
- Build your minimum viable product. Take it to the relevant departments.

# 11

# TRADITIONAL TRADE IN INDIA

The methods of trade have changed with the changing times. Technology has made things easier and we value a great idea equally as good investment or infrastructure, if not more. The new-age entrepreneurs are pulling significant markets and profits from the traditional businesspersons. While the fundamentals of the business remain the same, technology has changed their means of implementation. The key lies in balancing new technology with the traditional wisdom of doing business.

There are people who started from one taxi to build an empire in the transportation business. They are rich and successful in every right. However, smartphones ensured that those who wanted to follow their footsteps did not need to follow the same model. All they required was to act as a bridge between the service providers and customers. Technology is that bridge, be it hiring taxis or buying fruits and vegetables.

We have discussed how technology has the potential to transform the informal sector. This chapter deals with mixing technology with the traditional methods of business. Let us begin with a true story that explains why people think of business as a cumbersome task.

This is the story of a child who lost his father at the age of 12. His mother also departed for heavenly abode just three days after the tragedy. The boy was the eldest of three brothers. The one after him was just six-years-old, while the youngest one had still not left the cradle. The boy's challenges had just begun.

His relatives bartered household belongings for food and shelter for a few days. Soon, the boy left the youngest brother at one of his relative's place and moved to a big city. He began washing utensils at a tea shop for livelihood.

Adversities make people learn fast. The safety net around us keeps us weak. The boy learnt the business of selling tea within a year. He somehow arranged for a stove and necessary things to prepare tea. A time came when the boy was now running his own kiosk. Although it wasn't so quick. Later, the boy rose to the league of the most successful businesspersons of Bhopal. After his accomplishments, he turned to the devotion of Goddess Durga. A temple built by him still attracts many devotees.

The world knew this man as Pandit Shravan Awasthi. His education qualifications were barely restricted to writing his name.

His progeny continued the family business but they were also looking at new avenues. The next generation did not have to go through the same struggle. They always had other options. The experience is very close to me as the man was my maternal grandfather. He has always been an inspiration. His story shows that favorable circumstances may not always lead to favorable results.

The story also has the following lessons to improve how budding entrepreneurs should think.

1. Struggle is necessary to learn any business.
2. Learn to take responsibility.
3. Never shy away from jobs that improve your skills.
4. You can learn business under any circumstances.
5. It takes time and patience to learn.
6. Practical knowledge is more valuable than books.
7. You need not be rich to start a business.
8. Start from small investments.
9. To expand, understand the market.
10. Make new relations. Be honest with them.

The last principle was inviolable for my grandfather. Value addition and a good reputation are pivots of the present trend in business schools. People like my grandfather learn it from their lives. They know it is the mantra for success. Values and principles were far more important in traditional trade. They are relevant today. Chanakya is one of the most prominent intellectual luminaries of our past. I like him the most for these following reasons:

1. Give respect to vanity, do what a fool needs and tell the truth to the wise. This will make your business flourish.
2. Every friendship has some vested interest. Beware while making friends.
3. Happy shall be the one who does not shy away from seeking knowledge, doing hard work and dealing in money.

India's trade was premised on many such principles. Your behaviour will follow Chanakya's mantras. The secret of success often lies in small things of life. Reacting to a person's ego is slipping to his level. Many intellectuals have delved into human behaviour. There are two fools if you are debating with a fool. The Indian way of doing business focuses more on trade character. Your attachment to your buyers and their perceptions are assets of value.

Chanakya's second lesson emphasises on learning to recognise people. A business leader often needs to take hard decisions which may touch some people's raw nerve. Personal relations should never come in the way of trade. You must figure out your prospective friend's interests. A good team lives one dream. This happens only when interests are also shared.

Not everybody understands profit or money. This could be because of their background. We must never hesitate in the matters of money. Many young entrepreneurs deem money as the sole remuneration. You need to learn to deal with currency, whether you do it in classrooms or in the professional world. Time does not teach everything. Never rush into becoming a boss.

A leader must be first among equals. It is your start-up, and therefore, have no qualms in any task for its progress. Many young minds fall for the romanticism of leaving jobs or becoming their own bosses. These are superficial to my mind. You can free yourself from the job, but remain a worker for your own company.

## INDIA'S BUSINESS TRADITION AND ITS SHORTCOMINGS

You must know the place and its traditions before making it your base. We only look towards the West for knowledge. Our own past has a lot to offer. Our culture has honoured personalities and capabilities. India has been a country with caste system. This system was based on different skills. Each person is valuable and ordained with different skills. Some learn by reading, others from talks or viewing. Some love business more, while others love studying. Some like physical labour and some let their brains run more.

This subject calls for a different book. However, we will restrict ourselves to what a new entrepreneur needs. Recognise your personality and develop yourself. You are hungry for success if this book is in your hands. Reading this book means that you want to know the secret of success. This is enough to prove that you have it in you to realise your dreams.

Success has obstacles in India. Some facets of our traditional trade can also be hard to deal with. Same old methods persist even in this start-up era. We expect 'Digital' India to make things better. Indian entrepreneurs should keep the following things in mind:

1. Relations are above business and product.
2. Rank and recognition matter a lot.
3. Focus more on getting work than developing infrastructure.
4. There are challenges posed by government and bureaucracy.
5. Always value time.

### Relations Are above Business and Product

Considering India's diversity, it is difficult to generalise a standard behaviour which applies to all situations. Indian society is still knit in relationships. You should take time to develop contacts and relations as an entrepreneur. It is by meeting people or branding yourself in a way that connects you to them. You also need to take factors like caste, religion and region into consideration in India. They can benefit or harm your business. The people you are liaisoning with to reach different departments also matter. Sometimes, good relations are even more important than a good product. Mere public relations will not suffice in India. You will need to develop personal contacts at all levels. Don't rely on your team for this.

## Rank and Recognition Matter a Lot

Most companies in India follow a hierarchical system of governance. This means taking orders and transacting money can be a time-consuming process in India. Most decisions in Indian companies are taken at the top level. Therefore, no decision is likely to be passed without approval at the level of directors or owners. All the tasks, including physical labour, are well defined. Indian business honchos rarely engage in low-level tasks. They share very formal relations with their subordinates. Therefore, it is necessary to find out who you are dealing with.

## Focus More on Getting Work than Developing Infrastructure

Lack of infrastructure and insufficient supply chain management are impediments for foreign investments. It is easier to find work in India than to get a suitable infrastructure for it. Therefore, it is necessary to prepare beforehand while dealing with government orders. You can take the help of people who already have good infrastructure. You cannot escape paperwork and need to have a backup plan while doing business in India. This applies even if you are helping somebody to get work. Remember the old Indian dictum, 'One should not live beyond one's means.'

## There Are Challenges Posed by Government and Bureaucracy

Red-tapism and the resultant delays can be a big obstacle in doing business in India. It will test your patience. Payments can get delayed and you have to visit government offices several times. Your contacts will come in handy at these times. Though even government officials are often transferred resulting in further hassles.

## Always Value Time

Time management is still a premium quality in Indian work culture. Delays are normal. Though the times are changing fast but things like postponement of meetings on short notice are not surprising. You need to be tough to meet these challenges. It is not a turf for the short-tempered ones.

Many big business owners are not formally trained. They may be difficult to interact with. They have risen by building an ecosystem of their own and you can learn a lot from them. Let us now look at some social segments of the society traditionally known to be engaged in trade. These are known as 'Vaishyas' in the Hindu caste system. Some of their attributes are:

- Hard-working
- Good in keeping accounts
- Sweet talkers, good in developing relations
- Good understanding of profit and loss
- Acting as a bridge between the people's needs and market

These are necessary attributes to become successful in business. There are several castes like Lalas and Baniyas who have engaged in trade. In terms of region, India's prominent business groups are:

1. Gujaratis
2. Marwaris
3. Sindhis

## GUJARATIS

A famous Gujarati quotation says that you need not paint a peahen's egg! This means that a peacock's wings are beautiful by birth and need no cosmetics. The same applies to the Gujarati community for business skills. They have it in their blood. Most Gujaratis are confident in tradecraft. They not only fend for themselves but also create employment for others. This is the reason Gujaratis have made a name for themselves all around the world. They have no trade secret but they do not judge any business by their scale. A Gujarati businessperson is ever-learning and will go to any length for profit. Not that there has never been an unsuccessful Gujarati businessperson. But their rate of success is high because they have so many role models around them to follow. A conducive atmosphere for business helps them. Most Gujaratis prefer not to take up jobs. They are more inclined towards their own business. This is one reason why Gujarat fares among the Indian states for income generation. The state can be a model for rest of the country. Gujarat proves that there is no lack of business opportunities in India. All you need to do is seek. Some traits of a Gujarati businessperson are as below:

1. **Beginning early:** Gujaratis learns business since his/her childhood by observing people around them. Therefore, starting a new venture comes to them easily. The good thing about start-ups is that they do not need heavy capital. Their entire ecosystem is different. All start-ups should also learn from their surroundings when they are new entrants.
2. **Investing only for profit:** Money should only be spent to beget money. A Gujarati can assess profit beforehand. This comes from experience. New entrepreneurs can take help of market research. Business means profit to a Gujarati and profit is business for him or her.
3. **Prioritising self-reliance:** Gujaratis hate working for others. They aim to become their own boss. You are responsible for

work that is yours and you get opportunities to grow. Start-ups also begin with the same philosophy.

4. **No job or person is small:** Most Gujaratis relish equality. They do not view any job or person as small. To them business is profit, be it gold or junk. A Gujarati businessperson will respect all workers and attach importance to their work. They realise that respecting subordinates only enhances productivity. This is something all start-ups should emulate.
5. **Networking and strengthening your options:** Gujaratis are very good at developing contacts. They know any relation, big or small, can be useful. Maintaining contacts is vital for any business. You must always have options related to your work. Gujaratis never put all their eggs in one basket. Strong networking helps them.

## MARWARIS

The Marwari culture has a great pool of proverbs. One such adage says, 'Only money is master, all else disciples.' This implies the Marwaris grow up with the importance of money imbibed into their minds. Another proverb goes like, 'Even a utensil worth a dime should be thoroughly checked before buying.' It reinforces the value of money among the Marwaris. This also means that they attach great importance to even small jobs.

Large joint families are still common in Rajasthan and Gujarat. Their expenses can only be met if the family works together. This means a team is already there. Marwaris can follow their money wisdom in the toughest of situations. The modern method of enticing customers by throwing big money goes against the traditional wisdom of investing only in profit. Meeting with Marwari businesspersons will give you an impression of their image of being customer friendly. It is not fake. They are patient and sweet in their behaviour. They learn business and money management from an early age.

Both Gujaratis and Marwaris love their freedom. They are well aware about the market risks and also the needs of their customers. Early conditioning makes them more capable of taking risks. It is only when you jump into the water that you will learn to swim, no matter how many books you have read about it.

The Marwaris learn to take market risks early just as children of fishermen do not take long to venture out to the sea. They have a good sense of humour and are positive thinkers. They understand the psychology of buyers better than the others. The Marwaris are ever ready to embrace change. They find subordination difficult. This race is leading India's business fraternity since ages. Therefore, they have a good network all across the country. Their new generation has the luxury to learn from their elders. Some of the best traits of the Marwaris are:

1. **Encouraging entrepreneurship:** Most Indian parents are apprehensive of their children taking up business as a profession. The general fear of the uncertainty of the market still prevails. They think business is only for those who have some related background. They do not realise that anybody can learn business as it is no more restricted to traditional methods. Many Marwaris have the potential to turn their brands into a global entity. You can reach them on the internet. They all have one thing in common; business was the only career choice available to them and their families never discouraged them.
2. **Capability to take risks:** This is a field governed by competition and it is not always possible to satisfy customers. Entering a market with weak preparation can have serious consequences. Those with no family background in business lose their hearts early. Whereas Marwaris have the knack of taking small steps forward. They are not afraid of risks and are always looking for profit. The more risk you take, the better the profit you are likely to make.

3. **Habit of expansion:** There's a dictum stating, 'A Marwari can reach a place where not even a bullock cart can.' They are not averse to migration because they are ready to take risks. New beginnings don't scare them. Marwaris know that customers and products have no caste or identity. They are confident that their skills will not fail them in any part of the world. Start-ups can learn the art of scaling up their business from Marwaris.
4. **Hard work:** I have visited Maharashtra's Marwari-dominated areas. The weather can test your limits, both in winters and summers. But these hardships only make the Marwaris stronger. The relation between personality traits and the climatic conditions merits scientific study. The climate is challenging in many parts of Gujarat and Rajasthan. This is the reason you will not find lazy people here. This holds for the desert areas of Rajasthan. You can see the industrious spirit in most Marwaris. Their minds are not programmed for a mere nine to five job.
5. **Social amiability:** Marwaris value social acceptability. They mix up in any society as sugar does in milk. They can gain acceptance in any kind of social set-up. Marwaris are seldom seen as outsiders anywhere. Their cultural roots and amiability play a role in this.
6. **Serving society:** The Marwaris have strong community bonds. They stand by their own despite his or her social or economic status. They are benevolent in helping their youth by giving scholarships and jobs. There are many Marwari social welfare organisations. Marwaris' sense of duty is not restricted to their community. You can see charity hospitals, colleges and scholarships sponsored by Marwaris in many other parts of the country. Many famous religious places have shelters and other facilities built by Marwaris. This strengthens their social ties. Social perception is an important aspect of business ecosystem. All entrepreneurs must learn to fulfil their social responsibility from Marwaris.

## SINDHIS

The proportional contribution of Sindhis in India is extraordinary. Many businesspersons from the community feature among the world's richest people. They are related to their community. I have seen Sindhis from close quarters during my formative years in Indore and Bhopal. Hirdaram Nagar near Bhopal houses many Sindhis till date. Known earlier as Bairagarh, the locality has emerged as a major trade centre. Most members of the Sindhi community are traders by family background.

Sindhis are historically known to be committed, hardworking and disciplined. They are known to be a trading class. They have attained success in several fields after migrating from Pakistan in 1947 and have the tenacity to rise from the ashes. Sindhis respect their past and traditions. Therefore, you will find many proverbs defining their wisdom of trade. Faith in the wisdom of these proverbs and devotion to God counts much higher to them than business. Nothing happens without God's wish and whatever God does is for good, is their central philosophy. This premise keeps the Sindhis positive under all circumstances. Sindhis preach understanding a mission before taking it up. They urge to take a path that does not come in the way of others' happiness. They have a marvellous saying, 'Let us act in such a manner that we find the sought for gem and we continue to keep the friendship.'

This proves the Sindhi viewpoint for human values. Having faced many hardships, they know how to establish themselves anywhere. They have the art of attaining after losing everything. Below are some essential Sindhi traits that make them special.

1. **Self-reliance:** Sindhis hate dependence on others. Government jobs are not the first preference of their younger lot. They grow up in a business-related atmosphere like Marwaris and Gujaratis. This gives rise to entrepreneurial aspirations in them. They learn business along with their studies. Only such type of an early atmosphere paves the way for self-reliance.

2. **The capability to realise the importance of customers:** Customer is God; this is a cliché in the Indian market. However, few can match Sindhis in remaining connected to their customers. Any normal Sindhi businessperson will tell you that the bulk of his or her customers are decades-old. Valuing customers and catering to their needs is part of the trade culture of Sindhis. Good service and behaviour are necessary to keep customers, and Sindhis know it well.
3. **The right mindset for money:** Many people view Sindhis as penurious. However, most of them are devoid of any understanding of the importance of money. Sindhis know how to earn and invest money. They seldom face bankruptcy because they are not dependent on one trade. Sindhis are wise in their expenditure. They eat and wear what is necessary and not splurge money. Less spending means more profit. Even the richest of Sindhis follow this philosophy. Most people from working-class make expenditure plans before they have earned. Sindhis are different because they view extra money as a new business opportunity.
4. **Working at less profit margin for the big turnover:** Sell products and make money; this is the common thinking about business. However, entrepreneurs of today's era also aim at hidden profits. Sindhis were always good at recognising and tapping these benefits. They prefer big turnover with low margin. Their real success lies in the size of their market and consumer base. Small margins can mean big profit in a huge market. Sindhis are not averse to risks. They believe not in building shops, but markets. They have a reputation for the quality of their services and the prices they offer.
5. **Never say die attitude:** No work is small for Sindhis. They are hardworking, and thus can find dignity in any job. You can see them cleaning their shops themselves. They are never the prisoners of public perception. This small quality can make a big difference. Ego and show-off are signs of fools. Simplicity coupled with practicality is the best approach to

business of any size. I have seen Sindhi traders weighing their words. The community had to face great hardships during partition. Yet, it rebuilt itself. Their simplicity and approach to business is their biggest strength. They have an eye for the right opportunity and they are fearless because they never say die.

## COMMON QUALITIES OF GUJARATIS, MARWARIS AND SINDHIS

All business communities have some things in common. But in a diverse country like India, all of them are unique in their own way. These three communities are distinct, yet they emphasise on similar business practices. Everybody can learn from these practices.

1. **To begin early:** This may not be possible for people without a business family background. Consider the time you start as your childhood. Devote time for learning. Dedication can make anything possible. Learn the art of profit-making along with studies, if you are a college-going student. Take small steps. They teach you valuable lessons.
2. **The right mindset for money:** You can call them miserly or greedy, but these communities value money. Some people enjoy saving and making money as others do with spending. Adopting the right attitude for money will make you emphasise on the right use of money. You can implement new ideas only if you have saved money. All these communities are passionate about saving money.
3. **Smooth behaviour and the art of building a consumer base:** The art of communication is integral to any successful business venture. How well can you express yourself? How successful are you in winning the trust of your customers? You can find answers to such questions in the business practices of these communities. We can develop the art of communication, whatever be your financial or educational background. Listening to consumers is the key.

## DIFFERENCE BETWEEN TRADITIONAL BUSINESS AND DIGITAL INDIA

We have tried to understand India's traditional methods of business by discussing some of the most successful Indian trading communities. The business has changed with times. Attaining success need not be a decades-long process in today's time. We have examples who made it big in no time and that too at an early age. Product, medium and customers remain the same, whether you are selling online, in a supermarket or in some grocery shop. The difference is only in the scale and technology.

Those who can match their feet with time can produce great results. Businesses that are wedding modern technology to traditional means of trade are making it the most in today's world. Any business has two important aspects; practical and technological.

The practical aspects comprise your conversational and networking skills along with your attitude for money. The technological aspects include innovations and new methods of reaching out to your customers. The budding start-ups must think about the differences in traditional and online models of business. This is not to rank one model over another. Some products and services may demand either of these two models, there might be businesses which are done best by fusing both. Technology has made business easier in the following ways:

1. Reduction in incurring the cost of establishing a business
2. More effective opportunities for marketing
3. The need to win consumer trust
4. More reachability to the customers in less time

### Reduction in Incurring the Cost of Establishing a Business

Most traditional businesses worked in a complicated manner. New entrants found it hard to understand their working. They were handed over as legacy to family heirs. These heirs learnt business at an early age. Aspiring entrepreneurs from nonbusiness backgrounds did not have a level-playing field. We have discussed the changing trends of business in the Chapter 'Organising the Unorganised Sector'.

Modern businesses do not require a huge real estate and other infrastructure. Not much investment is necessary for online businesses. Unlike traditional businesses, modern online trade saves you from expenses like property rent, huge salary bills and procurement from the wholesale market. Companies like Amazon and Flipkart are using affiliate marketing to reduce expenses in keeping stocks. This reduces the need for inventory and decreases overhead cost.

The mere idea of making shopping easy for people can make you the owner of ventures like Bigbasket and Grofers. These models also need many qualities required in traditional trade like understanding the market. You must not forget that traditional businesspersons still rule the roost in the market. Technology is giving you an opportunity to act as a bridge between them and their customers. You are heading for a low-cost successful venture if you are thinking of benefiting them and their consumers.

## More Effective Opportunities for Marketing

Online businesses have great reach and they have a larger budget for digital marketing as compared to traditional businesses. Traditional businesses make strategies for local regions. They choose specific areas for online marketing.

Online businesses need to pay more attention to internet platforms like blogs, search engines, social media, etc. For example, Facebook page is a significant feature for business marketing. The digital world entrepreneurs have greater opportunities for marketing than their traditional counterparts. Yet, they can learn how to invest in marketing from the latter. The best marketing is one which does not sound like one.

India has many world-renowned outlets. Branding is at the core of its success. This branding is based on credibility. A customer remembers your brand if he or she is satisfied with the product and delivery. No amount of marketing will work if you lack this traditional attribute of credibility. Marketing means making an identity of your brand to attract customers. Traditional businesses use print and local communication mediums while start-ups rely more on digital mediums for this marketing.

### The Need to Win Consumer Trust

Traditional businesses focus their strategy and energy more on winning the customers' trust. They never like to turn them away. Your branding should be such that customers can believe you even with blind eyes. They must know that you will be able to deliver a good quality product. Traditional businesses have an edge in this respect as they give their customers a chance to examine the product before buying it.

Online entrepreneurs are also working hard to win the trust of their buyers. This is more necessary in a country like India where videos showing poor quality of online goods, edibles, often become viral. The quality of the product along with delivery will determine your success in the online market. Try to ensure good quality of service even if the margin is less. Remember, consumers' trust is your biggest asset.

### More Reachability to the Customers in Less Time

Online platforms are always open; consumers only need to spend a few minutes to buy. Whereas you will need to go shopping, see the product, even stand in queues and bargain to buy from traditional outlets. You must have seen people queuing even to pay bills in supermarkets. This gives the advantage of time to online businesses.

The motive was to draw the buyer to the shop in traditional business. In online business, start-ups need to win customer loyalty. This is where marketing and branding are important. Many online ventures are ruling the customers' hearts by providing products at their doorsteps. They are likely to remain relevant. No wonder that most start-ups begin with apps these days. They know if there can be shops selling the same products in the market, there can also be many apps providing similar products. The online media has large space but you must learn survival from traditionals like Marwaris, Gujaratis and Sindhis.

## THINGS TO REMEMBER

- The background does not count. You can begin even in the worst of circumstances.
- Traditional businesspersons can rise from the ashes because they are smart.
- Traditional knowledge and its implementation are beneficial.
- There is no guilt in being rich. Profit is good. You need not be shy about money.
- Serve customers' interests. Their convenience and trust are your biggest strength.
- Be your own boss before dreaming to become of others. Work as an employee.
- Learn about the system's weaknesses to succeed.
- Be patient. A good businessperson should have a cool head.
- He or she is soft-spoken and composed in any situation.
- Networking and strong relations are key to entrepreneurial success in India.
- Mating traditional business practices with modern technology is also the secret to success.

# 12

# AN ERA OF START-UP REVOLUTION IN INDIA

**'I see startups, technology and innovation as exciting and effective instruments for India's transformation.'**

– Shri Narendra Modi, Prime Minister of India

## *Case Study—Team Startup India and GeM*

India's young generation has read about the green and white revolutions only in textbooks. The power of the youth is strengthened through participation in such monumental economic transformations. The start-up revolution is one such chance for the present generation. This is just the beginning and we can already see some great results. All revolutionary initiatives improve gradually. There can be consequences which are difficult to anticipate. The initial success of the Startup India programme is the MVP of this scheme.

I participated in PM Modi's video conference on Startup India. This was a good lesson in understanding how to bring together young entrepreneurs from across the country. The video conference had a few representatives. Yet, it encouraged millions more. PM Modi has started many schemes like the Startup India, Government e-Marketplace (GeM), Invest India, Make in India and Skill India to support these young minds. It is a revolution because it is awakening new confidence among our youth. The increasing number of start-ups show an increasing number of people willing to innovate.

Organising the unorganised sector and developing social entrepreneurship is paramount. A lot still needs to be done in these fields. However, the country is moving in the right direction.

I am presenting below some excerpts of the action plan of Startup India. Let us first understand the motive behind the initiative.

Startup India is a flagship initiative of the Government of India, intended to build a strong ecosystem for nurturing innovation and start-ups in the country that will drive sustainable economic growth and generate large-scale employment opportunities. The government, through this initiative, aims to empower start-ups to grow through innovation and design. To meet the objectives of the initiative, the Government of India is announcing this action plan that addresses all aspects of the start-up ecosystem. With this action plan the government hopes to speed up the start-up movement.

- From digital/technology sector to an array of sectors including agriculture, manufacturing, social sector, healthcare, education, etc.; and
- From existing tier-1 cities to tier-2 and tier-3 cities, including semi-urban and rural areas.

The action plan is divided across the following areas:

- Simplification and handholding
- Funding support and incentives
- Industry-academia partnership and incubation

Some of the questions written on the Startup India Mission action plan, which one needs to answer are:

- What if your idea is not just an idea?
- What if it sees light?
- What if its born?
- What if you can get someone to believe in it?
- What if you can get someone to help you nurture it?
- What if you can set a clear path for it?
- What if it can travel?
- What if it grows and blooms?

- What if the entire world embraces it?
- What if your idea is not just an idea?

These poetic questions represent the dilemma of the young entrepreneurs. The business domain used to be dominated by a chosen few. These were clans where the upcoming generations were trained at an early age. This is a revolutionary time for small entrepreneurs as they can think of starting their business without legacy. This is not only a question of self-employment but also solving the country's problems. Many innovators and start-ups are doing the same.

Make in India is yet another milestone in the journey of start-ups in India. All these schemes are inter-connected. Businesses from all across the world are being invited to manufacture in India. The idea is to turn India into a manufacturing hub. It cannot happen without developing an indigenous talent pool that can run these manufacturing units. Investments can come from abroad but we cannot import infrastructure and skilled labour. Therefore, the Skill India programme can support Make in India.

PM Modi wants the young entrepreneurs to create a favourable business atmosphere in the country. Startup India is helping achieve this goal by attracting direct investment. As I have stated earlier, these are just the initial successes. These are still early days to assess the success of the scheme. But, it is safe to assume that we will witness a rise in the level of investment and start-ups.

PM Modi has also assured that Make in India will be a good experience for global investors. He is keen to improve infrastructure to fuel this process. Besides start-up initiatives, schemes like Smart Cities Mission are paving the way. This revolution is bearing fruits. India is marching ahead in labour and technology. India has always been a labour-intensive market. Now start-ups are taking this strength to a new level with the help of technology. Social entrepreneurship and technology in the unorganised sector is opening new vistas. We will soon see a new picture if these attempts remain consistent and the administration keeps supporting in the same way. Even those who could not understand the significance of the Digital India programme, can recognise the ongoing transformation if they see it in the light of schemes like the Startup India, Make in India and Skill India.

I am impressed with the pace of these changes in our economy, and therefore mentioning these positive aspects. Every change brings its challenges. It would be wrong to argue that there is no scope for improvement in implementing all these schemes. It will take some time. However, we are witnessing a new mindset in the country. Old habits die hard, be it individuals or a country. These habits decide our destiny. India has tried to become self-reliant ever since independence. But, many lacunae remain in the system, including the administration. Therefore, we find promises of efficient administration from the top leadership so enticing.

Keeping this in mind, PM Modi has called upon talent from other fields into administration. Even the Startup India team comprises such individuals. This team has contributed a lot to this book. I dedicated many of my shows to the functioning of this team.

## TEAM STARTUP INDIA

Launched by PM Modi on 16 January 2016, the Startup India scheme encourages small and big enterprises by providing loans, guidance and other help. The scheme aims at promoting entrepreneurship to increase employment opportunities in the country. The team behind the mission is impressive.

Dr Preetdeep Singh is the co-lead of team Startup India. He believes that this programme has ushered in a change in the mindset of the Indian public. It is bringing investors and startups together under one platform, and thus saving their time and energy. According to him, it is easier to shape entrepreneurial skills among the youth if universities and incubation agencies are brought together.

Training agencies and non-governmental organisations can expand their operations by becoming part of start-ups. Start-ups were always meant to be the focal points which can attract budding entrepreneurs. The government's efforts to increase the ease of doing business has made registration of start-ups easy.

Dr Singh claims that it is now possible to complete the process of registration of start-ups in just 20 minutes. The applicants only need to give company incorporation certificates or documents related to partnership. There is no need to submit investor or incubator-related details. The application requires information on product, innovation and the purpose of the start-up. You can connect with the Startup India team in 48 hours after completing your application. Dr Singh informs that entrepreneurs can avail learning models, Amazon clouds, call centre credits and 42 applications including related to HR management, GST and customer lead. All this is free of any charge. These facilities reduce the initial investment.

Explaining the functioning of the Startup India, its manager Palak Bhatia says that the 22-member team of Startup India mission works like a start-up. It solves problems reported by the start-ups through e-mails or in person, introduces new entrants to the corportate world and enables start-ups to work. The team helps any start-up that needs guidance on issues such as GST, license and tax laws. Startup India aims at providing answers to such queries in less than an hour. The centre and state governments plan new policies like regulation of drones and e-pharmacies for start-ups. The state governments also encourage start-ups and follow policies on new incubators, achievements and start-up teams, etc. This helps to improve the start-up environment.

According to Nishant Malhotra, the assistant manager of the Startup India, 20,000 start-ups have registered themselves with the initiative. Out of these, 2,500 are collaborating with the government departments and doing a business of around ₹400 crore. New start-ups need a market. Associating with the government departments help in taking on existing brands. Many departments like the Airport Authority of India, CRPF, BSF and the Defence ministry are welcoming more and more innovations. Nishant recounts many successful start-ups in fields such as ambulance service, education, air purification, waste management, plastic recycling, etc.

The Startup India website is an important link between the country's start-ups. It also makes the registration process easy. Its Senior Manager Pratham Varshneya explains that applicants need to give their e-mail Id and mention the area of their operations. This connects you to the start-up hub and the map. You can then access information about start-ups, mentors and investors in your region. Startup India also encourages innovation hunt. It involves identifying and felicitating new entrepreneurs. All these facilities link start-ups to new markets. Dr Pratham cites the example of innovation hunt by the Agriculture ministry. Out of 1,400 Indian agri start-ups, 1,100 took part in it.

Please visit Startup India's website if you are planning a start-up in India. I would recommend an extensive study of the websites related to other such schemes. I know many ventures which are trying hard but are oblivious of the benefits provided under the Startup India mission. I am sharing with you one such handy information on Startup India's action plan on tax exemption. Many young entrepreneurs got connected with the schemes after I apprised them.

## TAX EXEMPTION ON CAPITAL GAINS

- **Aim:** To promote the growth of start-ups and address working capital requirements.
- **Details:** Innovation is the essence of every start-up. Young minds kindle new ideas every day to think beyond conventional strategies of the existing corporate world.

During the initial years, budding entrepreneurs struggled to test the feasibility of their business idea. Significant capital investment is made in embracing ever-changing technology, fighting rising competition and navigating through the unique challenges arising from their venture. Also, there are limited alternative sources of finance available to small and growing entrepreneurs, leading to constrained cash funds.

With a view to stimulate the development of start-ups in India and provide them with a competitive platform, it is imperative that the profits of start-up initiatives are exempted from income tax for three years. This fiscal exemption shall facilitate the growth of business and meet the working capital requirements during the initial years of operations. The exemption shall be subject to non-distribution of dividend by the start-up.

## TAX EXEMPTION TO START-UPS FOR THREE YEARS

- **Aim:** To encourage seed-capital investment in start-ups.
- **Details:** Under The Income Tax Act, 1961, where a start-up (company) receives any consideration for issue of shares which exceeds the Fair Market Value (FMV) of such shares, such excess consideration is taxable in the hands of the recipient as Income from Other Sources. In Start-ups, where the idea is at a conceptualisation or development stage, it is often difficult to determine the FMV of such shares. In majority of the cases, FMV is also lower than the value at which the capital investment is made. This results in the tax being levied under section 56(2) (viib). Investment by venture capital funds in start-ups is exempted from operations of this provision. They shall extend the same to investment made by incubators in the start-ups.

Let us now discuss the most important part of the action plan. Understanding the world of business is vital for any innovation. It is a world full of creative and industrious people who will give a tough competition. Imagine a situation where you have worked hard on innovation only to find that it is already in the market. You can only test the strength of your product in the real world of the market. It is not only about remaining connected to the consumers but also with the other start-ups. Collaboration between two start-ups has worked wonders most of the times. It can solve many problems. Many festivals and interactions are organised by the Startup India. Here's how they have been mentioned in the action plan.

## ORGANISING START-UP FESTS FOR SHOWCASING INNOVATION AND PROVIDING A COLLABORATION PLATFORM

- **Aim:** To galvanise the start-up ecosystem and to provide national and international visibility to the start-up ecosystem in India.
- **Details:** A pivotal component for growth of start-ups is regular communication and collaboration within the start-up community, both national as well international. An effective start-up ecosystem can't be created by the start-ups alone. It depends on active participation of the academia, investors, industry and other stakeholders. To bolster the start-up ecosystem in India, the government is proposing to introduce start-up fests at national and international stages. These fests would provide a platform to the start-ups in India to showcase their ideas and work with a larger audience comprising potential investors, mentors and fellow start-ups. As part of the Make in India initiative, the government proposes to:
    - Hold one fest at the national level to enable all the stakeholders of the start-up ecosystem to come together on one platform.
    - Hold one fest at the international level annually in an international city known for its start-up ecosystem. The

fests shall have activities such as sessions to connect with the investors, mentors, incubators and start-ups, showcasing innovations, exhibitions and product launches, pitches by start-ups, mentoring sessions, curated start-up walks, talks by disruptive innovators, competitions such as Hackathon, Makerspace, etc., announcements of rewards and recognitions, panels and conferences with the industry leaders, etc.

## LAUNCH OF ATAL INNOVATION MISSION (AIM) WITH SELF-EMPLOYMENT AND TALENT UTILISATION (SETU) PROGRAMME

- **Aim:** To serve as a platform for promotion of world-class innovation hubs, grand challenges, start-up businesses and other self-employment activities, in technology-driven areas.
- **Details:** The Atal Innovation Mission (AIM) shall have two core functions:
  - Entrepreneurship promotion through Self-Employment and Talent Utilisation (SETU).
  - Innovation promotion to provide a platform where innovative ideas are generated.

The main components proposed to be undertaken as part of the mission include the following.

## ENTREPRENEURSHIP PROMOTION

- Establishment of sector-specific incubators including in PPP mode (refer #14 of this action plan).
- Establishment of 500 Tinkering Labs.
- Pre-incubation training to potential entrepreneurs in various technology areas in collaboration with various academic institutions having expertise in the field.
- Strengthening of incubation facilities in existing incubators and mentoring of start-ups.

- Seed funding to successful and high growth start-ups innovation promotion.
- Institution of Innovation Awards (three per state/UT) and three national level awards.
- Providing support to state innovation councils for awareness creation and organising state-level workshops/conferences.
- Launch of Grand Innovation Challenge Awards for finding ultra-low-cost solutions to India's pressing and intractable problems.

## *Case Study: GeM—Government e-Marketplace*

New ventures used to struggle to work with the government. The government's purchase and tendering system had many loopholes. We have rectified this through the establishment of the Government e-Marketplace (GeM). This is the online space for government purchase dealings, enabling small start-ups to sell their products to the government. The GeM is a proverbial gem as it has helped many start-ups. The first case study of this book owes its success to the same platform.

I had the chance to meet many officials of GeM. People like S. Suresh Kumar (Additional CEO), Chief Financial Officer (CFO) Rajeev Kandpal and Product Manager Anurag Awasthi provided valuable information. The GeM is strengthening schemes like Make in India, Startup India, Digital India and Skill India. The government plans to shift its entire buying process to this platform. The information shared by the GeM officials is also available on its website.

GeM is working under the ministry of commerce and industry, where common user goods and services can be bought. GeM is a dynamic, self-sustaining and user-friendly portal for making procurement by the government officers.

Public procurement forms a very important part of the government activity and reform in public procurement is one of the top priorities of the present government. GeM is a very bold step by the government with the aim to transform procurement of goods and services done by the government ministries and departments, public sector undertakings and other apex autonomous bodies of the central government.

GeM owes its genesis to the recommendations of two groups of secretaries made by PM Modi in January 2016. They recommended setting up of a dedicated e-market for different goods and services bought or sold by government/PSUs besides reforming Directorate General of Supplies and Disposals (DGS&D), the finance minister in his Budget speech for FY 2016-17, announced setting up of a technology-driven platform to facilitate the procurement of goods and services by the various ministries and agencies of the government.

DGS&D, with technical support from National e-Governance Division (Ministry of Electronics and Information Technology) has developed GeM portal for the procurement of both products and services. The portal was launched on 9 August 2016 by the Commerce and Industry minister. Procurement on GeM has been authorised by General Financial Rules by changing the government rules. The GeM is a paperless, cashless and system driven e-marketplace that enables the procurement of common use goods and services with a minimal human interface.

## GeM Advantages for Buyers

- Rich listing of products for individual categories of goods and services
- Search, compare, select and buy facility
- Buy goods and services online, as and when required
- Transparent and ease of buying
- A continuous vendor rating system
- User-friendly dashboard for buying and monitoring supplies and payments
- Easy return policy for sellers
- Direct access to all government departments

- A one-stop-shop for marketing with minimal efforts
- One-stop-shop for bids or reverse auction on products and services
- New product suggestion facility available to sellers
- Dynamic pricing
- Seller-friendly dashboard for selling and monitoring of supplies and payments
- Consistent and uniform purchase procedures
- Facilities provided by GeM to the start-ups
- Product list for individual, prescribed categories of goods and services of common use
- Look, estimate, compare and purchase facility on dynamic pricing basis
- Market place for buying a majority of common user items
- Single-window system for aggregating demands and ordering
- Transparency and ease of buying
- Useful for low-value buying and also for bulk buying at a competitive price using verse auction or e-bidding
- Continuous vendor rating system
- User-friendly dashboard for buying and monitoring supplies and payments
- Return policy
- GeM brings in transparency

GeM eliminates human interface in vendor registration, order placement and payment processing to a great extent. Being an open platform, GeM offers no entry barriers to bonafide suppliers who wish to do business with the government. At every step, SMS and e-Mail notifications are sent to the buyers, his/her head of the organisation, paying authorities and sellers. Online, cashless and time-bound payment on GeM is facilitated through integration with Public Financial Management System (PFMS) and State Bank Multi Option System (SBMOPS); web-services integration is being extended to payment systems of railways, defence, major PSUs and state governments. Seamless processes and online time-bound payment, which is also mandated by the Department of Expenditure, has given confidence to the vendors and reduced their administrative costs involved in pursuing officers for timely payment.

The GeM and Startup India have prepared a new start-up environment. It is preparing new entrepreneurs. We need to pay more attention to industrial education. Skill India is also an important initiative. An increase in start-ups will also lead to an increased demand of skilled workers.

This is an era of start-up revolution because the government has taken into account the interests of the start-ups. Be it linking them to government schemes or helping them with tax sops. Indian youth is now coming out of the mindset of perceiving a secured job as their ultimate aim. We need good hands in governance but it equally requires capable entrepreneurs. I have traversed through Uttar Pradesh for a programme I did for *Amar Ujala*. I found that youngsters already knew about Skill India, but there is scope for better implementation. Yet, it is a good beginning and a foundation stone for the start-up revolution.

# 13

# SEVEN LETTERS OF S.T.A.R.T.U.P.

India is the motherland of many great talents. Shakuntla Devi, also known as human computer was one of them. Her life is a saga of great motivation that everyone must know about. The mathematics genius was famously quoted as saying, 'Without mathematics, there's nothing you can do. Everything around you is mathematics. Everything around you is numbers.'

As a student of mathematics, numbers have always fascinated me. It is perhaps for this reason that I am enumerating seven things you must know for success in start-ups. Each one of them is derived out of the alphabet of the word 'start-up'. These seven aspects are derived out of my interactions with the seven prestigious experts of this field.

Seven colours make a rainbow, seven chords make music, seven days make a week, seven continents make the world and seven beautiful letters make a start-up.

This quote mentioned 'Friends'. But, a start-up is no less than a friend for any young entrepreneur. The seven experts I mentioned are specialists in the following seven fields.

- **S** – Statistics and Strategy
- **T** – Trading and Business
- **A** – Administration and Authorities
- **R** – Right and Wrong
- **T** – Training and Education
- **U** – Ups and Downs
- **P** – Projects and Partnership

Both the government and the start-ups need to pay attention on these important points. Statistics are vital for accurate market analysis. Not every entrepreneur can be a number wizard, but one can seek the help of the specialists. Your strategy should be based on sound data.

You will also need a good understanding of trading practices. Even a great innovation is useless without it. Even a small idea can do wonders if you know the art of business. We need to support better trading for start-ups. However, start-ups should also be well prepared.

Policies are formulated in the legislative bodies but are implemented by the local administration. Therefore, it is important to connect with the local authorities and understand their vision. GeM is a good initiative linking young entrepreneurs to the local governing bodies. We need more such efforts.

Oblivious of the existing guiding factors, most start-ups invest a lot of time deciding right and wrong. Many schemes and mentors can save you hard work. The Startup India mission is one such programme. We need to take it to the lower strata of the society.

There are a lot of questions about our education policy. Our archaic education set-up also needs innovation. The start-up sector cannot bloom without the right training mechanisms. The failure percentage of start-ups can reduce if they are better equipped to handle all the links in the chain from the market to the end customer. We need to impart practical knowledge in our schools and colleges. The start-ups should not wait for assistance and make their efforts instead.

Many young entrepreneurs are impatient for success. Ups and downs of the business world can take its toll on mental state. Trade is akin to a battle field. Your brain is your best weapon. It must remain cool under all circumstances. We need to promote industrial psychology in this country. Start-ups should also not shy away from motivation and counselling sessions.

We have discussed the prospects of a partnership between start-ups and the government in welfare projects. Be it power, roads, water, security or policing; start-ups have immense opportunities. Project like *Namami Gange* is still awaiting better innovation.

I hope you will find the following interviews with different experts useful. The start-ups are the new-age phenomena and insights of these seasoned masters of their field will help you assess the future in a better way. A right assessment is the key to a successful strategy. Here are these seven experts:

- **Dr Bimal Kumar Roy** (Padma Shree, Former Director, Indian Institute of Statistics)
- **Dr Mahesh Gupta** (Chairman, Kent RO)
- **Deepak Singh** (Senior IAS Officer)
- **Ajay Muttreja** (Advisor and Mentor, FICCI Start-up Committee)
- **Dr Vinod Tibrewala** (Chancellor, J.J.T. University, Rajasthan)
- **Dr Ritu Sharma** (PhD, Industrial and Organisational Psychology)
- **D.P. Mathuria** (Executive Director of National Mission for Clean Ganga)

The subject of statistics can be difficult to comprehend in the beginning. Mathematics, in any case, in not everybody's cup of tea. However, pay heed to Shakuntla Devi's quote. The world around you is all made of numbers. They are there to be deciphered. Statistics are integral to any start-up's journey. Here's what Bimal Kumar Roy had to say about the subject during an interview for *Innovate India*.

## S—STATISTICS AND STRATEGY

### Innovation Digging Its Path through Statistics

Dr Bimal Kumar Roy (Padma Shree, Former Director, IIS)

Today we live in the information world and much of this information is determined with the help of statistics. If an information is conveyed, to prove it right one needs statistics and data.

## Innovation and Statistics

Innovation first starts with your conviction, belief, dream and vision, this is the start of an innovation. In this procedure there is one important thing, that is the observation and information you are gaining and whether both of them are supporting your conviction, belief, dream and vision. So statistics drive everything. Now how do you conclude that from the surroundings, from this observation, whether your dream is a truth or just an imagination? There is a difference between your dream and reality. Your dream becomes real and bringing the dream to reality is triggered by statistics.

## Current Situation of Statistics in India

As a statistician, I would say that the work is in progress. The government is also working in the same direction. It requires knowledge to know where proper planning is needed, which sector needs the most importance, so before government decides on how to plan, how to invest their resources, what will be the importance for the future; you need to know what is the ground reality. Depending on that you put your political priority. Yes, it is the government's job, but political priority along with the current situation or the history of the country in all aspects is what you call data. Data must be more specific and more accurate or it could be very general also. So the Indian government takes help from a statistician, they have statistical service; I think there are 500–600 ISS officers. They help them out. Interaction with the academician is there but they should increase it. When the academicians will be taken into confidence, it will help the government immensely.

## Key Areas Where Statistics Are Playing a Vital Role

The first sector is the Finance and Insurance sector. How do you fix the premium of insurance unless you have enough data: How did the accident happen?; Who caused the accident?; How many accidents happened?; In which group did the accident happen? and; What was the loss, was it a loss of life or just injury? So unless you have all the information, you cannot fix the premium. So we do statistical modelling putting all information as an input, and the output comes for what can be insured and what premium can be fixed, and to bring out the output one needs statistical methods. Investment bank uses this method, so we use all these data predictive analytics.

### Possibilities for Start-ups

The start-ups should have some statistic ideas; it must involve areas like studying history, current market, etc. It is also a million-dollar question as to what makes a start-up successful. So I like to study if someone would be interested to promote that: Why does a start-up become successful? But I need help in getting the data.

### Possibilities of Studies in Statistics

If you have the data then it's analysis is easy, but getting this data is hard. Twenty years back, very few industries used statistics; except the process quality, nowhere was statistics used, but now it's being used in many facets such as finance, investment and insurance.

### Start-up Helping Other Start-ups

Mu Sigma is a very successful start-up. One of our students started it, now it's a global power. They do the market analysis, they give consultancy to industries about where one should invest. Rights and wrongs are the only things that one should know and statistics tell you that. So if your idea is futuristic, then statistics is the only tool.

We have many celebrities in sports, cinema and other fields, but we have very few in academics. This can encourage more students to come and join this beautiful world of numbers.

## T—TRADE AND BUSINESS

### Make the Best Trades, Money Is Secondary

Dr Mahesh Gupta (Founder, Kent RO)

Failure is the first step to success, just focus on how strong your ideation is! And then to sustain yourself in the market, take each day as an opportunity to come up with an innovation. Leaving no stones unturned and overcoming all the tough challenges in life, Dr Mahesh Gupta, today, is the founder and owner of the huge business group, KENT RO. His achievements are not new to us; he had already become a rebel in the water purification industry as early as the 90's. He has today become an epitome of success defeating his failures.

In 1998, Dr Gupta entered health care segment and launched the first domestic RO water purifier. Competing with the leading national and international brands, KENT RO Systems Ltd is today the leading and most dynamic water purifier company in India, commanding a market share of about 40 per cent in RO water purifier segment. For his contribution to the water purification industry, he is known as the pure waterman of India. Here are some important points from his interview.

### Better Technique and Innovation Creates a Market

When we launched KENT RO Purifiers, other strong brands already existed. Our purification system costed ₹20,000 each. Other purifiers were available at ₹3,000. But there was a remarkable difference in the technologies. The other brands' reverse osmosis could not eliminate soluble impurities KENT's RO did. And believing only in this difference, we kept on moving and flourishing.

Many a time, we were not entertained as we had a costlier machine than those existing in the market. But we remained confident enough, and accepted this challenge and continued our marketing. To convince a customer door to door to purchase an

RO system, which was far costlier than the existing one, was the biggest challenge for us. But we sustained that situation and this was our victory.

### Creating a Brand

When KENT RO was established back in 1998, we wanted, that whenever pure water is talked of, KENT RO shall always be remembered. And for this, 20 years back itself, we coined it with the name KENT RO. Today, even if people buy any other RO water purifier, they say that they have purchased KENT; to see KENT becoming synonymous to RO, makes me happy.

### Ground-breaking Marketing Tricks

We believe in innovation. We have more than half a dozen patents to our credit. With an ambitious growth plan and state of the art technology, KENT applied remarkable marketing strategies. We recognise Hema Malini as the face of KENT RO. This has complimented her too. The poise organisation has also sponsored Kings 11 Punjab, which again adds to its innovative strategies.

We have innovated in the selection of media also. Besides, one should always believe in long-term strategies. An example of this is, we had campaigned in 2006 with our famous tag line '*KENT deta hai sabse shudh pani*'. But even after so many well-wishers told us to change the tag line, we did not. Our basic focus was to provide pure water and it remained our central point of strategy forever.

### Don't Stop, Keep Innovating

Even though KENT RO is an established brand, we are innovating continuously. Since our inception, we have been improvising our product. Even today, only two or three per cent of people use RO for drinking. So I feel, the major challenge for me lies in making the remaining 97 per cent get equipped with pure and healthy drinking water through KENT RO. Yesterday, we commuted on bull carts, today we roam on cars and tomorrow we will travel in rockets! This is how fast we are changing!

### Tips for Start-ups and Innovators

An innovator should have a belief in his solution that he is providing to the market and only then can he imitate the same belief and confidence in the eyes of the customers. Failure is a by-product of innovation; success being the prime. So one should learn from failures and focus on success. To succeed every day is a new challenge for young entrepreneurs. Whatever new you innovate today, will be old tomorrow. So you should be ready to brainstorm your mind with new ideas each day.

## A—ADMINISTRATION AND AUTHORITIES

### No One Who Achieves Success Does So Without Acknowledging the Help of Others

Deepak Singh (Indian Administrative Services)

Smart move by an administrative officer is important for the successful implementation of any innovation. All the innovations and start-ups would go to waste if an administrative officer doesn't understand it, and gets involved in making it helpful for the society on grassroots level. Along with innovations, an IAS officer is a responsible authority for the welfare and administrative policies. Making all such things possible, a dynamic officer has received tremendous appreciation for his innovative efforts for the tribals of Madhya Pradesh. Deepak Singh played a crucial role in many districts of Madhya Pradesh. As the district magistrate (DM), he has a keen interest in innovations and he encouraged many start-ups for social entrepreneurship.

### Innovation as an Administrator

Being an administrator I've realised that we are the bridge between all the efforts by the government and the common man of the country. It was such a great opportunity for the tribal people when the government launched NAREGA and the Forest Act, as it provided the landless tribals their forest and they got a better life through the convergence of many schemes. As far as my innovations are considered, it's very difficult to assess your work. Still, there are many schemes and efforts by our team and government that made me realise that there are many opportunities available for an administrator to innovate for the upliftment of the society.

### Apparatus by the Administrator

Deepak worked out his idea by developing water resources for the tribal people and merged a few schemes of horticulture and agriculture department into it. The steps were time-consuming but they improved the living standards. They are in a better position and some blocks are so developed that they are selling their fruits and vegetables to big cities like Mumbai. The biggest award for such an effort is that other districts should also follow your path and it happened with this scheme.

### The Expectation from Start-ups

Whenever I think about implementing any scheme, I put myself at the place of the target beneficiaries and try to think like them. Being an administrative officer, I always look for talent which can support us in the successful implementation of these schemes.

### Schemes and Public Welfare

Merging different schemes to make it useful for the tribals was time-consuming, the process required speediness and extensive knowledge about schemes and the target areas for the authorities. Sufficient information of the schemes and methods of implementation was important for the administration to make the idea successful. Extra coordination between different departments and time to time orientation programmes for all the administrative authorities is the need of the hour to make this purpose possible.

Administrators have to work on implementing multiple schemes at the same time but they are seldom able to do it. Working at ground level and close association with the public is very important for execution. Identifying skills and weakness of the beneficiaries, and to ensure their involvement is also an important responsibility of an administrator.

### Encouragement to the Start-ups

Youth must keep a few things in mind if they want to get into start-ups and become an innovator. They should be more focused on employability than education. Youth should also know about the benefits of the schemes introduced for them and get involved in its successful implementation.

### Government and Start-ups

A memorandum has been signed between the Government of Madhya Pradesh and the United Nations Development Programmes (UNDP), to cooperate in the implementation of a programme; building an institutional structure to provide marketing support and capacity-building for entrepreneurs under the Mukhyamantri Yuva Udyami Yojna in Madhya Pradesh by providing important and specific training to 5,000 entrepreneurs to build their capabilities in relevant areas of entrepreneurship development. Also, this programme has been collaborated with IIM Indore to design and conduct focused training modules for entrepreneurs.

### Exploring Start-ups in Tourism

While there are many historical monuments in Dhar (we did this interview when he was the DM of Dhar), the whole district and nearby areas also have beautiful tourist sites like Mandu, Maheshwar and Mandaleshwar. There are a few countries today where tourism plays an important role in the country's economy, like Mauritius and Singapore. Few new job vacancies can be taken out in the field of tourism, such as coordinating with people to bring people here, to coordinate with resorts, restaurants, etc. Burhanpur and Dhar, both are very important in terms of tourism. We have taken several steps to preserve these tourist spots and make them accessible to the tourists. The young entrepreneurs are very much expected to try in tourism. State governments are also helping young entrepreneurs and upcoming start-ups. Local administration is playing an important role. Government platforms like GeM are favourable for these new start-ups.

## R—RIGHT AND WRONG

### The Superior Man Understands What Is Right; The Inferior Man Understands What Will Sell

- Confucius

Ajay Muttreja (Mentor and Advisor to FICCI Start-up Committee)

India has the third largest number of start-ups. One of the essential steps towards promoting entrepreneurship and self-reliance among the youth is Startup India programme. But still, have you ever thought where we are lacking behind. Is it propelling innovative solutions and creating employment? If not, what is missing?

The need of the hour is that whenever an idea is generated, implementing that idea is necessary to make it work and the implementation requires an implementer.

### The Right Timing for Start-up

One always wanted to know whether it is the right time to start something of your own or the current scenario of the market.

To which I feel that India is at the cusp of evolving into its true potential of entrepreneurship. Start-up ecosystem and culture of accepting failures is evolving. The craze for entrepreneurship and start-ups has influenced the rural areas. I expect a few lakh new smaller start-ups will jump into this ecosystem soon. At least, 30 per cent will emerge from the semi-urban and rural areas.

## Innovation and Start-ups

Turning a novel or useful idea into a solution that adds value from the customer's perspective is innovation. It should have a viable business model.

## No More Capital Trouble

The new entrepreneurs face trouble for funding, but our start-up mentor, through his advise, makes it easy to generate funds. Most of the new start-ups explore funding from the investors at a very early stage. If the start-up has a unique technological advantage with the secret sauce to innovate (and create barriers for competition), there is no shortage of funds for this start-up. The key essential for start-ups is to focus on customers' voice and feedback and get acceptability of the innovation by getting a few customers.

## Big Funding Agencies

- Venture capital (foreign and Indian)
- Indian Family Investment Funds
- Private equity
- International agencies including World Bank, United States Agency for International Development, Department for International Development
- Central and state government bodies (e.g., Technology Development Board of Department of Science and

Technology, Biotechnology Industry Research Assistance Council [BIRAC]); Banks (e.g., YES, AXIS)
- Multinational corporations (e.g., Intel, Facebook)
- Indian corporates

I am associated with many of them. New start-ups can get funding for their business from family and friends, besides Angel Networks (e.g., The Indian Angel Network [IAN] and TiE). These big funding agencies should be approached only after you have gained customers and there is a clarity of repeat business with sustained revenue growth.

**Strategy Designing**

Brainstorming sessions with yourself for a perfect design of strategy of your start-up is a must. One needs to be honest with the intrapersonal to develop a robust 'road map' and they are:

- What is the problem that you are trying to solve? What are your observations?
- What do you see your potential user doing?
- What are they saying?
- What do you infer they are thinking?
- What do you infer they are feeling?
- How real is the problem being solved by you?
- What is your solution?
- How is your solution better than the others?
- If you have found no other solution to this problem, please share where and how did you search for the existing solutions and the others being developed.
- Is it worth solving this problem?
- Is the solution worthy enough to be taken forward? What investments do we require for it?

**What Will Be the Returns?**

- to the user

- to you
- to the investors
- to the government

## Big Mistakes a Start-up Commits

- Rigid on their idea, don't alter their offering
- Underestimate the importance of right hire and dedicated mentors
- Weak road map for business sustainability and scalability

## Tips for the Budding Entrepreneur

- Positive attitude
- Good listener (absorb like a sponge) and flexible to change
- Attract and hire better talent and treat them as partners

## Copying Is Not Cheating

There is nothing wrong in copying. Chinese companies started with a similar approach and they are now focusing on innovation and global market adoption. Today, India has over 40,000 start-ups with a good ecosystem and a boom of consumerism and digital explosion. In the next two years, we will see a few breakthrough inventions in India to meet the big demand for the unexplored markets in India, Africa and other developing economies.

## Government Programmes

Over 500 initiatives of the central government and many state governments are there, many of them are impactful, but the possibility of betterment is always there. It should be further penetrated into smaller towns and rural areas. We should learn from the mistakes and success stories. I can help in bringing my learnings and insights as I have been fortunate to work with many of them.

## T—TRAINING AND EDUCATION

### Do You Want Results? Train Harder

Dr Vinod Tibrewala (Chancellor, J.J.T. University, Rajasthan)

We are the world leaders as far as the number of youth is concerned but we are far behind in the quality of the youth. This doesn't mean that our youth lacks potential, but they lack quality education. Though the government is introducing schemes, but still, most of the youth is deprived of the right way of professional education. Learning is an ongoing process and we need a completely new picture of education in India. We need innovation in education too.

### We Have Numbers but Not the Quality

We have the maximum number of youth in the entire world. In this way, we can consider ourselves as world leaders but we are not. There are many small countries in the world which are leading the world economies and we are far behind in this competition. We are nowhere in the competition. Why are we struggling for development even with the largest youth population in the world? This is because it is not about the numbers, but about the quality of the youth. I'm not saying that our youth lacks potential, strength or dream but it lacks quality education and the right guidance.

### The Need for the Innovative Education

We are still imposing conventional education system on our youth. They have to learn those things also which are not related to their core interests. Up to a certain age, basic knowledge about all subjects is important but to impose it during colleges and institutes is not in today's education system. We are adopting technologies and systems from around the world but our education system remains the same as left by the British at the time of independence. Most unfortunate thing is that many of the international universities are running their online courses in India but we are still following the conventional way of education. Today's need is subject-specific education with apt opportunities for practice. It's not about getting a degree, it's about getting the skill to create products with zero defects along with the degrees.

### What Could Be Done

When I say employability, my focus is on specific skills which may make a student employable even during his or her academic course. The market needs skilled people and not only the certification from some institutes. I don't say that all institutes are not innovating the education system in India but the majority is on conventional track. UGC and government have to take some steps forward for the betterment of the education system in India. I must appreciate new skill development or vocational programmes introduced by the UGC. The number of institutes are increasing day by day but what we need is the quality of the institutes. Vocational courses are a good move but again this is just a drop in the ocean. UGC has to give more freedom to the private universities for introducing new ideas.

### Don't Always Look at the Government for Help

The Government of India has started various schemes with good intention. These schemes should reach the real beneficiaries, that is, the youth of the country but not any middleman. Earlier, a Mafia was working on such schemes that used to do all the technical formalities and bring out various funds from the government. Now the time has come when we should stop blaming the government for everything. Social entrepreneurship is the need of the hour and I've taken up this challenge and trying my best to innovate education in the country.

### e-Learning and Video Classes

e-Learning and video learning is not the future but the present. All the developed countries have already used it and they are also providing opportunities in India. We should also start working on it. For example, a good professor or lecturer is confined to a certain institute and only a few privileged students can reach his lecture. If we start live streaming of these lectures or the e-classes of these lecturers, than thousands or I must say, millions of students would be benefited by it. I always emphasise on the practical platform also. Such students should also try to do practical work at various factories or companies on whatever the student is studying. Our university is trying it's best under whatever freedom is available from the government to a private university. Courses should also be redesigned for new learning techniques. Conventional courses are putting an extra burden on the students. We should design new courses with a specific training programme.

## U—UPS AND DOWNS

### If There Are No Difficulties in Life, It Means You Are Dead

Dr Ritu Sharma (PhD, Industrial and Organisational Psychology)

Life should be like a roller coaster ride, ups and downs make it exciting. Cases like that of the Cafe Coffee Day owner always disturb young entrepreneurs. Well, we have always lived with a misconception that whenever a person is suffering from some mental disorder, then he needs to be taken to a psychologist. And many of us don't even know that there is a subdivision within the psychologists as well with specialisation in different fields. Organisational psychology is of great importance for start-ups or entrepreneurs at an initial level or in a difficult situation. Always remember that the reason why half of the people aren't able to succeed in life is that they hypnotise themselves into believing that they can't accomplish their goals. It is a mind game they play with themselves.

## Don't Be Discouraged with Others' Foolishness

I think there are a lot many ideas available, but I cannot see perseverance, sustenance and productibility of any idea. I think it is a great initiative by PM Modi that he is supporting so many business ideas. To a certain extent in media, it is shown that there are a total of these many business ideas and that these many are a flop, but how many of us tried to learn who was the person behind the business? How prepared was that person while initiating the business? No business owner can be successful in a single day. They have seen those downfalls. But what matters is how many of them will get up and continue with their business. Make in India is a wonderful initiative, India has such a variety of world-famous things. Starting a business is not important, sustaining it is. Among today's youth, nobody has a small goal, everybody has a bigger goal. So at the initial level with a bigger goal; your business will be a boon because it's a noble idea. But what is there in your idea that will sustain it?

## Assist Yourself before Assisting Others

We must know what our locus of control is. How much do we blame others for our failure and how much do you want to know about your failure and why it happened? If the businessman realises that his failure occurred because of him, then he will be able to work it out. But for that, self-introspection is very important. We critically evaluate others very quickly but how quickly do we critically evaluate ourselves. I don't have to look at the business idea to suddenly become rich; I must take small sustainable steps.

## Industrial Psychology in Start-Up Era

It is the irony of Indian society that people do not understand what the organisational psychologists are all about. We have seen clinical psychologists training employees; we have seen counsellors doing training for employees. We have to understand that these people are specialised in certain fields. An organisational psychologist is someone who will help the employees to improve their performance. He will look at the individual aspect of the organisation like how to motivate people, how to drive people, organisation development and training. These are the specialised fields the organisational psychologists especially work on. You need to sit with this person and plan in case you have a small number of employees because he is the person who will help you on how to engage your employees, and make them more effective.

### The Motivation for Industrial Growth

First of all, you have to have clarity of goal before you can drive the others. An ambiguous mind cannot drive 10 other people; it will only increase ambiguity in the environment. For instance, you will show a vision to your employees that in three to four years you have to reach here, but when that goal is achieved, then what will be the next stage. So the clarity of goal within you is very important. And the plan is the thing that needs to be concrete rather than just working on anything. To have that knowledge that can help you grow and sustain in that particular business, that is something very important. In a society today, you need to learn about how to run a business and what are the integrities of that business. Gain some experience. Today you go to any big organisation, the child of the head of the organisation goes definitely for an internship before becoming a CEO or vice president.

### Depression in Organisational Psychology

I have earlier said that at the initial stage, the idea will receive a boon but after a certain time it becomes stagnant because no new ideas are being contributed in it. Lack of planning is the major reason that leads to depression. And the second is having too much expectation without any planning. Let me give you an example. If you ask a child what he would want to study then he says engineering but after engineering, if you ask him what he wants to do then he doesn't know. That is the same thing as mentioned above, you have pulled yourself to one creative thought, but you haven't created your series and long-term goals. Unless you have them, you won't be able to deal with the depression. Perseverance is something that will help you get up and work on it. For that subject and to be successful in that field you must have passion and the enthusiasm that you like this thing a lot.

### Leaders and Followers

I see leaders are the people who have this exceptional intelligence, perseverance, energy and an exceptional understanding of the people around. A leader should be a person whom the people around would like to follow. That means that one should be so learned that people should think that they are still learning from him/her. I have seen leaders who want to capture all the power as a possession. And then, there are leaders who want that whosoever are working within him must grow. And I think the second one is a better leader. Because, whoever will work under the second type of leader will never feel suffocated. As the leader has achieved his growth and he knows his success story. So he is working as a team. A leader should know the capacity of each individual and somewhere down the line, he should be able to motivate others.

## P—PROJECTS AND PARTNERSHIP

### Partner-up to Create Meaning and Value

D.P. Mathuria (Executive Director of National Mission for Clean Ganga)

For the world, rivers become the lifeline of the civilisation but in the Indian context, rivers resemble the Indian culture; not only in providing livelihood to the population which is residing on the banks but also in terms of their religious beliefs, their ethos, their daily ways in which they live their life.

## Innovation for *Namami Gange*

I feel that nowhere in the world you'll find people taking their daily bath or washing their utensils or taking their livestock for various other purposes to the banks of the river. The government has been conscious of this and accordingly came out with a flagship programme of *Namami Gange*; this programme has outspent ₹20,000 crores. And when we speak in terms of linkages of this programme with innovation, there is a very strong linkage, you'll find a lot of documentary evidence and literature accounting that a large amount of pollution is contributed by many areas. One of the prime objectives is to abate this pollution which enters the river in various ways.

There are contemporary and traditional methods to treat this pollution by the construction of sewage treatment plant, by constructing a network of sewers, by intersecting the drains and carrying the sewage.

## Innovate India and *Namami Gange*

Traditionally, the Indian system has a lot of innovative knowledge in terms of how to treat this pollution. The beauty of this innovative concept is that these are decentralised techniques, in a sense that in a way you collect the entire sewage from a place and carry it to a common point, in big quantity and treat them. Another approach can be that you tap the pollution at the time it is being generated and treat that pollution and let that clean water flow through the system. And decentralising the treatment are the focal points where these innovative techniques and technology can make an impact when it comes to clean Ganga.

## Innovation Required

A few examples of these innovations are the indigenous vegetation, which has the capacity, through their root system, to absorb the pollution. Root system is a house where a group of bacteria eat up all the organic matter and even stabilise it, also absorb toxic heavy metals and this is a very successful system. Sixty per cent of the pollution in Kolkata city has been treated by this wetland system. So there is a need for many start-ups to do some research, and develop and identify those species which are effective in treating that particular kind of toxicity.

The Government of India has alloted a budget of ₹16,000 crore for cleaning the Ganga, in which ₹1,000 crore is for sewerage infrastructure to deal with industrial pollution.

Another equal amount has been made available for research and development capacity ability and innovative techniques. We are encouraging a lot of these innovative projects—there is a concept of constructed wetlands. We have sanctioned one project in Vrindavan, Mirzapur, Farooqabad. Another important aspect of innovation is training manpower to cater to the sector-specific requirement.

## A Major Contributor to Pollution

Eighty per cent is contributed by our municipalities itself. When it comes to innovative techniques in industrial sector it becomes a very important area in which extra efforts can be put in, because industrial production releases many kinds of toxic waste which are then released into the river.

Recently, we discussed with one of the scientists from Singapore; they are implementing a system of toxicity detection particularly for the industrial sector. So this kind of innovative practice has a very good scope of replication. (Here, Mathuria is talking about H2O Mantra's Dr Shailesh who's the first case study of this book.)

## Opportunities for Start-Ups

We are encouraging the start-ups and innovative schemes under the research and development component of *Namami Gange* programme. We have got a scheme under which the technology component can be applied to us, I mean that the start-ups can provide us with a solution for a particular identified area and can propose its system or technique. A start-up can also propose a commercial part of its concept and those concepts can be scrutinised by the expert body and recommended for demonstration purpose. If a start-up can prove the results in the first month, it becomes eligible for reimbursement in the costs, so this is how we are encouraging start-ups in the non-traditional concept of abatement to pollution. Even if we claim that we can reduce pollution by this technology by 40–50 per cent, then we encourage them.

## Tips for Start-ups and Innovators

Start-ups must realise that the government will not do everything by itself, it has to be a social movement. If such start-up solutions are provided to us then we are ready to look into it and we do encourage them to participate in our programme. If the start-ups and innovators are sure and confident of their technology then, definitely there is a big scope in *Namami Gange* programme to encourage them, to implement them and serve the cause. These experts are talking about their respective field's work. But you can get an idea of how the people at the top think. Development is a continuous process with many challenges. These challenges are the minefields of opportunities. A successful start-up is capable of tapping them.

## THINGS TO REMEMBER

- Understanding statistics and interpreting them is necessary for good research.
- Don't try to be a master of all trades. There are experts for specific tasks. Take their help.
- Understand business before becoming a businessperson. Learn to buy and sell.
- Right practice will ensure success. Prepare before you enter the field.
- Maintain good relations with government officials. Research government schemes. Offer them solutions to social problems.
- Look for opportunities everywhere. Start-ups have great chances of success even in villages and small towns.
- Wrong decisions are only the stepping stones for the right ones. However, you can minimise them by taking advice from the experts.
- Investors are always available for true and an effective idea.
- Ups and downs are as integral to business as the heartbeat is to the body. Be positive about them.
- Participate in government welfare schemes and avail their opportunities.

# 14

# SUCCESS IS THE SUM OF SMALL STEPS, TAKEN DAY IN, DAY OUT

**'Be not afraid of growing slowly; be afraid only of standing still.'**

This ancient Chinese proverb offers great insight into the process of progressing in life. Most start-ups are conceived by young minds. They are full of enthusiasm and hungry for success. This is their real strength but only if channelised in a proper way. It is better to tread slowly than moving too fast and falling flat. You need to build your dreams brick-by-brick. Small steps can scale the biggest mountains. These small steps, in your case, should be directed at preparing yourself. You can avail opportunities only if you are prepared to seize them. Those with foresight, assess future possibilities before deciding for their present. The understanding of basics will help the youth establish their business. The more you sweat while preparing, the better will be your results.

Mental preparation is necessary before establishing any new business. Apart from chalking out a road map, you must also visualise it in your mind. Test not only your business but also your attitude.

Much is said and written about creativity and passion. But how much do we know about them? We all know about research but it is still not well-utilised in India. India's research and development is plagued by plagiarism. Having this clarity can make the rest of the journey easier. The following five things are good parameters for self-evaluation.

1. Creativity
2. Passion for the profession
3. Research
4. True innovation
5. 5W's and 1 H of start-ups

Apart from these factors, keep in mind the common reasons for failure of many start-ups. Some are listed below.

## CREATIVITY IS DEFYING THE CROWD

Creative or innovative thinkers are not unheard of, they exist among us. We all have innovative ideas in our mind but only a few unlock it or become successful. Why? I got the answer with a very simple incidence. My friend, who is in a government job, called me and told me that he's taking a one-year leave and going to pursue some professional course. He had researched well and invested a lot of time for searching the right course. I was having an 'Aha' feeling for him but he was not sounding happy. He called me because he was confused. He is a family man with so many liabilities. His family despised his decision. Even his friend circle wasn't too happy about it and questioned it. I told him that fortune favours the bold and as per my opinion, he was on the right track as he was fulfilling the basic definition of creativity—defying the crowd.

Have you faced a similar situation in your life? Of course, we all have faced it at a certain time or phase in our life. I advised my friend to go ahead with his decision as defying the crowd is the basic definition of creativity. It's a scientific approach and science is based on well-established theories and experiments. No doubt if he'll continue with his hunch, he'll be successful.

If one stops him/her from pursuing his/her dreams then they obviously won't be able to achieve their dreams, but they will also fall into the same crowd of creativity opponents.

## Creative or Innovative Thinking

It's an important subject in cognitive psychology and many researchers have worked hard on defining it. Few common points every researcher agrees on are:

- Novel useful idea
- Rejects previously accepted ideas
- Requires intense motivation and persistence
- Results from organising unclear situation in a coherent, clear and new way
- Creativity can be developed and promoted

Last point is the most important as it clearly indicates that creativity is not only related to giftedness or some kind of ultra intelligence. Creativity is a goal-directed thinking which is unusual, novel and useful. Many of such creative thinking becomes so important that they influence the whole human civilisation and are called historical creativity. The Mona Lisa, the Laws of Thermodynamics, Theory of Relativity or the development of business houses like Microsoft, Apple, Facebook, etc., were never possible without these simple steps of creativity. Good thing is that you can develop this ability at any point of time.

## Think Like an Innovator

According to cognitive psychology, creativity requires a confluence of six distinct but interrelated resources: intellectual abilities, knowledge, styles of thinking, personality, motivation and environment. The last three factors are of prime importance.

Numerous researches support the importance of certain personality attributes for creative or innovative thinking. Some of the important attributes are willingness to overcome obstacles, willingness to take sensible risks, willingness to tolerate ambiguity and self-efficacy. One can develop these attributes with practise, but the reverse practise will generate only fear and a tendency to quit.

In my friend's case, if he'll not take the sensible risk and take opposition positively, then he'll develop a tendency of quitting all the possibilities and finally, the creative thinking process will be locked.

## Motivation and Environment

Motivation doesn't necessarily mean an advice from outside, listening or reading to other's view point. They might talk sensible but it is quite possible that their own life would be a mess. Only your actions and rewards for it will keep motivating you. Remember that motivation is something which keeps moving you in the mid of obstacles and opposition. It could be your will power or many a time, support by someone who himself or herself defied the crowd. One can have all the internal resources to think creatively, but without some environmental support (such as a forum for proposing those ideas), the creativity that a person has within him or her might never be displayed. Look around what kind of people and situation you have. Most of the time the contradiction between our thinking and environment creates a disturbance and we lose all the willingness to move forward. It doesn't mean you should leave the people or place but you should learn to remain unaffected by their acts.

## Investment in Creative Thinking

There is no age for learning and there is no end to it. In India, most of the people stop learning new skills or education after getting a job. Many researchers suggest that highly intellectual and successful people never stop learning. This point should be understood in reverse, that is, these people are highly intellectual and successful because they have a tendency to keep learning new skills. My friend's case is the same and now I'm amazed while writing this that such small things stop people from becoming innovative or creative. Real investment is not the property, cars or other costly things, but the improvement or enhancement of your intellectual property and that is possible with a constant learning attitude.

## PASSION FOR PROFESSION: PATH TO SUCCESS AND SATISFACTION

Things which get you rewards always feel near to your heart or you can call them the passion of your life. From the very childhood, people's appreciation for your efforts make you feel good about certain things. For example, it may be drawing, dancing or singing which gives the child a feeling of respect when family members appreciate. Rewards and appreciation by the people make them realise that they are good at it and they find their way for the same. Here we are talking about the process of converting this passion into a profession as one who understands it will get the joy of success and satisfaction of achievement.

Identifying interest or passion is not that difficult, but nurturing it as a profession is far more difficult as it requires skill acquisition and a constant guidance. One who gets it, certainly explores the particular area and achieves as per other skills. Always remember that talent is a set of many skills, as passion alone can't lead you to success. For example, you want to be a successful singer, than only good voice and musical diploma won't work for you. These are the basic necessities but you have to have knowledge about the entire music industry, connections in the field and awareness of the reality shows or other platforms to exhibit your talent. So is the case with each and every field, even with every idea or innovation in a particular field.

Here, we've to understand that being talented and exhibition of talent requires two different sets of skills. Reward and appreciation are the constant motivations for moving further throughout life. People who manage to acquire both sets of skills get success. Success is nothing but the constant reward generation or satisfaction about your current situation.

Profession is something we engage in for earning a livelihood. We all need money to survive, but most of the time survival processes lack the passion and that's why lack the reward and appreciation process also. This is the reason why all the companies run employee reward and appreciation programmes to keep them boosted. These efforts are just for the sake of company's growth and so that the individual may feel good for a period of time, but at the bottom of his heart the missing satisfaction always creates discomfort and that's why most of the people feel caged or imprisoned in their respective professions.

One who finds his or her way from passion into profession, will get the joy of success as they are not dependent on somebody else for their rewards. Passion into profession is a self-rewarding process. Most of the time, profession is chosen on the ground of social and financial grounds. People are not passionate about curing ailment but they know that the doctors get respect and good money. It's a fact that all the doctors may be of great use to society, but they are not equally rewarded or equally successful or equally satisfied in their lives.

Identifying passion is the first step and then acquiring all the possible sets of skills is the next step.

- What pleases you?
- What are the things you can do even without getting any money or reward?
- What kind of people make you feel jealous? (That's an odd way but it helps you in identifying your true passion.)
- What kind of subjects can you read or watch on the internet tirelessly?
- What are the things that make you forget the time lapse?
- What goes on in your imagination?

Answers to some of these questions could help you in understanding the seeds of passion within you.

I write seeds of passion and not true passion, as interests and hobbies alone can't lead you anywhere and this is the most common mistake made by people in identifying their true passion. Always remember, passion does not mean merely understanding your interests and hobbies but the process of acquiring all sets of skills related to it. The most successful people are the most passionate about their work, and they are almost never defined by a single skill. They are a fusion of skills, often not even exceptional skills, but they've made their fusion exceptional. Steve Jobs was not the world's greatest engineer, salesperson, designer or businessman. But he was uniquely good enough at all of these things and wove them together into something far greater. So is with any of the successful entrepreneur, artist, journalist or sportsperson.

I've seen many great artists in my life who are not as successful as their talent deserves. So is with people who have great connections and strategies to get success but equally great skills are missing in them. It should be a proper fusion. Many a time, small talent and fewer marketing strategies could work out beautifully but fusion is the basic necessity. I've seen many great writers who have great writing skills but reaching the publishers and understanding the publication industry is completely missing, such people are certainly wasting their talent. Start-ups and innovators should also identify their passion and then convert it into the profession. Always remember that just profit hunger won't lead you anywhere. You can become an ideal once you identify your passion; convert it into your profession with the fusion of the various skill sets required.

## RESEARCH IS THE MISSING LINK OF INNOVATE INDIA

Learning by watching others is the thumb rule for any kind of learning and so is with the start-up or new entrepreneurship learning. Unfortunately, we do have many academic degrees in business sphere and a practical or research based approach is still lacking. If we talk about the complete education system, we would lose the core goal of addressing the start-ups or innovators or the upcoming entrepreneurs. We can discuss the importance of research work in the sphere of new business development or start-up development.

- **Importance of research:** We all know that research is the base of innovation, but research is equally important for business development also. Although we have industrial psychology, not many start-ups are able to get the benefit of it, in fact, it is confined to the big business houses only. Start-ups already struggle with their budget and investment issues and in such a condition it's hard to afford another expenditure of hiring an industrial psychologist. But at a certain level, hiring experts is a wise investment.
- **Need of research:** Nothing can define the importance of a well-rehearsed approach and a constant positive thought process. Conventional study hardly gives any idea about the real business world. In such a condition, one requires to learn from his/her mistakes or with the support of others. In this way, it becomes important to make a proper research study on the success traits of business strategy.
- **Motivational books versus research:** We have many books, motivators or special programmes which talk about the business mantra, but these are the source of very basic and superficial information. It can help in instant gratification or an instant relief from the struggling situation but ultimately, one will remain on the same platform.
- **Scientific research for start-up:** Everybody has the same environment but some are doing great and most of the dreamers are still waiting for luck factor. Luck factor is nothing but the right direction at the right time and the right place. Psychology deals with the factorial (factors affecting) analysis and case studies. A deep research in this direction is important to analyse the commonality to deal with the basic challenges.

- **Basic challenges and wastage of energy:** Anxiety, depression, fear of failure, thirst for achievement, etc., are the hurdles which affect the growth of an individual and if he or she is trying to establish his or her start-up, then it would certainly affect the entire process. These problems can't be resolved with a regular psychological approach. We have to find out the common issues which lead to such situations. Hypothetically, it might be just lack of right direction, but with proper research, we can find out the root cause by comparing only a few case studies.
- **Procedure for the research:** We have plenty of information about the rise and fall of the start-ups but we never tried to come up with some generalised thought. The most beautiful part of scientific research is that it can be replicated or be applied in any given condition or situation. Such a research would certainly help in strengthening Indian entrepreneurship as a whole.
- **Make your own research study:** We grew up with exchange of ideas. We learnt from our mistakes and this is the way we have learnt everything. I have no idea who will come forward for such an awaited research work for start-ups or innovate India but till then, I advise all the start-ups to make their own research. Try to find out the pros and cons, read as much literature about your respectable trade as possible. One must also focus on the general psychological factors to keep the spirit up in all ups and downs and tough situations. Last but not the least, one should learn from others' mistakes and success too.

## TRUE INNOVATION AND NOT PLAGIARISM

Human civilisation has progressed through inspirations. The new society has developed with improvisation of traditional inventions. Science revolves around the principles given by Einstein and Newton. Research is practically done which was earlier theoretical. Science has evolved a lot over the years. Think, what would have happened if we had kept on revolving around the principles given by the great scientists of the early age? There would have been no progress. We had to move forward by research and improvements in these principles.

NITI Ayog has recently broadcasted a report raising deep concerns on the current scenario of water conservation in the country. The question that now arises is why water although a natural resource, even rich nations are not able to cope with the problem, forget about eliminating it. In India, the condition of science has not leveled up for a while and the major reason behind this drop is the lack of originality. Our own research is very limited. We have so many problems to face but there is no planning for systematic implementation of those plans.

## Lacking True Innovation

The basic theme which we are following is to copy the techniques of countries around the world. Whether it is our education system, our entertainment industry or our lives, we are influenced by the Western countries. Yes, we have made our place in the field of generic medicines. That is, inventing cheap medicines which have less or no side effect. But in recent times, India has vastly developed in one field, the space science. Chandrayaan is a big success for India as far as Mission Mangal is concerned.

Despite this, we have been far behind in research in other areas. We have the best institutes to boast, but even institutions like IITs have been accused of plagiarism. I do not want to keep those cases here, but we have to understand the status of these excellent institutions too. We have already had a long debate about school education. In schools, textbooks are restricted to only theoretical knowledge.

The teachers who are teaching them too believe that copying and pasting is studying. It is said that educated people in India are unemployed, but it is important to understand who here is actually educated.

## Startup India Is a Hope

I consider Startup India to be a great initiative. This is a scheme that focuses on the youth's innovation rather than the degrees. Incubators are being set-up so that they help these start-ups to deal with business challenges. Now, the worrisome part is that even here copy–paste is gradually taking over originality. In the name of innovation, young people make some modifications in an already existing foreign technique and idea and put their name to that innovation. There is no shortage of qualified students or researchers in the country but we are lacking in giving them the right opportunity. This is the reason why the qualified youth migrate abroad for research and further study. That's why I consider Startup India as a great initiative as it has encouraged reverse brain drain.

Though I've already given a detailed chapter about it in the book but I'm mentioning a few areas again, in which we desperately require some indigenous innovations.

1. **Waste management:** The elimination of pollution from natural resources is the first step we should take. Stop the misuse of wind and water. Nothing is going to happen just by putting a poster or running a campaign. It is a matter of awareness amongst the people that the government should create.
2. **Education management:** First of all, there is a need to understand the meaning of education. Today, there are many excellent institutes in our country. Just increasing the number of colleges and institutes to develop talent will not help. There is also a need to pay attention to what is being taught there.
3. **Management of principles of science:** The two major careers in India are either cricket or working in films, both would get you nationally or internationally famous, but the youth should also think of how much this nation requires science and innovation and indulge for its betterment.

## The Trendsetter

Singapore, for example, is a country with shortage of water. Due to lack of natural resources, it depends entirely on rain water. In such a situation, Singapore has done a lot of hard work and research to deal with this challenge. Along with bringing awareness through water to school education, Singapore has done a great deal of its investment on water saving and reusing techniques like rain water harvesting. We must learn from Singapore, whether it is the reuse technologies of water or their water reservoir system. That's why I considered Dr Shailesh Kharkwal's story as the lead story of the book as it shows the true success of Startup India. It has reverse brain drain, true innovation and exchange of technologies between the two countries.

## 5W's AND 1 H OF START-UP THINKING

We have read about the 5W's and 1H in journalism only, but these six questions give you a solution for all the confusion.

These basic questions are equally beneficial for resolving your confusions and indecisiveness for starting a new business or a start-up. Asking the right question and getting the desired answer, is the key to thinking clearly and wisely. Success is not an instant advantage, but a continuous and long-lasting process. If these questions are initially made a part of your road map, then you may already be ready for facing many conflicts and challenges ahead. The 5Ws and 1 H are Why, Where, When, What, Who and How? In a start-up, these would come in the form of the following questions:

1. Why a new business or a start-up?
2. When should I start?
3. Who will be my team mates?
4. Where will I get the funding from?
5. What are the challenges I'm going to face?
6. How to overcome it?

## Why a New Business or Start-up?

Doing any new work seems very heavy and confusing. This is exactly the same as after passing a 10th or 12th class exam, you used to get worried about the next set of exams. This is not limited to school education; in fact, this conflict unfolds at almost every level of life. We either get education in some area or use our natural talent to make our livelihood arrangements.

Now it's in your hand to attempt or not to attempt this real-life exam. If you'll attempt it, you'll go to the next level, otherwise you have to be satisfied with your current position and situation. Those who want to make their own identity in life believe in attempts, and at this point you start realising, why you should start your own business. This is not just limited to business but also applies to various fields like education or skill development. Being passionate about making great money and wanting to own a brand is the basic desire for all aspiring start-ups.

## When Should I Start?

Common dream of the start-up era is to become 'your own boss'. For most of the youngsters it always remains a dream as they might be aware why they want a start-up but they never really start working for it. Here comes the next crucial question, when should I start? Obviously, you'll start from your current situation but that creates dilemma for everyone with certain common questions. How can I leave my current job or work? Will it be a success or not? What if it's a failure? One should analyse his or her current status and ask themselves, am I dissatisfied with my current situation, and if yes, then why? Always remember that for your happiness, you are the sole person responsible. Nobody else except you, can change your situation. Neither your family nor your friends or a person you are working with can make your dreams come true, unless you take a stand for change.

After taking the stand, the next step is to choose the right business. Your experience with a particular business, your hold in the market, your expertise, your personality, your age, etc., are important factors to analyse before choosing the right business. The most common way to choose right business is to do the same thing which you already know or others are doing successfully, as you can learn from them. But the best way is to come up with an innovative style as market always welcomes an innovative idea.

### Who Will Be My Teammates?

Once you've made the internal commitment to your business, you'll be requiring a good team. Hire action-takers who can get the job done. No business has ever taken off based on an idea. It is the execution that transforms an idea into a legitimate, revenue-generating business. You want to build a team that's capable of accomplishing things instead of just spouting off ideas. Before you think about anything else, consider candidates for the hard skills that they possess. You need to cultivate a network of supporters, advisors, partners, allies and vendors. If you believe in your business, others will too. How I'll get these will always remain a question if you won't go to the people with your ideas. Believe me, the market is waiting for such innovation and ideas. Your focus should be on a team of like-minded people who differ in their skills: like one can be strong in marketing while the other could be in PR exercise or accounts. If initial partners are from various fields then this would enhance the success rate of a start-up. Always focus on a small team otherwise every gain will get drained out in managing teams only. Increase your team with an increase in the business.

### Where Will I Get the Funding From?

To grow your start-up you probably need outside sources of capital. If you bootstrap (self-funding) and remain without external funding for too long, you may be unable to take advantage of the market opportunities. Now the big question is—from where will you get the funds for your start-up? I met many investors during my *Innovate India* project and they all said one common thing, this is a question of least importance. This could be surprising for many of the readers and so was for me too but the reason is very simple and logical. Investors say we have all the money to invest for a good idea, what's important is an innovative business idea. Even in this book, Ajay Muttreja has given his advice on the funding issue. Funding is secondary; your primary focus should be on a successful minimum viable product.

The Government of India has also launched a ₹10,000 crore start-up fund in the Union budget 2014–2015 to improve the start-up ecosystem in India. In order to boost innovative product companies, the government has launched Bank of Ideas and Innovation programme. Government backed Pradhan Mantri Micro Units Development and Refinance Agency Limited (MUDRA) starts with an initial corpus of ₹20,000 crore to extend benefits to around 10 lakh small and mid-size enterprises (SMEs). You are supposed to submit your business plan and once approved, the loan gets sanctioned. If you comply with the eligibility criteria, government grants as a funding option could be one of the best. You just need to make yourself aware of the various government initiatives. Crowd funding, angel investors or networking in the business organisation will also help in finding the answer for this question. Startup India team is also helping for the same. They provide consultants and mentors for the same.

### What Are the Challenges?

Most of the initial shocks or business woes are the basic challenges for growing a start-up. Always remember, every new business demands time. You have to set a time frame and fund for your business. If you have not made your road map properly, then your energy and time can be ruined and it can be a major obstacle in moving ahead. Disagreements among the core team or other member's distrust towards the business can also affect your confidence, so always be ready to work on every aspect yourself. Likewise, due to lack of funds, start-ups may lose many major possibilities, it is important that you stay connected to the start-up and business network. If your idea is good, then many big investors may ask for a large share against the money they invest in your start-up. In such a situation, you may become an employee in your own company. However, always remember, less shares in a big company (market value) is far better than more stocks in smaller companies. Big funding can also give a great boost to your business and marketing strategy. A major reason for the breakdown of start-ups in initial level is the lack of information about new styles or understanding about the big business modes. We will discuss it in detail at the end of this chapter.

## How to Sustain Your Growth?

You may succeed in resolving all the W's mentioned above but this one H alone is equal to all the W's. One can sustain in the market by matching up with the market speed and capturing the opportunities as fast as possible. Most important exercise for the same is to invest on your innovative mind. Join the courses, attend seminars and meet the experts, read as much as possible about your field. This will certainly make you more competent to face the obstacles. If you stop learning and innovating after the initial success, than you will sooner or later face a major setback. Network locally, nationally and via social networks. Join networks like your local chamber of commerce or other relevant business groups. When attending networking events, ask others what they do and think about how you can help them.

Most people don't plan, but planning will help you get to market faster. A business plan will help you gain clarity, focus and confidence. A plan need not be more than one page. Keep upgrading your plans with every success and sometimes, it may be required in case of a failure. As you write down your goals, strategies and action steps, your business becomes real.

It's important to remember that you are not alone. If you want to be your own boss but you still feel stuck, reach out and connect with the other entrepreneurs in a variety of ways. You may be surprised by the invaluable experience sharing with them.

## MAJOR MISTAKES USUALLY DONE BY INDIAN START-UPS

According to the IBM value, 90 per cent of Indian start-ups fail in the first five years. The reason behind this problem is the lack of exact needed innovation. We show that we are innovating but actually we are copying others. Here, I will try to point out some serious issues responsible for the failure of most of the Indian start-ups. Let's start with a factual thing which shows the contribution of Indian innovators in the world of innovation. If we talk about only Asia, then during 2015–2016, India has filed only 1,423 patents in comparison to the top of the list, Japan with 44,200 patents. We are lacking in filling more and more innovations in the world forum. It's not that we lack talent but the real problem is the identification of the talent and nurturing innovations.

In the last few years, the scenario of Indian start-ups has drastically changed now that the big investors are not showing interest in Indian start-ups. We have facts for the same but instead of looking into the factual part we must focus on the real problems with Indian start-ups. We should get prepared to stand with the top start-up cities of the world. Silicon Valley, New York City, Los Angeles, Boston, Tel Aviv, London, Chicago, Seattle, Berlin and Singapore are nurturing the start-ups and innovators. Let's talk about some brief areas where the Indian start-ups should work.

### Involvement and Interest of the Customer

Most start-ups think of themselves and not about the customer. Customers' profitability, liquidity growth, productivity, gross margin, revenue inventory, turnover, cash flow, brand equity, customers acquisition, retention, speed of transaction should also be kept in the mind. Innovation comes when you solve a problem that the customer can't solve. Understanding the customer is important. We are more into copying successful start-ups; like when Uber came we had Ola and other apps, so is the case with Flipkart after Amazon and many more copied versions of such successful innovations. Frankly speaking, we haven't done any big innovation ourself so far.

### Lack of Financial Understanding and Management

Biggest reason behind the failure of Indian innovator is the negative cash flow. We run our business for the sake of profit but the Indian market is a little different especially while you are working with the government. It runs on cheques and credits, but until you are not sure about the recovery of the money, stay away from such business until you don't have money in the backup. You need cash in hand for the next business and if you lack the working capital, then complete focus will be on recovering the market investment. You won't get investors all the time. Many successful Indian start-ups have failed due to this negative cash flow. GeM has given some opportunities but things should be more transparent in government projects and its payments. Transfer of officers and change of government creates serious problems for start-ups, while working for government projects.

### Scalability and Expansion Factor

Market acquisition is important but with loss leading strategy it can be dangerous. You should have a profit road map. Many a time, margin is compromised for the sake of expansion and this could also lead to wrong results. Prepare first for the profit, otherwise, complete energy will be sucked out by the repairing strategies. There are start-ups which have profitability, margin and regional strength but still their business lack scalability, customer retention and recurring cost model. One would have to have a continuous revenue-generating customer for a sustainable growth. Start-ups should work on recurring model with the existing customers instead of running out for the new one. This model gives them a real base and strength for scalability.

## Start-up Team and Management

A successful start-up requires high potential, high performance and high-skills teammates. Continuous competency mapping and competency assessment is required. A successful start-up should have a team where teammates can transform ideation into execution, and then reality. For this purpose, you should have a team of the most talented people around you. Lack of good teammates, highly efficient people is another reason behind the failure of many Indian start-ups. They were not able to assure engagement of manpower and their output for the company.

## Marketing Strategy

Product positioning should be done only after identifying the real market. You should know your perfect customer and perfect market. Along with this, knowledge about perfect product and imperfect product is also important. Then comes product planning, segmentation, market demography, market psychographic study and single signal identity. It means that one should know its strength, whether it's the newest, problem solver, convenient, cheapest, best value, most prestigious, maximum features, most reliable, etc. There are many ways you can identify your start-up. After identifying it, your position should be perfect according to your strength. With this you should package, brand, market and present your product and services in the market. This could be supported by a scheme policy and back-end work.

Presenting product as laggard or a latecomer in the market always has limited or no growth at all. Don't fall into the line, create your own line. For that, adoption curve of the market should also be well understood. Along with these points, one should be prepared for the competitors' eye on their start-ups. For that, you have to create a market barrier with the help of intellectual rights filing, patents, proprietary technology, etc. Startup India helps young entrepreneurs with all these things.

## DIGITAL MARKETING FOR START-UPS

### Beware of Fake Likes and Subscription

Social media is a strong tool for promotion but it's crowded and we are not aware of the right approach for the same. We are more concerned about social media likes and subscription but how the claimant is generating it is hard to understand. Always remember, no promotion is always better than fake promotion. Right content and right approach is very important for a successful promotional exercise. Today the record says, an average Indian is spending 200 minutes per day on social media and in the coming years, this time spent will see a great rise. In such a scenario, attention span is at its lowest, and one must focus on effective and short ways to get registered.

### A Picture Is Worth a Thousand Words; a Video Worth a Million

A picture says a thousand words! Surely, this proverb came into existence when videos were not there. Now the time has changed and the need to reach the whole world is far greater for all the big or small business houses. Whether you are running an NGO or a start-up, that requires reaching the target audience, you need to have a good promotional plan. Videos are the most promising promotional strategy for all kind of promotional tasks.

## How to Reach the Audience Effectively

There are times when you see short films or documentaries that may move you and increase your interest level for a particular product or project. First of all, a good demographic and psychographic research is very important for producing a good film. You can take the help of genuine professional companies for the same. Here, the team of professionals study your target audience and then plan the content of the film accordingly.

If you are making generic films which are interesting for all kinds of viewers then it would also be a good strategy. For example, you can create a general short film on some subject of prime importance and showcase your company or product in its small part; it gives you a great reach. You can also get associated with popular YouTubers or Facebook pages for the same. There are many examples where start-ups are promoting themselves with popular motivators on YouTube.

## Need of Digital Marketing Start-ups

Not only in India but digital marketing has a strong scope worldwide. But the scope is only for those who have a sound knowledge of it. Few people know how to run Google adword and Facebook promotions. They proclaim themselves as digital marketers. But actually, digital marketing is beyond these. With time and increased number of smartphone and internet users, almost everyone is on the internet. And through digital marketing, you could easily connect with them. According to a source, till 2020, India needed 20 lakh digital marketing professionals and till date, only a few thousands exist (actual digital marketing professionals). There is a strong need and scope for digital marketing agencies, professionals and start-ups in the coming time.

## Beware of Fraudsters

Investments in digital marketing are on the rise, and expected to reach $300 billion in 2020. However, media experts insist that 30 per cent of the investments do not see the light of day due to murky digital marketing ecosystem. Clearly, there is a need to track genuine ad views in a foolproof manner. There is an onslaught of bad inventory in the system. Fraudsters have been able to get away with it because there is no end-to-end tracking that is being done, either by businesses or agencies. The fraud is typically carried out by creating fake ad traffic using content-scraping websites or other environments, getting bots to click on the ads, launching ads outside of a user's view, or creating other fictitious mechanisms to deliver advertisements that are not seen by consumers.

## Choose the Service Provider Wisely

The new saying is that you throw a stone in India and it will fall on the roof of a digital marketer. Every next guy claims to be into digital marketing, but as a client you should make sure that the people you are looking for your promotions should not work on the above-mentioned strategy of fake likes and numbers. You shouldn't pay them complete money in advance. You must focus on the outcome of the promotional activity. The best way to ensure you establish a partnership with an agency that will produce results is to find one that has a good track record of doing just that. Established digital marketing agencies should be able to show you some of their past work, and how they were able to work together with a company to achieve its goals. Obviously, an agency that can tout itself as award-winning or has an impressive client list of big brands will be the most attractive, but this doesn't necessarily make them the best fit for your business.

## THINGS TO REMEMBER

- Creativity means standing taller than the crowd. The majority may not agree with you.
- It is always beneficial to evaluate your thinking in consultation with experts.
- Identifying your passion is half the battle won.
- Research your area of interest. You can take help of research agencies.
- Imitating has its limits. However, doing so in a smart manner can bear some fruits.
- Never shy of questioning yourself. Seek your answers before moving ahead.
- Practise writing down answers. This will strengthen your road map.
- Invest in yourself. Spend on seminars, books and experts. This is a lifelong investment.
- Attain deep knowledge of digital marketing. Beware of fake operators in this field.
- Your creativity, innovation and passion are your real assets. Invest in identifying and polishing them.

# 15

# TEN STEPS TO DEVELOP THE RIGHT MINDSET FOR OWNING A START-UP

Every field has its own requirements and challenges. Understand the various phases of establishing a new start-up to develop the right perspective. The world and its march forward through the annals of time are governed by human thinking. Likewise, environmental crisis and the spectre of a nuclear catastrophe are its other facets. Your viewpoint makes or breaks this world. This applies as much to your dream of a start-up. Only right thinking can bring positive results. However, what is right thinking? How do we attain it? Can it be developed? All successful people paid attention to a few basics and reaped wonderful rewards.

The legend of Sheikh Chilli is viewed as negative by many. I disagree; in fact, I advise people to follow him. Sheikh Chilli is not wrong in dreaming. It is his inaction that makes him a joke. Imagining the fruits without putting labour is his undoing. Being a Sheikh Chilli with right preparation can make you a winner. Let us refresh that story once again.

Once a man hires Sheikh Chilli to carry his earthen vessel. The man, with a reputation for daydreaming, puts it over his head and starts imagining. He foresees getting two dimes for this work. 'I would buy an egg which will hatch into a hen. Soon, I will own many hens and I will sell them to purchase a goat. The goat will turn into many goats, which will then fetch me a cow.' The train of thoughts in Sheikh Chilli's mind has no brakes, once started.

From cows to horses, Sheikh Chilli becomes a rich man in his dreams. 'One day, I will have a big house and a beautiful wife with many children. Sitting at the lawn of this house, my wife would call me to meals. But I will be smoking hukkah and will say no.' He nods in his dream to say no, which leads to the falling and breaking of the earthen vessel, thus shattering his dreams as well. He could barely save himself from the wrath of his employer. The story is often quoted as an example of ambitions that are devoid of efforts.

You can prepare your inner Sheikh Chilli to escape this fate through preparation. Sheikh Chilli failed because he had a long-drawn business plan that was governed more by greed than professional thinking. His vision is driven by the desire for an opulent life. Who doesn't want to become rich? But one must know the path to riches. Sheikh Chilli's plans move from one stage to another. Therefore, his mind makes him more imaginative than practical. Yet, he has enough wisdom to not dream of buying horses straight after selling eggs. His imaginations are entrenched in a certain degree of realism. Sheikh Chilli lacks in persistence of this thought. Second, he was incapable of imagining only one step at a time. More importantly, he should have been focused entirely on his current task of lifting the earthen vessel.

Many young entrepreneurs lose focus in the present as they are too much invested in the future. One should give his or her 100 per cent even if it is for an employer. You cannot improve your future prospects without giving primacy to your present tasks. More than wealth, team and brand, you are your best asset. Nobody can take away your innovative mind from you. This confidence makes you a winner.

The need is to turn Sheikh Chilli's dream into a start-up vision. It is possible through the right mindset. Stop seeking reasons for success and failure outside of yourself. Follow the 10 steps given ahead to develop a more innovative mind. This does not require extra efforts. Instead of learning to do things right, you must save yourself from doing wrong things. This is possible through affirmative thinking and a strong character. Dream big like Sheikh Chilli, but also work hard on them to turn them into a reality. Practise can make anything possible. Learn to practise the following 10 steps:

1. Practise to let go of slavery
2. Practise experience
3. Set up an aim
4. Conquer your fears and worries
5. Love thy struggle
6. Take right decisions
7. Mingle with people
8. Understand the importance of time
9. Be important
10. Have a strong will power

## Practise to Let Go of Slavery

You will start dreaming of your own venture only after you have practised to get out of slavery. You own your actions once it happens. Fear of failing to lead is one of our biggest weaknesses.

Right approach can help overcome this shortcoming. It is always the psychological aspect of enslavement that bothers us. For example, nobody likes to be dependent for fulfilling their basic needs and desires. Servitude in the professional arena takes away all the fun of the job. We feel stifled when others take decisions of our life. More the mental subjugation, greater will be our frustration. This frustration reflects as vexation in our daily behaviour at home and office. It may soon turn into depression.

All doors of progress are shut if one develops a habit for this kind of slavery. Such people get accustomed to their boundaries and never attempt to go beyond them. However, the more you vouch for the security of these boundaries, the more insecure you become. You must have noticed we are always less afraid while driving ourselves, whereas being driven by another amateur driver can make us anxious.

We are more confident and conscious of our well-being when we drive our own lives. On the other hand, self-doubt induces a false sense of security in patronage. Most of us blame others for all things ailing our life. This feeling takes away our control over the vicissitudes of life.

The moment you surrender this control, you start treading the wrong path. This is succumbing to the servility of life. Life begins with dependence for all of us. But those who are the real winners of life move towards self-reliance. Rest only resign to the shackles of life.

Those who repose faith in their capabilities to accomplish any task are finally unfettered from these chains. Nobody can deny that success requires struggle. However, this struggle cannot be imposed. A truly independent person learns to relish and thrive in hardships. These are the kind of people that become an inspiration for lesser mortals. We all know there are only a handful of such people in the world. Others merely try to follow their lead.

The desire for recognition is another cause of mental slavery. True seekers know that accolades follow those who have attained inner-freedom. However, courage is the first precondition for any kind of independence. Develop this courage so that your mind does not accept enslavement as the final truth.

Do not follow the author's words blindly. Ponder over the structure of your life and beliefs. You will realise most of your limits are self-imposed. You are afraid to break those limits because you are unaware of your potential. Remember, you are losing time with each passing second. Utilise every second to gain real freedom and you will see every moment is full of ecstasy.

## Practise Experience

Any start-up begins with inexperience. This makes the entire process even more interesting. Budding entrepreneurs learn from their contemporaries. They read books, train with experienced people or get on-the-job training. However, learning from mistakes is the best way to improve.

We keep widening our know-how in the area of our expertise. Our expertise is essentially enhanced by experience. Therefore, experience determines our success in life, or the lack of it. If you take new experiences as part of an exercise, then progress is a continuum for you.

Even bad experiences make you a better person. As they say, anything that does not kill you, makes you stronger. My friend's disappointment with his car paved his way for learning a new skill. A skill that might make a difference between life and death at some time. Breaking down of a car is a small incident but the underlying principle applies equally to the biggest disappointments of life.

Any failure drives you towards recognising your shortcomings and acknowledgment of weakness is the first step towards overcoming it. Whereas, a good experience is a confidence booster. Opening your arms to both sort of experiences drives your life towards a positive direction. Wasting energy in worrying instead of sorting your troubles is a recipe for disaster.

This attitude will never let you control your life. Fear will only aggravate your woes and it will keep on chasing you until you start facing the cause of your worry.

The practise of welcoming new experiences is very important in life. Remember, you are a student of life until your last breath. There are no bounds to knowledge, as there are no limits to learning. Your experience is indeed your only true earning in life. It is the bedrock of your personality and confidence.

Obviously, a familiar path is always easier to tread. A friend of mine is fond of traveling. He is well aware of the problems that a traveler faces and the preparations that are required for a journey. His habits have made him confident of any journey. The same thing applies to any field of life. You cannot experience everything under the sky in a limited lifespan, but you can certainly learn the basics of an experience. You can learn that difficulties only polish your abilities. The ability to feel something new is God's grace. Whether you want to open your being to newness or continue walking on the beaten track is your decision. But perfecting the art of experience is imperative for a good personality and a successful life.

**Set up an Aim**

The purpose behind your start-up and what you want to attain within a given time span, is your aim. Meeting small ambitions add up to the realisation of the big goal. It is necessary to practise setting up your aims and work hard to make them a reality. What is the purpose of life? This seems to be the moot question for any thinking individual. Some find their purpose early while others have to wait. However, most of the people never find it.

Nevertheless, each individual, consciously or subconsciously, wants to find why he/she is here. Those who waste their life loitering aimlessly, end up blaming their fate. You are what you want to be; you are doing what you have made yourself capable of doing. We are an aggregate of our dreams and desires. Our experiences and circumstances are responsible for what we are. However, many people have realised impossible ambitions through the power of imagination and dreams. To set a target, you must not be disoriented from the true path of your life. You must be as focused as Arjuna was while taking an aim at the eye of the fish.

What ambition we set for ourselves depend on our nature. Our ultimate aim would always be vague if our thoughts are astray. Start concentrating on everyday targets to remain steadfast on the final purpose of life. It will require a lot of patience and perseverance.

You need to look at how you do your daily chores, are you into the habit of procrastination and do you manage your situations with patience. You can only set your aim after you understand yourself and the trajectory of your life. Observe how you utilise your time. Are you simply passing your days or remain in a hurry? Note down all these traits in a diary. You must learn to effectively manage your time. Mostly, we do not delve deeper into these questions. Our efforts in organising life are momentary. A spirit of improving schedule comes over for a day or two and then passes. Life continues on its usual course.

The discerning of this usual course of life is very necessary. Contemplate how you spend your time. This will give you an idea about where your life is heading.

What are the tasks that take up most of your time? What jobs do you do with your heart? Answers to these questions will reveal the areas of your core interests. Feel for an ambition that emanates out of your passion. Make it a part of your daily life. Learn, plan and take help to achieve it. This practice can deliver surprisingly positive results. I can say from experience that putting your heart out in a mission makes things happen in our favour. Sometimes, you find opportunities coming your way or you may meet people who you need the most. All these coincidences are good omens. Nothing is impossible once you learn to set your goals right.

## Conquer Your Fears and Worries

Most of us grow up with our ghosts of fear. The fear of failure is among the most common ones of these fears. Like none of those who talk of ghosts have actually seen them, the ones pointing at your failures have also not tasted success in their lives. The fear of professional failure is worse than failing itself. It dissipates your energy. Overcoming this fear opens many new doors of opportunity.

Fighting your fears is nourishing them. You just have to observe as they come and go in your thought process. Mere observance can stop their nourishment.

Fears are of many kinds; some are long-term and deep-rooted fears. Others emanate out of our insecurity for the future. Fear of ghosts is one of the most common type of deep-rooted fears. We hear ghost stories in our childhood. TV, films, literature and folklores further condition our minds towards this fear. This fear refuses to leave us even when we become a responsible adult. Religion also takes root in our psyche similarly. More people would bet on finding a ghost in solitude than finding God.

This shows that fear arises from negative thoughts. Negative emotions are normally balanced by positive mental stimulations. However, when negativity dominates all other thoughts, fear takes over our being. Reading about fear can be of some help but not until you start developing a positive mental frame.

One of the best ways to dispel fear is to immerse yourself in an activity you enjoy. All other mental processes cease, when you are fully involved in a work. For example, playing a sport or watching a movie insulates you from negative emotions for a time being. The disarrayed thoughts are the only reason of fear and there is no alchemy for fearlessness than to get rid of useless mentation. The moot point, therefore, is how to get rid of these uncontrollable chain of thoughts. The first step is to realise the need to control your mental chatter. Try to meditate on your inner conversation without trying to control it. Thinking about not thinking is a thought in itself. Therefore, the best exercise is to let your thoughts flow unhindered. The only thing you have to do is be a detached observer.

Normally, one thought triggers an involuntary chain of mental prattle. This process makes you either happy or sad. We fear the future because it is uncertain.

Love for your work will take you forward in the learning process. We discussed in the beginning of this chapter the futility of mental chatter. Either thoughtlessness or positive thinking are the panacea for this deep-rooted nature of mind.

The first option is ruled out in this mundane world and it is a tall order to achieve that state. Positive thinking can come only if you take interest in your work and persist with improving your skills. Some people admit failure even before they have begun the fight. Expecting positive results can prevent this tendency.

You can succeed in any field of your choice. However, you must know how to be the master of your mind. Controlling your mind is almost like playing a musical instrument. Meditating on your thought process will help you to get rid of your real and imaginary fears. This practice will make you realise the true value of your abilities.

## Love Thy Struggle

I encountered different stories of struggle during my projects related to start-ups. Many of these experiences are recounted in this book. All these case studies have one thing in common; struggle, which most of us shy away from.

The eminence of struggle applies equally to all human beings. It is an essential part of the journey of life. No civilisation would ever have thrived without their tenacity to struggle. To get out of your comfort zone is a struggle in itself. We have discussed about self-confidence. Lack of self-belief gives you a feeling of struggle. It is also borne out of a feeling of wantage. Even feeding their family is an ordeal for many people while to others, it might mean finalising a deal of millions. Every fulfillment entails struggle. Avoiding it means you are settling for no attainment in life. All the glories and accomplishments recorded in history are sagas of struggle. Those who have circumvented the path of trials have restricted themselves to mediocrity.

All chapters in school and college curriculum end with a series of questions. Students are expected to answer these 'problems'. It is a kind of a measure to judge whether a pupil has understood the lesson or not. The higher you move in standards, the harder do these problems get. The same applies to the struggle of life. Greater obstacles mean more struggle, but they also signify that you are moving higher up the ladder of life. Escaping this natural process will result in the same fate as that of the stunted caterpillar.

### *Rabindranath Tagore writes in one of his poems*

> LET me not pray to be sheltered from dangers but to be fearless in facing them.
> Let me not beg for the stilling of my pain but for the heart to conquer it.
> Let me not look for allies in life's battlefield but to my own strength.
> Let me not crave in anxious fear to be saved but hope for patience to win my freedom. Grant me that I may not be a coward,
> feeling your mercy in my success alone;
> but let me find
> the grasp of your hand in my failure.

### *The Heart of God: Prayers of Rabindranath Tagore*

Tagore clearly knew that there just isn't any salvation without the pain of struggle. Do not crave to be saved from struggle but develop the patience to withstand it.

Preparing yourself for the strife is the only way forward in life. You can develop this attitude by taking on the mundane challenges of everyday life. Observe how you respond to difficult situations. You will realise everything you possess is the outcome of some struggle. Learn to take every affliction as an opportunity to grow. Otherwise, the drudgery of life will fill you with despondency. It will end all your potential to succeed.

The sloth makes our mind restive. You will always find hard-working people more at ease with themselves than those who shy away from labour. Every task that stretches your limits is an excellent opportunity to make you a better person. You will find satisfaction in the lassitude involved.

Contemplate why what is a tall order to you might be child's play to another person. You also possess many attributes, which others will find hard to attain. One can keep on complaining for the unfairness of life as a ruse to circumvent the path of struggle.

However, there is no other option but to walk on it. All great people had the will power to strive amidst the worst of tragedies. Never lose heart and keep your morale high. Accept the reality of struggle with a smile on your face and you shall be indomitable in life.

## Take Right Decisions

Your life is a result of the choices you have made. Hence, it is paramount to understand that the right decision can only be taken in the present moment. Life is here and now and so is its vital force. It is only the present situation that influences our power of discretion. Rational decisions can only arise from a well-composed mind. As Swami Yogananda Paramhamsa said, 'Live in the moment and see the beauty of all before you. The future will take care of itself.'

The cacophony of brainwork can distract you from the right path. It reduces your capability to take decisions. A heart shrouded with fear and doubt can seldom reach the right conclusion. Most people summon their experience to reach any important decisions. We all seek good advice before making an important move. It is a subtle attempt to seek confirmation to our own conclusions. All advice contrary to our decision is difficult to accept. In fact, criticism only weakens our resolve to stick to our stand.

Psychologists agree that bitter memories and fear of their repetition in future hamper our decision capability. Your own experience would tell that there are as many mouths as there are opinions to every issue. It only adds to the confusion in the ultimate calculation.

I know many people who cannot just get over making plans. You would always find them making business plans or discussing a change of profession. They have been paying such lip service for years yet their intentions remain unrealised. They are the people who yearn for change and yet fear it. The inertia of status quo prevents them from taking any significant decision.

Decisive people know that the path to success is full of challenges. There is a risk involved in every challenge. Mark Zuckerberg, the founder of Facebook says, 'The biggest risk is not taking any risk. In a world that is changing, the only strategy that is guaranteed to fail is not taking risks.'

Even the most sagacious of decision can fail, what matters more is the efforts you put behind them. You can do any task that has ever been accomplished. Each human being has the potential to achieve the unachievable.

To have doubt means at least a part of you will accept the challenge. But confusion stands in the way. Trust your intuition to clear the path. The real irony of life is our inability to act despite knowing what is right and wrong. You shall not need any advice to tread on the right path. Whenever faced with the predicament of doing or not doing, always chose the latter. Start by doing what is necessary; then do what is possible; and you are doing the impossible. The dilemma signifies the inner urge to accomplish a task. Otherwise, mind can straightaway reject the idea. It is often the apprehension of unfavourable consequences that shrouds our decision-making capability.

There is, at least, a chance of positive change in doing a thing; inaction borne out of perplexity will bring failure. Reconsidering a decision for petty gains can spell disaster. The mechanism of decision-making is often described as thinking from heart or brain. Do not confuse heart with the biological organ in this context. It refers to the emotional centre of our psyche. It is nothing but the constant flow of thoughts, memories and emotions. Whereas, brain is the logical part of our being.

Most people feel a constant struggle between these two centres of consciousness. As Einstein said, 'The heart says yes, but the mind says no.' Well, there is no definite solution to this paradox until you become enlightened to transcend beyond both. Until then, use the faculty of mind to analyse, assess and interpret the issue at hand in the light of your experience and the advice of others. Contemplate if the conclusion thus reached is in conformity with your intuition. I say the first hunch in any matter to be the voice of heart. Weigh the inputs of your heart and mind and use free will to reach a conclusion. Remember, nobody can take decisions on your part. Take responsibility for the steps you take in life.

Taking decisions is difficult in the world of start-ups. You often have no scope for experimentation. There is a lack of experience. Your first instinct can be your best guide under such circumstances. That your path has succeeded in the past is immaterial. It is a unique situation that you will deal with. Therefore, there cannot be any right or wrong. The success of your decision will depend on your groundwork. Thus, gain self-confidence to back your decisions.

## Mingle with People

Your start-up's success hinges on your inter-personnel skills. Reach out to new people to exchange ideas and find new possibilities. If you are meeting the same people every day, visiting same places, doing same things repeatedly, you will only get what you have been getting. Keep doing these things if you are happy with what you have achieved. Otherwise, change is your only option.

The inertia of daily circle of life inhibits our tendency to meet new people and venture out to new places. It is a normal psychology that we prefer familiarity over unknown scenarios. It is just as we prefer known paths to the unknown ones. Treading on a new road always involves risk and effort. But it teaches us how to explore the journey. One becomes confident of finding the way on his own.

The same principle applies to interpersonal relations. There is not much difference in the mental process, whether it is searching for a path or interacting with people. We feel more comfortable in the company of our close acquaintances. Whereas, there is always some hesitation in opening up to strangers. This unease of breaking our comfort zone limits the scope of enriching our personality. We feel somewhat unnerved whenever the situation demands breaking of this zone.

Many people pander at the opportunity to join unfamiliar gatherings. It has more to do with edginess than lack of will. However, you must also have noticed that memory retains only new experiences. We only remember things unusual to our daily pattern of life. Any break from the routine is welcome but mind wants to escape the efforts involved in it. You must be resolute to prevail over mental qualms for giving space to new sensations.

You must not enter new situations or meet new people with preconceived notions. It is like turning those experiences into picture frames hanging on the walls. Free the walls of mind from all such frames of prejudices. No man is good in real life. All human beings are a complex mixture of both the traits.

There is no point in judging a person who has no bearing over you. You cannot conjecture about a person or place without knowing. Whether your experience is good depends on your point of view. Spend your precious energy only on people that have a positive effect. Be approachable to everybody, even to strangers. Share your life with them and learn from their experiences.

Do not forget that they are as apprehensive of strangers as you are. It would be better, if you take the first lead in breaking the ice. I have spent many journeys without mingling with my co-passengers. Whereas, many whom I opened up to, became friends for life.

Being extrovert adds to your self-confidence. It opens new doors of opportunities. It is like forming a network of relations as a spider weaves her web. As Max Gunther writes in his book *The Luck Factor*, 'A spider strings many lines to catch passing flies, and the bigger her web, the better she eats. So it is with those who would catch good luck. And with exceptions, the luckiest men and women are those who have taken the trouble to form many friendly contacts with other people.'

Whenever you miss an opportunity to meet a new person, you could be denying yourself innumerable moments of fortune. You are wasting your social skills by doing so. A chance moment could prove to be the biggest break of your life. Attending one simple gathering could transform your life.

You should be involved whole-heartedly in any such exercise. Test your communication skills on all such occasions. It will make you a better person. This is not only about seeking opportunities but also polishing your personality. Such experiences make you capable of facing any new situation.

## Understand the Importance of Time

Failure to meet deadlines will always cast aspersions on your success. Proscastrination will put you in a situation like that of an examinee who hasn't prepared till the last moment. A successful start-up must have a time frame for tasks. Planning our time must be part of our personality.

The concept of time has intrigued humankind since time immemorial. Still, common knowledge about time is superficial. We understand time only through what we read or listen. Time is not restrained only to the ticking of your clock. There is a world of difference between understanding time and experiencing it. A superficial comprehension remains constrained to measuring time in the given dimensions, whereas living is a different dimension altogether. Learn to experience every passing moment. This moment, the very breath, the present scene in front of your eyes is the present manifestation of time. The bygone is bygone and future has still not risen. We impose our impressions of the past on time. This leads to a misleading concept of time. The time is much more than a periodical ticking of clock. The thing we call age is nothing but accumulation of spent moments.

Some of these moments stay in our conscious memories. However, a constant dwelling in the past ruins the present. Many people hanker for memories as they associate past glories to them. There are many who relish even past wounds. This is a gross injustice to life that is here and now. Use experience to better your present instead. We use the experience gained through practice in implementing it at present. Once you have learnt the basic notes of music, you play the full tunes. Once you have learnt driving, you implement the skills on road.

We burden time with our journey of thoughts. We load it with memories and aspirations. Whereas both the past and future do not exist. Mixing your present with illusions of the past or future will deter you from effectively planning your life. One might ask how to plan, if you do not conceive it. How do you create something new without imagination? The question holds merit. Its answer lies in who controls you inner being. You can channelise your imagination towards creativity only if you are its master. Otherwise, the same faculty might lead you astray into narcotic hallucinations. It will only weaken your ingenuity.

This is clear while making plans. You need to know the relevant subject before chalking out future designs for it. Based on this knowledge, you assess your capabilities and the challenges involved. The step of implementation follows this assessment. This is how you should move ahead. However, only a few people possess such clarity of insight. Most plans end up as they were not exactly meant to. It is because some experience muddles with our present. If the experience is unpleasant, it fills us with worries about the future of the plan. A positive reminiscence might turn you over confident. Expecting your moment of victory in advance may add to the pressure of performance. It may also give rise to anxiety that will always be detrimental to your cause.

All these mental cobwebs stand in the way of proper utilisation of time. You must contemplate how your life is connected to time. You are a product of conceptions formed by mental conditioning. Your character is made by the suggestions you have imbibed from the outside world. This process continues until our last breath. You transcend time the moment you understand its true nature. You cannot waste a single second when you are conscious to the flow of time. Wake up to the present moment. Observe the footmarks it leaves on your conscious nature. Every single secret of your existence lies hidden within this very moment. It is the determinant of your karma. Do not lose yourself in the continuous mental chatter. It is the biggest contempt to time. It is akin to slumber of soul that can render your whole life pointless. Dreams come only when we are asleep. However, your whole existence is a dream, if you are not aware of the present moment. You have not realised your full potential unless you do not command your thoughts.

## Be Important

Finding solutions to the people's problems and making their lives easier is the main motive of any start-up. You can only do so if you have the trait of a problem-solver. Be it start-ups or your personal life, only those who are of some use, gain prominence in any field of life. To be of some use is the talisman of success. We understand the importance of mutual interests in all our relationships. The moment you rise to notability, people are all in praise for you. They feel honored to interact with you. This is not for selfish gains; it is the collective nature of humanity to worship the rising sun.

You can understand this tendency by a simple example. A simple plumber or electrician becomes the most important person when you are dealing with power or water problems at home. You feel reverence for these simple workers in many such situations. It forces you to cajole them for an early visit. Notwithstanding their profile of work, you would find such workers are busy most of the times. From a utilitarian point of view, it is our requirement that makes us important to society. The amount of respect one finds in society is proportional to utility. The principle is simple; necessity begets influence.

This principle of utility applies to personal relationships. You can or cannot be indispensable to the other person. Sometimes, you may be needed because of your special qualities.

The society needs people who can bear its responsibilities. Self-doubt prevents us from meeting these responsibilities. Your present deeds will only decide your future worth. So start making a list of your valuable qualities without losing time. Think how you can contribute to your family, society and the workplace. Pay attention to the things that can make you a favourite in the eyes of the others. These can be tiny gesture. I have come across many people who are not very successful yet they are the heartthrobs in their circles. Several people are in demand during family festivals like marriages as they accept responsibilities.

It is necessary to diversify your capabilities, if you want to be beneficial to the society. Everybody is born with at least one specialty. Do not remain restricted to dreams while watching others excel in their areas of skills.

Dexterity in any job will require perseverance and a thorough study. However, little knowledge is worse than no knowledge at all. You are neither proficient nor in a condition to accept your ignorance in this state. Such people are only good at boasting.

They always shy away from proving themselves. We are losing precious life force with each passing moment. Not using the precious time for self-accomplishment is gross injustice to the whole existence. Walking on this path can get you to the real purpose of your life. Only a man with a purpose can devote his life for a cause. The world bows to such dedicated souls. Never cease to explore your utility to existence until you find your purpose. Success and admiration will come your way.

### Have a Strong Will Power

All the practices mentioned above can never be realised without will power.The good news is that it is possible to develop will power. It is even more necessary than understanding the business principles for establishing a new venture. The start-up ideas are often new and disruptive. Therefore, there are no precedents to meet the challenges involved. A strong will power is our only guide in such situations.

Only you can decide what you want from life. You are the best judge of your capabilities and shortcomings. Nobody can assess the areas where your efforts need improvement and areas where you can excel. You know what is right or wrong for you.

Success demands hard labour. It is borne out of struggle. All of us know it from our personal experience. We know of our desires and the way to realise them is through will power. In its basis lies the practice of remaining steadfast on your path while resisting distractions.

I read a book titled *Icchashakti Aur Uska Vikas* (Developing Will Power) during my school days. It was a concise book containing Swami Buddhanand's writings. It had a profound effect on my life. The book taught me how will power is at the basis of our existence. Everything you do in life is determined by will power or the lack of it. In the words of Swami Buddhanand, *Abhishtaki siddha auranishta se doori hi mazboot icchashakti hai* (strong will power is getting the desirable and avoiding what is not).

Many factors contribute in motivating you towards doing any job. They can be company, our own thoughts or family values. Try a simple experiment. Place your palm on the ground. Try to block all commands from your brain to your hand and then try lift it. You cannot move it. Not even your hand can move without will power, leave apart great achievements.

Man is a bunch of never-ending desires. Every fulfillment begets a new desire. We want something every second of our lives. Passing an examination is the biggest thing a teenager might ask from God. However, the yardstick would be different for a millionaire businessman. Buddha said for a reason that desire is the root cause of all sorrows. Still, most among us spend our lives chasing desires and losing.

A desire is the thirst for bliss. Accomplishment of an ambition gives us the moment of that bliss. But it isn't eternal. Soon, the surge of happiness recedes and the mind moves towards another desire. An unwavering perseverance ensures success in fulfilling ambitions. The bigger you aim, the more hard work, patience and faith it requires.

People with strong will power are ideal in all fields, be it arts, science or politics. Aspiring to set an example is a good motivation. You can choose the field of work on your own. Will power grows as you gain expertise with practise and enhances your interest in the job. Ineptness and fear are the biggest reasons for aversion towards any work. It takes a strong resolve to perfect any skill. Small things in life can contribute hugely in driving your commitment.

Setting too many ambitions at a time will give rise to doubts. It can even result in despondency. We need to figure out how we are spending our energy every day. Excessive use of cell phones or television can be a huge distraction for any productive work. Remember, vital force is the fuel of our being. You can put it to make your life beautiful or waste it in trifles. Understand the worth of this life that you have been bestowed with. You should feel gratitude towards existence for every second that you live. Such attitude will do wonders to your will power.

Strong determination means to complete a task that is worth doing at any cost. It is the self-control to stop yourself from committing a wrong deed. The capability to judge good is inherent in our consciousness since birth.

Are you not aware that healthy body is the first condition for a blissful life? You also know that good health comes from regular exercise and balanced diet. Likewise, the laws of energy and importance of its utilisation is a fact. Those who cannot work for their interest despite this knowledge can only be called weak-willed.

Many among us make a resolution to start regular exercise from the next morning, but resolve fades in the face of sloth. I have seen many people pledging to quit their addictions. They even try to follow suit but only to fail after a few days. Each failure to keep your resolution further weakens your determination. The moment you make your resolutions, your earnestness grows in all fields of life.

Start doing what you like without losing a second. Don't waste time in quitting that which hampers your growth. Small things form our habits and our character is the sum total of our habits. You cannot be an emphatic personality if you are not firm on your words. A strong-willed person exudes confidence in his decisions. You have nobody else to blame for your failures if you are not determined. I have seen many talented people leading an unsuccessful life because they don't have the tenacity to quit their addictions. Will power affects both our body and mind.

It is necessary to know what makes you weak. Why do you lack strong will? The way to attain a resolute character opens the moment you focus on this question. Lack of will emerges when we deem the task at hand as impossible. Prepare yourself for your goal. Learn from people who have already fulfilled that ambition. Remember, the fear of failure is worse than failure. Mentation on your ambitions is futile. You will need to wake up and start walking on your chosen path. The fear of failure can soon become a permanent trait of your personality. Backtracking from a challenge becomes your response in every small and big venture you face. Fear and self-doubt never leaves weak-willed persons.

It is necessary to set deadlines for every task you undertake. It can do wonders to enhance your will power. Start with small chores of daily schedule like bathing or getting ready for workplace. Your confidence to accomplish big goals is boosted if you are successful in keeping the time limit of these small things every day.

We have discussed the importance of failure and struggle in the realisation of your aims. We know that failure is a stepping-stone towards ultimate success. We live in a world full of talented people. There is no end to expertise in every sphere of life. But we have to remember that even they have faced their share of failures. Learn to respect failure as a natural part of the process and no task shall remain unsurmountable for you. The moment you are confident enough to accept any challenge, you become a strong-willed person. You learn to keep away from all the negative aspects of life.

## THINGS TO REMEMBER

- Only successful personalities make for a successful entrepreneur.
- You can attain such personality under any circumstances.
- Focus on small things in life before making big plans.
- Your personal behaviour and reaction to other people reflect in the way you do business.
- You build your character brick-by-brick. Watch your habits and improve them.
- Your health, personality and time are your best assets. Working on them is of paramount importance.
- Struggle is hallmark of progress. You are missing something if you haven't encountered struggle yet.
- Meet new people and visit new places. Don't limit your circle.
- Develop qualities that can make your family, society and country better. Make a list of traits that can improve others' lives. Keep updating this list.
- Talent is always respected. Develop your skills.

# 16

# FIVE BOOKS TO INSPIRE SUCCESS

Mentioned below is the summary of five books which can help you reach your goal. You should read these books in the same order as discussed in this chapter. Most of the books are filled with foreign case studies which may not be easily relatable. The difference between the business cultures of India and countries like the USA and China is also clear. Therefore, their success stories may not be entirely relevant to our context. Yet, the basics of a successful business remain the same all around the world. Though we are witnessing original innovations in increasing numbers in India, it is also true that most start-ups try to replicate the model of the Silicon Valley enterprises. Therefore, it is necessary to understand these books in the light of India's business atmosphere.

Most successful start-ups are led by people who have either worked for another start-up or have experimented with one of their own. The eureka moment in terms of start-up ideas is extremely rare. You will need to nurture and develop your idea. Befriend these books. More so, if you have no experience of business or working for a start-up. These books will transcend you to that world. You need to be psychologically in that zone while planning a new business venture. Many unforeseen situations await your journey. Learning from these books can prepare you for such trials.

Reading about others' struggles not only inspire you but also reduce your fear of failure. Although books have their own limitations as most of them only highlight the decisive moments of the protagonist. These are either the most dramatic turns of the story or junctures that decide the fate of the venture. The stories told in these books may not tell much about the daily habits of their central characters, their general behaviour or how they react to success and failure.

These are the aspects one needs to grasp. It is for this reason that delving deep into bulky books can sometimes be boring. Yet, books can have a life-changing effect. This transforming ingredient in any book is its central message. For example, *The Alchemist* by Paulo Coelho says even impossible dreams can be realised if we persevere and pay heed to omens.

However, conveying this message in as many words is unlikely to move many hearts. Therefore, the writer has to take you along to the journey of that shepherd boy and you start identifying with the characters of the story. You would have witnessed that all good books have a lingering effect. But it does not stay forever because we are witnessing the truth through the character's experiences and not our own. Only you can write your story.

## THE PRINCIPLE OF 1:4:40

Most of us yearn to be role models, we dream of lives which can make for an inspiring story. However, your life is unique to yourself and no book can fully encompass it. More important is the underlying principle governing your real-life story. It will apply to other's lives also. I was taught during my theatre days that to act in 1 play, you should read 4 first, and to read 4 plays, see 40 first. This logic applies equally to the world of start-ups and innovations.

Work with at least four start-ups to start one of your own. You can be part of its governing team or an ordinary employee. A struggling start-up can teach you far better than any professional institute. Learn the positives as well as the negatives of that venture. Give your best to it. I do not suggest that you should change four jobs. You can work for one and understand the rest.

Likewise, read about 40 established start-ups related to your field. Devoting time to this exercise can become the most rewarding experience of your life. The principle of 1:4:40 merits a separate book. All I am emphasising here is the point that it is just one principle that finds expansion in any book. The narration is made interesting through storytelling. This also helps in getting your point across.

Books can help you prepare to make decisions. Many books narrate the right or wrong decisions which made the difference and also the reasons behind them. You must pre-decide the literature and reference as part of your preparation for a start-up. There are some really good books, you will find helpful in this phase. However, reading them will consume significant time and energy. Since reading and understanding books are my job, I have presented summaries of some such books in the coming chapters.

Yet, I recommend that reading should be your necessity and not merely a hobby. After all, books are food for your thoughts

The five books I have summarised are as follows:

1. *Zero to One* by Peter Thiel
2. *The Lean Start-up* by Eric Ries
3. *The $100 Start-up* by Chris Guillebeau
4. *The Start-up Owner's Manual* by Bob Dorf and Steve Blank
5. *Rework* by Jason Fried

All these five books have been written with different perspectives. Yet, they share some underlying principles. I have written this chapter only after testing the principle of 1:4:40. I researched at least 50 books before zeroing on the above-mentioned books. I attempt to give their gist simply. You will be able to get the essence of these international bestsellers in one chapter. These summaries will give you the knowledge that these books seek to impart. You are free to read them in full.

Our professional education still relies on old-fashioned courses. This book and this chapter will give you deep theoretical insights. As I stated earlier, these books are similar and I have taken care to not sound repetitive. The essential points have been concised.

## SUMMARY OF *ZERO TO ONE* BY PETER THIEL

Peter Thiel, the author of this book is an entrepreneur. He has compiled his series of lectures on start-ups and presented their improved version in the form of this book. The book created ripples and is considered among the best pieces of literature on start-ups. This book has nothing unique to offer. However, it encapsulates the most essential feature of any successful business. It is to introduce something new to the market, an innovation which is not yet there. Most people try to compete within the existing ambits. For example, they would think about a showroom with a new theme and at a profitable location while entering the garment market. Very few innovate on the fabrics or designs. This is what Peter terms as thinking from zero to one. Making a horsecart out of horse is '1 to N' growth. Whereas, thinking about manufacturing a car instead of a horsecart is 'zero to one' mindset.

The book focuses on the right meaning and definition of innovation. Innovation, by definition, means creating something new, a 'zero to one' approach. Look at what is missing in the existing world and what can be done to fill the gap. This would be the beginning of the 'zero to one' viewpoint. People line up to imitate or change original innovations. This is what Peter calls '1toN' journey. While there is nothing wrong in this approach, it won't take you to the level of 'zero to one' innovators who are always remembered.

I liked this book because it talks not only about business methods but goes a step ahead to discuss innovative ideas and innovative minds. It focuses on the need to research and experiment to do something new.

Peter Thiel can claim an authority over the subject as he showed the power of 'zero to one' thought through PayPal.

He was also among the first investors in Facebook. An innovative mind can take your dreams to new heights. The market is full of books that claim to teach marketing, salesmanship and planning.

This one stresses only on moving from 'zero to one' or doing something new.

There are two aspects to this book. Readers might feel it is only about existing start-ups or the ones on the verge of taking another leap. Most of the examples cited by Peter in this book fall into similar categories. Therefore, beginners may find it difficult to comprehend the book. However, you will be able to develop an innovative mind at the beginning of your professional journey itself, if only you can understand the mantra of this book.

The most important principle that the book propounds is to go beyond the existing competition by offering a product or service which nobody else can.

The following three dictums of the book are noteworthy:

- The biggest leaps in progress are vertical, not horizontal.
- Monopolies are good, for both business and society.
- Founders need a vision to take their business from zero to one.

**Lesson 1: The Biggest Leaps in Progress Are Vertical, Not Horizontal**

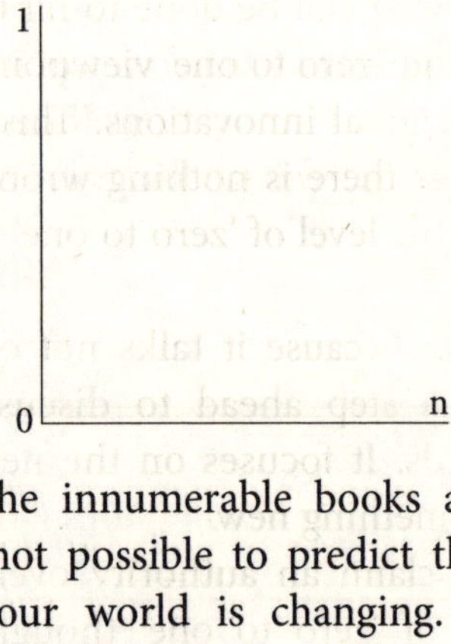


Notwithstanding the innumerable books and movies on the subject, it is still not possible to predict the future. More so, considering how our world is changing. An overwhelming majority in the business world comprises people who only capitalise on the existing technologies and markets. These are the ones who tread from '1 to N', meaning progress. This movement involves a lot of competition and seldom gives distinction as you are only following the existing trends. At most, people will reach 100 from 1 or grow to n times. However, few entrepreneurs introduce new products or services. This is the journey from 'zero to one'. The market follows such people. They are the ones who set the trend.

Steve Jobs is one such example. He introduced smartphones at the time when most of us where content with phones with button keyboards. Steve Jobs revolutionised the world of mobile phones. Soon, the market was flooded with smartphones of all kinds. Some improved upon features like cameras, some dwelled on competitive prices while others concentrated on branding. Several other smartphone companies emerged and progressed. However, the difference between Steve Jobs' Apple brand and the rest differentiates horizontal growth from the vertical one.

To embark on the journey of 'zero to one', Peter Thiel urges you to ask yourself a few questions. He motivates you to focus on future challenges and think about the possibilities of the changing world. Some of these questions in the Indian context could be: Will we exhaust all our energy resources? If yes, then what will be the alternative? How will the world look like without water? PM Modi has envisaged *Janshakti4Jalshakti* (people's power for saving water) with a similar vision. The government can provide a conducive environment, but the initiative will have to come from the youth, still unemployed. Imagining a better future can lead you from 'zero to one'.

### Lesson 2: Monopolies Aren't Bad. They're Good for Business and Society

Are you a Microsoft client? I am. There are high chances that you would also be. Almost 75 per cent of the computers are operating on Windows. Is such kind of monopoly wrong? Peter does not think so. In his view, only the first entrant and the one who evolves can create a monopoly. Do you still use Yahoo or Bling search engine? Most of us don't. The search engine business is heavily monopolised by Google. This is among the reasons why Google can spend a good amount of money on improving the user experience. The company has maintained it's dominance and is only moving from strength to strength. It is now working on futuristic projects like driverless cars. Companies like Microsoft and Google are still thinking in terms of 'zero to one'. They will most likely also monopolise the product markets they are creating. What are you thinking? Imagine a better future and create a monopoly market of your own.

### Lesson 3: If the Founders Don't See, a Company Can Never Go from Zero to One

Monopolies are not created overnight. It requires a great product and a diligent team. It needs vision. A clear vision makes it possible to ensemble a capable team and gain monopoly. Peter Thiel himself worked for years with a team of 50 members. He did not achieve dominance in the payment gateway business overnight. All disruptive entrepreneurs are geniuses with a maverick streak. Peter also feels one needs to be quirky and a bit eccentric to complete the 'zero to one' journey. Only this attitude enables you to be in that imaginative zone where new ideas happen. The power to think ahead of the present realities gives you a futuristic vision.

Peter Thiel says in the book, 'Shoot for the moon. Even if you miss it, you'll be among the stars.'

This book calls upon its readers to not become part of any race, but be in their league. Become the one who the others think of chasing. Begin from the top. History belongs to those who complete the 'zero to one' journey. Many progress from '1 to N', but rare are those who choose the path of 'zero to one'.

Be far-sighted and prepare for future challenges to take on this path. Early beginning and hard work will help you along the way. Peter Thiel teaches by his example. The assertions in his book are not new. Yet, the branding and marketing ensured a top slot in the list of books on start-ups.

## SUMMARY OF *THE LEAN START-UP* BY ERIC RIES

A start-up begins with uncertainty. It is almost impossible to exactly replicate an idea into execution. Sometimes, results might exceed expectations while ideas may turn out to be pipe dreams at other times. The author, Eric Ries, shares similar experiences in this book. He could see many shortcomings in his start-up IMVU. However, this did not deter him from introducing his product to the market. Ries believes in the Build-Measure-Learn model.

The most important thing for any start-up is the vision. A clear vision leads to strategy. A good strategy constitutes a business model, road map of the product, partner's viewpoint and knowing customers as well as competitors. Your product can change often. You can also modify your strategy for good reasons. However, your vision should remain the same. Failure only means the need for a better strategy and execution. Knowing your weaknesses and improving upon them is the only path to success. Ries suggests another way of understanding customers and their needs well.

According to Ries, one should not waste time in theorising strategies and introduce the product to the market, even if it is far from perfect. The approach should be to gradually improve the product by strengthening the customer feedback system. Experimenting with small groups or in small places can also help. Ries suggests testing the market with a low-quality prototype of your product.

Ries cites the example of Nick Swinmum's start-up Zappos. It was bought by Amazon for $1.2 billion. Nick wanted to sell shoes online. However, he didn't buy them and instead asked permission from different shopkeepers to take photographs of shoes displayed in their outlets. Nick then uploaded these pictures to his online platform. He was only testing if people would be keen to buy shoes online. He had a clear vision and strategy and the results are evident.

In his book, Ries underlines the need to choose the right customers and reaching out to them. Your strategy should focus on identifying people who need your product the most. He recounts how he knew his product had scope for improvement and yet, customers never complained. So much so, that he dropped the idea of upgrading the product. The underlying lesson suggests that you are making a product for the buyers and not for yourself. Any successful strategy should be receptive to market feedback.

Ries counsels finalising a minimum viable product after you have implemented the above model. Taking customers' feedback is necessary. The writer also mentions Toyota's mantra of 'Genchi Gembutsu' (go and see for yourself). It is imperative to go among end users for any 'lean start-up'. According to Ries, this was at the core of Toyota's success. The book cautions against 'analysis paralysis', meaning the tendency to launch products without proper research.

The book also discusses start-ups like GoupOn and DropBox to illustrate how effective implementation of a great idea even at a small level can bear fruit. These start-ups realised the importance of customer feedback. Most start-ups fail because they give precedence to their idea over customer need. You should begin by asking yourself if your product is at all required. Most successful ventures do not hit jackpot at the first shot, be it Zuckerberg or Steve Jobs.

An idea is necessary but it should be informed by the market's and customers' needs. The book teaches to treat a start-up like an experiment. Give your idea time and focus on MVP.

Many start-ups fail because they focus more on grand launching and investments. Others become self-obsessed with their idea, ignoring what the buyers want. Question your idea not with if you can make it, but with should you make it.

Traditional management skills may not work for a start-up. A conventional approach entails:

1. Market research
2. Formulating a strategy
3. Delivery of product

However, Eric suggests the following steps for innovative products:

- Build
- Measure
- Learn

Eric prescribes repeating these processes until you come up with a minimum viable product. It is a product to be initially launched with some unique features. It will help you to measure your product in the market.

Eric says you can either pivot or persevere after measuring the market response. Persevere if the response is positive or else pivot and introspect to improve your product. These are some valuable learnings of the book. But the absence of Indian case studies and a huge difference between the Indian and the US start-up ecosystem make it somewhat less relevant to the Indian entrepreneurs. The basic principles enshrined in the book are worth emulating though.

## SUMMARY OF *THE $100 START-UP* BY CHRIS GUILLEBEAU

Want to do business but not clear where to begin from? Ask yourself—what is your passion? How can it be used to benefit others? Try to identify that missing factor from people's lives and think of how you can fill the gap. You can do so by being a roaming entrepreneur.

This is what Chris Guillebeau tells you in his book *The $ 100 Start-up*. As the name suggests, the book teaches how to start your business in minimum resources. Although the examples cited in the book are not connected to India, yet the principles mentioned are really powerful, in fact, necessary for any successful business.

Most books on start-ups are written in developed countries where digital is the way of life. Such literature mostly deals with the challenges and doubts faced by the youth of the first world. India is treading on the road to progress at the international stage. The journey is powered by the entrepreneur spirit of its youth. It is, therefore, necessary to put this book in Indian perspective.

This book is particularly useful for those who:

- Want freedom from 9 am to 5 pm job
- Have less investment
- Want to follow passion while enjoying freedom
- Have less than five members on the team
- Have no great special skills

Chris seeks to give direction to your dreams while suggesting ways to make a practical business plan. He emphasises the importance of clarity on the following three things before starting any venture:

- Product or service
- Customer
- Way of transaction

These look like basic points. However, Chris uses them to talk about how doing business has become easy in the changing world. Identifying customers and ways of transactions were not always easy. Technology has made things easier. You can reach customers world over through digital marketing. Online retailers like Amazon and Flipkart provide online selling platforms. There are many transaction gateways for easy payments. Setting up a business no longer requires heavy investment and hiring big teams. All you need is a buyer and an understanding of the convergence of your passion with your business.

The YouTubers, publishers and micro-businesses do not require big factories. They run big businesses online. Huge markets and buyers are available in the virtual world. More and more young entrepreneurs are finding solutions for their problems and minting profits.

To identify your passion is common advice. But what if your passion lies in watching movies or listening to music? In other words, you also need to understand what market demands. According to Chris, you should try to find the area of convergence between your passion and market demand. This will give your passion shape to drive you to success.

Music buffs can become a part of radio or the online music industry. A passion is something beyond a hobby. Almost everybody loves music but those with passion will go deeper into learning and understanding it. It is those kinds who can make a career out of it. Think carefully, why should you get paid for your passion?

### Skill Transformation

Everyone has some skill. You need to tune it to your passion to make money. Skill can also be developed to suit your passion. The love for books can be transformed into the vocation of publication by learning skills like typing, translating, designing, etc. I have always loved cartoons and chose cartoon as the subject for my doctorate. However, I have to develop relevant skills to become a cartoonist. I will have to develop this passion to suit people's demand to earn money. This applies to all trades.

### Add Value, Get Freedom; More Value More Success

Helping people adds value to the business. Pay heed to what people want. We all want money, love and fame. Think of adding value to people's lives by reducing their burdens. People want to get rid of anxiety, worries and debts. Many start-ups are giving services related to lifestyles. There are many successful examples of ventures providing financial advice. Giving people business ideas, helping them grow it, relationship counselling are some related fields. In short, Chris tells you to think beyond your profit and innovate to make people's lives better. He also stresses the importance of the latest technology. According to him, technology makes lives better. You should anticipate the coming technological trends.

## Magic Formula

Summing up, Chris gives a formula:

Passion / Skill + Usefulness = Success

Recognise your passion and develop related skills. If both are added to the demand or utility decided by the market, then success is guaranteed.

Chris also urges to understand the difference between features and benefits. For example, looks and production value are the features of a YouTube channel, content is the benefit to the consumer. A product must have some benefit for the consumer.

## One-Page Business Plan

Business plans are important. However, Chris thinks many people unnecessarily waste precious time making these plans. He feels any good business plan should be short and clear. Learn to write your purpose in one sentence. Chris believes in the importance of planning, but he also tells you not to overwork on impractical plans. A hundred and forty words is a good limit to concise your mission statement. It can help you think about the first two specialities of your business: product or service and consumers. Put these two together to formulate your goal.

Get started immediately in six steps:

1. Commit to a product or service.
2. Build a simple website (can be a basic template, consider WordPress).

3. Come up with an offer.
4. Establish a payment method (consider PayPal).
5. Let the world know what you are offering (advertising, start on social media and go from there).
6. Repeat 1–5 over and over until you find success.

### Setting-up a Business in a Single Day

The way to kickstart a venture in a day is to become your advisor. Chris enumerates some simple principles to make it possible. Ensure that you have entered the market with specific expertise. If you come across as a business consultant then clarify which aspect of the business you specialise in. Make sure your consumers know what they can expect from you.

Chris focuses on attaching value to your service. People don't take cheap things seriously. They can question the quality you are providing. Ensure that your price reflects your product or service. In other words, he is telling you to attach a high price to your services as a consultant.

### Roaming Entrepreneurs

They are the laptop-wielding beings who relish the world of internet. Contrary to conventional managers stuck in some corporate office, these people work from anywhere. Chris cautions becoming a roaming entrepreneur only if it is required. After all, consumer satisfaction is non-negotiable.

Chris says that identifying common space between your passion and consumer needs, making your interest useful to people, and a short yet clear plan is the key to success.

## SUMMARY OF *THE START-UP OWNER'S MANUAL* BY BOB DORF AND STEVE BLANK

This book is for you if you are not a professionally trained businessperson. Although it is neither concise nor an interesting read, yet it gives you some valuable lessons in adopting a phased approach to draw customers. It can help to identify customers and teach methods of extensively researching the market.

The book underlines the difference between a big venture and a start-up. A large part of it is dedicated to earmarking your customers and market. However, authors Steve Blank and Bob Dorf begin by making the point that start-ups cannot be run on the same strategy as the big businesses.

The book mentions several start-ups that started with great preparation. Authors tell us these start-ups did everything that any big business would do to put the first foot forward. However, they consider it a mistake. They believe big companies already have a base and they know their customers. They don't have to find new markets and possess a database of customers. Therefore, small businesses cannot emulate them.

The book is a bit bulky but explains business details with command. I maintain that old business principles may not hold good for modern start-ups. The book categorises start-ups into web/mobile channels, including IT sector ventures as well as app and internet-based businesses, and businesses which sell products physically like garments, food chain and furniture, etc.

This book discusses the strategies to reach customers in great details. We will try to summarise it in terms of some principles.

Tasks like registering a company, branding and arranging for funds come at a later stage. Most people think these aspects are all that are required to be taken care of. According to this book, this conventional method of setting up a business holds good for entrepreneurs who are entering an established market and know who the consumers are. Start-ups have to do an extensive research to find their place in the market. As the saying goes, 'The more you sweat in peace, the less you bleed in war,' the book also emphasises on toiling before actually entering the battlefield of market. The authors recommend starting with an introductory product to identify the consumer base.

Start-ups need to begin by working on customer development. This should be done in a phased manner. The book advises moving to the next phase only if you have got your answers in the first phase.

It prescribes for preparing in four phases:

1. **Customer Discovery:** develop hypotheses and test them with customers
2. **Customer Validation:** test sales, see if people will buy, and see if you can scale up
3. **Customer Creation:** marketing
4. **Company Building:** transition to a sustainable enterprise

Every phase can be repeated as per requirement. You may need to change the strategy at any phase. This is not a failure. Don't be so attached to one particular method that you find it difficult to adapt. You have to make your product as per the customer and the market. Trying to do it another way around would be futile.

### Phase 1: Customer Discovery

You need to understand your customers. Don't develop preconceived notions about them. The book says that your customers will not come to your workplace. Instead, you will have to reach out to them. A start-up should aim at a smaller market and try to develop a minimum viable product accordingly. The purpose of MVP should be to attract initial buyers. It draws the attention of developers to the product's unique selling proposition (USP).

A product can always be improved based on the initial customer feedback. The authors emphasise the need to focus more on improving the important aspects of the product rather than working on beautifying it or adding features. The idea is to enter the market with a workable product and consolidate it based on customer's feedback. Don't waste time on giving your everything at the first step itself. This is the difference between start-ups and big businesses.

### *Business Model Planning*

The book mentions a business model canvas as an important guide for any company to make money. It is taken from Alexander Osterwalder's *Business Model Generation*. To put it in perspective, the authors advise taking a research-based approach and progress gradually. The research evaluates our efforts and keeps us abreast with reality. The research should focus on important aspects.

There are many components of the business model canvas.

#### Value Proposition Hypothesis

Go to the customers with a passable product. Evaluate it based on customer feedback. Make necessary improvements. Focus more on customers' stories than on apparent merits of your product.

#### Customer Segment

It concerns solving customers' problems, necessities and passions. Buyers will be marked. For example, end user, influencers, recommenders, buyers, etc.

#### Customer Archetypes

It is a common term in business parlance. Ideal customers are profiled based on factors like who they are, what are they trying to achieve, what motives determine their behaviour, how they think and buy, where they buy and what decisions do they make.

It is necessary to prepare a customer organisational chart or an influence map based on these factors.

#### Channel Hypothesis

In the case of material products, you must know the details of channels through which they reach the buyers. Choose the most appropriate channel for your product. The authors advise you to select a single, most efficient channel. Ponder on the pros and cons of the various channels for web/mobile-based products.

### Market-Type and Competitive Hypothesis

This tells you which market is suitable for your product; an established market, a new market, an expanded version of an existing market, a re-segmented market, etc. You can understand competition better once you know your market. This information prepares you to enter the market.

### Customer Relationships Hypothesis

This is regarding winning over customers, retaining them and developing a relationship with them. The authors enumerate the following ways to achieve this: get, keep and grow phase. Get awareness, interest, consideration and purchase. Keep and grow focuses on selling more products to existing customers.

Think of different strategies to connect to the customers. Don't be wary of testing these plans. It is also important to retain your customers. Try to make your customers spend more.

How will you manage yourself and the company, if your plans do not work? The book calls upon to think over this contingency. You will need to enlist all partners required on different fronts. It should be clear what you want from them and what they are supposed to get in return.

### Revenue and Pricing Hypothesis

This hypothesis involves the following questions:

- How many items do you plan to sell?
- What is the revenue model?
- What will you charge?
- What is the evidence that you should keep moving in the same direction?

Do not just use this tool for one-time planning. Update it once a week. This will ensure a record of your company's progress.

*The Size of the Market*

Following is the method to assess the size of the market:

- **Total Addressable Market (TAM):** The world where your product resides (the group of your customers)
- **Served Available Market (SAM):** People you can reach through your selling channel
- **Target Market:** The most appropriate customers for your product

You will need to research in this respect. Get access to the latest figures: from reports, press notes, libraries and other sources. It is difficult to create a new market. Therefore, evaluate the existing one. Know more about competitors.

You will have to evaluate how well you understand the problems of your customers. Find some answers like how important is this problem for your customers? How many customers are talking about it? Is it important enough for them to discuss with their friends?

You can find these problems in five steps.

1. Design experiments for customer evaluation: short, simple, objective, a pass/fail experiment aimed at collecting data and gaining insights. In short, gaining feedback from customers. There are many ways to do it. You can prepare your test based on your customers and their needs.
2. Besides trying to understand your customers, keep visiting seminars, trade shows, launch programmes of other set-ups. It helps you to understand the existing challenges and the ways to overcome them. The authors of this book also propound the five ways to solve customers' problems.
3. Testing your solution: After testing the problem, this phase is about trying the solution. There are five steps recommended by the authors.
4. Update your business model and team: See how new information fits with the old hypothesis. Decide if there is

a need to pivot your strategy or is it better to move forward. Discussing your learnings with investors and the management is also part of this step.

5. Is your product fit for the market? You need to ensure that it suits the market. Do many people need it? To what extent does it give a solution to the consumers? How many people are going to buy it?

The most important question in the process of customer discovery is: Who are your customers and how do you reach them?

The main motive of the book is to make the point that restricting yourself to your plans is not enough. You need to consistently experiment and research the market and your consumer base.

**Phase II: Customer Validation**

It means testing your product at every stage (keeping in mind the costs as it is still not the time to scale up or expand your company). The authors divide customer validation into four steps.

Phase 1: Be ready to sell.
Phase 2: Go live. Try to sell.
Phase 3: Refine your product. Establish your company.
Phase 4: Analyse. Adapt your strategy or move ahead.

You will need to step out of the office and hit the real market in this phase. A minimum viable product needs to be finalised after knowing the customers. You cannot move to the other phases before going through it. Hit the market with a punch line after deciding your MVP. The punch line should be able to catch the imagination of the masses. It should make clear why people should buy your product. The first step is important. Therefore, I am going to explain its hypotheses in some detail.

The authors tell you to enter the market using the same hypotheses and keep changing them as necessary. According to them, this is also the time to connect with the sales professionals. The road map to the sales channel should also be clear by this time. You will need clarity on the expectations from all sides while opting for sales partners like agencies or digital platforms.

This phase is about identifying the customers and validating them. You need to take their feedback and change your product accordingly. Work upon the shortcomings in your MVP as suggested by the customers.

You should be abreast with all the customer and product-related information by now. Collate them and decipher them. Continue with the same strategy if you are happy with the product. Change either your product or your strategy, if results are not encouraging.

In short, review everything. You may find it difficult to go back to the drawing board. It may indeed be tiring after such hard work. This is the time when you can think of taking a break for a week or so. You deserve it after such hard work.

### Phase III: Customer Creation

The first two phases are about finding and validating customers. You come up with MVP for them. The third and fourth phases involve entering the real market. You will need to not only find an answer to questions but also implement them.

This step precedes knowing and developing your customers. You run the risk of wasting money if you haven't prepared enough in the first two phases. These are the stages to attract venture capital. These are also the stages when investors will show interest in your venture. There are always investors ready to bet on the right idea and the right preparation. You need to present your groundwork. Your business model should be repeatable and scaleable. The product should provide a solution to the problem faced by your consumers: the one that can enter the market with a bang.

### Phase IV: Building the Company

Most people start thinking about this phase at the beginning itself. The instinct is to begin by establishing a company before learning and finding prospective customers. This will lead to a conventional company which is reluctant to learn and find new customers. You had invested time to build an ad-hoc product and know your customers. Now is the time to enter the big market with a real product. You are past the search mode and are working in mission mode. You will now take the help of experts to introduce your product to the market. It is also the time to expand your team and take the initial success to another level. The authors tell you to hire good people, the ones who can identify with your aspirations.

Do not think of beginning with a big company. Do not overspend on office, team and large scale production in initial phases. It is important to understand customers and market. Focus on customer discovery. Research on the various hypothesis and note them. Implement these hypotheses on a large scale after validation. Building MVP is also necessary. The books leave you with a message that research is the backbone of good entrepreneurship.

## SUMMARY OF *REWORK* BY JASON FRIED

This book finds a place in my list as it focuses more on the initial thought process of establishing a company. The author, Jason Fried, is a successful entrepreneur himself. He writes from his own experiences. The book offers a solution to the biggest impediment any start-up can face. Most founders of new start-ups are into the process of entering an entirely new world. They are motivated by the success stories that they have read or heard of. Their aspirations can fructify only if they adhere to the principles of learning and work ethics. The principles that this book earmarks are as follows:

- Look at your own life's problems.
- Work on the basics.
- Strive to stand out in the crowd.
- You get nothing by working aimlessly.

**'When you don't know what you believe, everything becomes an argument. Everything is debatable. But when you stand for something, decisions are obvious.'**

– Jason Fried, author

Fried has addressed the problem faced by most entrepreneurs. One does not set up a business just to become rich. Don't be an entrepreneur for show-off but also understand the fundamentals of business. This is exactly what most learned people will tell you.

The writer begins by suggesting that instead of turning an idea into a business, you should begin with a side business. This makes sense because it takes time to learn new skills. Consider your part-time business to be a success only if it fetches you money. Your ultimate goal is to solve people's problems or make their lives easier and make money along the way. The fact that you are making money testifies that people need your product or services.

## Look at Your Own Life's Problems

The author is a successful businessman and has also worked as a business consultant. He has seen many of his clients struggling to manage many projects simultaneously. He then decided to focus on his web app development. Today, his web app products have turned into a big enterprise. There is no life without problems. Identify them and build a product to solve them.

Fried asks you to stop your efforts at once if you want to do business only for the sake of it. Most people think on this line only. They start by investing in office and staff. Little do they care to know how their competitors are providing solutions to customers. All start-ups should invest good time in this market research.

The author has been through the phase when business ideas are galore in conversations with friends. There are new plans virtually every day. But they prove ephemeral because providing a solution is not at their core. Planning a business only from the perspective of earning money won't bear much fruit. I consider it a good exercise to observe problems around you and keep thinking about solutions.

This process gradually enables you to solve big problems. Make it your habit to add value to your business. The writer cautions against making impractical plans. Stand for what you have decided and learn to fight against adversities. There will always be distractions like scepticism from friends, jealousy, etc.

### Work on the Basics

The writer gives an example of two coffee shops near his home. The menu of the first shop was full of options. However, the taste wasn't particularly great. The second shop had modest interiors and only four coffee variants. Yet, people thronged the place. Fried was among the loyal customers of this coffee shop and learnt his lessons.

Concentrate more on substance than style. Glossy packings and sprawling shops would make little difference if your product doesn't win hearts.

Most start-ups are in a hurry to buy an office and hire staff, even when they have the option of sharing space. Instead of hiring customer care staff, you can take their calls and e-mails yourself. This means some extra effort but it saves you precious money.

You can manage your time to do as many tasks yourself as possible. Better still, look for free-of-cost options. After all, *jugaad* is India's way! This advice is only for the initial phase. You can always expand once the business picks up. Confining to *jugaad* always is also counterproductive.

Fried suggests honestly presenting your start-up and not in a boastful manner. Don't try to portray what you are not.

Any lie about yourself will only be counterproductive. Most startups overhype their profiles. This poses a question mark on their credibility. Be honest to your customers. You don't have to overspend on the image in the initial phase.

## Strive to Stand Out in the Crowd

To make a mark in a crowded market is the biggest challenge for new entrepreneurs. They are up against big players who already have a claim to the market share. Following them will only make you their miniatures. Fried suggests a way to take on the established competitors without spending extra money. He cites many campaigns in which one brand makes fun of another. To target your opponent's shortcomings and giving an alternative can be a good strategy. Think of the ways you can economically do the same.

Dr Shailesh Kharkwal is one example among my case studies who has understood the basics of branding well. In the water filtration market, the fundamental of branding is safe and pure drinking water. He has been able to compete with big players through effective branding.

Kharkwal knows most products in his field are based on RO technology. The World Health Organization (WHO) and India's National Green Tribunal (NGT) have pointed out its ill effects. Kharkwal has focused on non-RO technologies. Many of his products have gained traction. In short, your business should focus on low-cost innovative solutions.

## You Get Nothing by Working Aimlessly

The author cautions against wasting time and energy. This is an important piece of advice. It is especially aimed at those entrepreneurs who make their colleagues and subordinates work overtime. Slogging out extra hours does not necessarily mean better efficiency. It may negatively impact the work environment though. One should strive to be more focused instead. Identify distractions during working hours and weed them out.

Desist from writing unnecessary emails to your employees. Too many meetings are also not recommended by Fried. He reasons out that inviting 10 people for an hour-long meeting means wasting 10 working hours. Call meetings only when necessary.

Fried wants to emphasise that the energy and happiness of your employees are your well-being. Pressurising them will only harm your cause. Working aimlessly will not get you anywhere.

The author busts some preconceived notions like:

- Not everybody can do business.
- Setting up a business needs loads of money.
- Big office and team are a prerequisite for a successful business.

The problem is that most start-up proprietors want to become Steve Jobs or Bill Gates in no time. However, you will also have to strive like them and match their skills. Start with a venture that teaches you the art of earning money.

It is great to dream of your enterprise. But it will always remain a dream if you don't learn the ways to succeed in it. The author offers wise counsel in this regard. He disagrees that people can learn from failures. According to him, they is only a lesson in what we ought not to do. However, you also have to know what you need to do. This is something only success can teach.

Mark Cuban is a big investor and a successful entrepreneur. He attaches great importance to learning from books. Cuban credits his success to books like *Rework*. According to him, this bestseller encourages readers to get going on their big idea and stresses the point that you don't need a refined plan or a lot of resource to start a successful company. It's all about trial and error.

In a review for the book, Cuban writes, 'If given a choice between investing in someone who has read *Rework* or has an MBA, I'm investing in *Rework* every time.'

Here are the main points of the books discussed in a nutshell.

- Mere dreams are not enough. You also need entrepreneurial skills.
- Find a common ground between your passion and market demand.
- Think of giving something to the market. The money will follow.
- A good product is the one which makes lives easier.
- Do something which others haven't thought of.
- Write down everything and learn to do a professional market research.
- Put down your strategy on paper.
- Start from small scale.
- Learn as an apprentice before starting your venture.
- Learn the tricks of marketing, sales and branding yourself.
- Start from a small and effective team that identifies with your ideals.
- Don't stretch too much on the wrong strategy.
- Learn to improvise your strategy.
- Understand the market and customers to plan a good product.
- Learn from your success. It teaches you what to do.

# 17
# THE LUCK FACTOR

**'Luck is what happens when preparation meets the opportunity.'**

This quote presents a broad definition of what we call luck. But it still needs some elucidation of the scientific and psychological aspects. But why are we discussing luck here? Since we have emphasised the importance of research and science for start-ups, let us try to see the concept of luck in the same light. I consider this an important chapter for the same reason. Understand two things before knowing the factual aspects of luck; luck is an important factor for any business and you are very lucky that you have the desire to chart your own course and this book is in your hands. How many of us have the tenacity to fight for our dreams? This is the reason that only a few are able to make a mark in the Indian start-up segment despite such a vast pool of talent.

Most people accredit their situation to the luck factor but it's a delusion. We find easy ways to escape from the efforts and will power required for creativity and innovations. Success and luck are not the same things but most people mix these two factors. Many successful people consider themselves unlucky and many unsuccessful people can find many ways to feel lucky. Achieving your personal goal (i.e., whatever big or small task you have undertaken) falls under the category of success and remaining happy in all conditions is the luck factor. One who's happy is lucky and according to Max Gunther (author of *The Luck Factor*), lucky people are not just optimistic but happy. So be happy and don't let your creative thinking be affected by the environment. Just a willingness to tackle the obstacle and self-motivation will nurture the desired results. It's a science and science works on proven theories.

Successful people seldom think about this luck connection. Although you can hear them sometimes acknowledging their destiny. Many students often ask me about the role of luck in success. My first answer is to make them realise that being born as a human is a great fortune in itself. As far as circumstances are concerned, no success story has ever been written without adversities. You are prone to upheavals even after you have attained success. Few can match the success of Steve Jobs as an entrepreneur. But he died because of the misfortune of cancer. You can only judge your fortune in hindsight. It doesn't matter much while you are working towards your goal. Since most of us believe in prayers, it is pertinent to understand your life journey from the prism of destiny. This chapter aims to present a gist of various research findings on this topic.

We credit or blame our luck for almost every important development in our lives. But seldom do we understand what it means. We wish other people good luck almost every day and pass on the buck to the same luck when things go bad. There are some interesting research findings on the subject. The gamblers are the most researched lot for their luck. They risk everything on providence. I consider those with the greater win percentage fortuitous. Not that they never lose, just that their success rate is higher. Life is also akin to gamble for some with similar parameters.

During childhood, I always considered one of my friends as felicitous. He had an expansive house and his father owned a car. In contrast, I grew up in a less illustrious locality and was doing different jobs from an early age. Then came a time when my friend's parents got separated. His mother could not survive a fatal disease. To cut the long story short, it changed my perception for the same friend. I felt lucky that I was not him. My own circumstances looked much happier now and I felt gratitude towards God. It is human nature to consider happy-looking pictures as lady luck's blessing while adversities become a curse of misfortune. One must realise that somebody's bad luck can be another person's chance. Looking at the less privileged people will make you think about yourself more.

Our circumstances guide our lessons in life. Most factors are common to the entire humanity. We accept them as social reality. These realities decide our response to the various situations. However, there are some who break these shackles and realise their true potential. The world marvels at their luck and pays obeisance to their talent. In reality, it is small decisions that shape their luck.

We measure our luck with opportunities that come our way. The more we can avail, the favoured we feel. All of us know the importance of action. Yet, hidden fear of destiny remains alive in some corner of our heart. This fear makes us believe in providence. Nobody can control destiny is a cliché. Understand the true character of destiny. We define it only after it has passed.

It is the outcome that decides everything. Even the perception of the outcome may vary for different persons. For some, fortune is money while others cherish health as their greatest blessing. Some curse their Gods for not having children while others rue their progeny's lack of talent.

This leads us to conclude that all of us have a life mixed with good fortune. You must understand what it means to be blessed for seeking blessings. Our lives are a sum total of our actions, that too of this birth only. It is not the doings of some forgotten incarnation that you can blame.

Once a businessman and a beggar came to see a saint. The saint asked them to come one-by-one. The businessman sought the blessing of expanding his trade to many more cities. The saint complied. When the beggar's turn came, all he asked for was that people of 10 streets give him alms instead of just one. He also got the boon. This means that both the businessman and the beggar were fortunate when they left the enlightened man. What do you think?

Our level of thinking decides what is best for us. I often ask students praying for good marks why they do not ask for something bigger if God is listening to them? However, good marks would solve their immediate problem. They move from one desire to another. Our luck is decided by what we want. Only consistent efforts can turn the course of your destiny. One meeting can change a life, but only if somebody has bothered to make that meeting happen.

One research on this topic suggests that the more people you meet, the luckier you get. Likewise, lady luck showers more blessings on amiable, generous people. It all comes down to what luck means to you. Decide for yourself and gear up to transform your destiny. I can never forget what I once read at one mausoleum, *Baadab baanaseeb, beadab badnaseeb* (courtesy brings you luck). You are lucky if you are patient and strong enough to welcome adversities. Nobody can match your misfortune if you are not ready to fight for a better destiny.

## THINGS TO REMEMBER

- Luck is important and you are very lucky.
- Success or failure is not the measure of fortune.
- You are the luckiest person if you are happy with the present.
- Fortune always favours a positive mind.
- You awake the lady luck by meeting new people.
- Your destiny is shaped by your personality and tenacity in the face of adversities.
- Unfavourable circumstances can also bring good luck.
- Only the ones favoured by fortune have time to struggle.
- People who take on challenges invoke good fortune.
- Results cannot decide good fortune. Small failures are often a stepping stone to success.

# 18

# THE SUCCESS FACTOR

We have little time to reflect on our inner being in the glitter of today's materialistic world. However, no illusion can hold forever. A day comes when the reality of chasing a mirage dawns upon us. We realise that it was as futile as chasing one's own tail. This wild goose chase sucks away all the vital energy and life becomes a perpetual cycle of self-serving delusions.

Seek the real meaning of life while your body and mind are healthy. Otherwise, lassitude will never leave life until it overtakes your whole existence. We all attach great importance to materialistic possessions. Have you ever pondered over their relevance in your life? Mere boxes of tin that run on wheels seem to define our ego. A car, a good house and a reputable job have become the ultimate aim for most people. All these things were made to serve humans. Somehow, we serve the lifeless materialistic possessions. Your body wants sleep but your pocket wants money. And the conflict never ends. In fact, the richer you are, there are more chances that you will grow into an insomniac. The velvety beds become pallets of thorns if there is no peace of mind. We do not seem to learn any lesson from misery of the powerful that have fallen from grace, owing to their lust for money.

There are people who have earned more money than required for their future generations. This greed leaves them with little time to stop and relish life. Yet, they cannot stop craving for more richness. But where do you find true richness? Cut through the gluttony and you can find it at this moment. You do not have to gain it; you already own it. The question is of looking within for real treasure. Your consciousness will shine, once you remove the dirt of ignorance. This inner radiance attracts the entire world.

One must know the real meaning of success in life. It is more than just prosperity or recognition. To some, success might mean living up to their ideals. From a common perspective, we can say that the real success should have two necessary ingredients; blissfulness and service to others.

Our mind identifies success with the emotion of victory. You work hard for your ambition because you visualise the moment of bliss that would entail its fulfillment. Just remember the moments when you have tasted victory. Success in small events like some school competition or some sports can be exhilarating. Sometimes, we also identify ourselves with the success of others. Like, when we are totally absorbed in some crucial game of cricket. In summary, our mind savours success because it fulfills the desire to experience bliss. We all want to win, whether it is a game of chess or the battlefield of life. This inherent yearning for victory causes the contemplation of our aspirations. All our dreams are an outcome of our present circumstances. We all want to become what we are not today.

Success is not possible without struggle. Victory comes only to those who fight hard. As Emily Dickinson said, 'To comprehend a nectar, requires sorest need. The triumph counts most to those, who have learnt to love their struggle.'

All limitations are only in our mind. Small vision restricts your dreams. Your whole life is spent clutching to the status quo once you have realised them. But you cannot win against the fundamental principle of change. The same life that was once your dream becomes grief, if you do not evolve with time. As humanity continues its march forward in time, the pace of change keeps increasing. This makes adaptation a key ingredient of success in today's world. You must have seen many fortunes changing in your life. Learn to accept change. Make conscious efforts to make it a better one. Therefore, we can say that adaptability and struggle are the two vital aspects of success.

A successful person is pleasant and confident. The secrets of success are revealed by regular practise.

Success also means security. One cannot feel proud unless secure. How can a person whose family is not safe be termed as successful? We also associate a sense of achievement with fulfilment of our elders' expectations and providing for the necessities of the younger ones. But they can seem like a failure if you take them as a burden. Success is incomplete unless you fulfill these responsibilities. Those who shirk their commitment never get a taste of success. Raising a child could be the biggest achievement for parents. Likewise, a smile on the face of your parents could be worth over thousand gains. This is a time-tested fact. People who take their responsibility seriously are successful in relationships. These responsibilities could be financial, emotional or psychological. In a nutshell, anything that brings satisfaction is success. Success becomes a habit once we understand its true meaning.

You can understand the whole concept of success through a simple example. Suppose you have to reach a destination. Now, you know the route or, at least, the address of the location. Things are simple in the former case, as you only have to move on the road. In the latter case, take the help of others. You seek directions from strangers or friends. Whether you undertake the journey in car or on foot would depend on your circumstances. Success, in this case, is reaching the destination. The same thing applies to life; if you do not know the way, seek guidance.

Seasoned players can manage success or failure better because they have already undergone the same experience. Whereas, novice players have to learn to keep their cool in both circumstances. This learning takes time and patience. The efficiency of your learning depends on your receptivity. The importance of a capable guide can never be overemphasised. You will lose time and energy if misguided by somebody along the way. The risk of straying from the path is always there until you reach the destination. However, it is sometimes good to be lost in the right direction. You should never lose patience.

Life is also a journey in the dimension of time. Your health and competence are the medium to accomplish your aims. You will need to nurture both physical and mental capabilities. Clarity of mind is imperative for success. If you know what you want to do in life, then you know the address of your destination. Now, you only need to find the route. Nothing can stop you from reaching your goal once you tread on the road. You only have to guard against the negative impulses. Reaffirm your desire to fulfill the ambition whenever pessimism overwhelms your resolve. Ask yourself, 'Are you doing what you always wanted to do?' Contemplate with the relaxed mind if no clear answer emerges. Deviating from path can lead to mental fatigue. However, avoid methods of instant gratification for relaxing your mind. Try to motivate yourself with positive thinking that inspires you to stay on the course. Make a list of the reflections that rejuvenate your spirits. The moment of rediscovering the sense of direction within the self is liberating. A constant composure is the hallmark of a person determined to realise his or her goal.

The famous Hollywood actor Jim Carrey said, 'I hope everybody could get rich and famous and will have everything they ever dreamed of, so they will know that it's not the answer.'

Study the life of those who have already achieved what you are longing for. They are an important signpost of whether you have chosen the right path. Be ready for the next mission as soon as you have accomplished one aim. This is the only way to dynamic living. As famous Welsh novelist, Gwyn Thomas stated, 'But the beauty is in the walking, we are betrayed by destinations.' A dormant mind becomes listless just as stagnant water stinks. Success is not a destination, but a road that you are on. Being successful means that you are working hard and walking your walk every day. Feel gratitude for the existence that has given the power of chasing your dreams. The journey itself becomes the biggest reward when you are on the right track. If thorns along your way teach lessons, the moments of rejoicing recharge your batteries. The constant lust for pleasure will make you insecure and lethargic. I have seen many people slipping into drug abuse just because they lacked a clear vision in life. The state of intoxication is only a temporary retreat. It does not solve the real challenges of life. A time comes when drug habits take control of your life and you feel helpless without them. You become a narcotics addict because you do not have strong motivations in life. It plunges you into the darkness of despondency and takes away all hope.

Your body is wearing with each passing moment. Every breath you take is one small step towards the ultimate destiny of death. Life is not a blank cheque. We only have a limited time to make a mark for the generations to come. We have discussed that social utility is also a manifestation of real success. Presenting an ideal, redefining the limits of your chosen area of action makes life worthy. We can only test an ideal personality in entirety. Many film heroes exemplify perfection on-screen but they are the opposite in real life. Such people are not the personalities one would like to emulate. You should be a paragon, an epitome of excellence in the eyes of the world. This is the real criterion of success. Remember your aim is not to belittle other people, it will only bring frustration at the end.

Do justice to self-image and the world would acknowledge you. We all want to be known as generous and amiable person. We try our best to behave like one. Many people donate millions in charity. All of us know, in theory, that honesty, generosity and love are enriching values. Then, why are most people bereft of these qualities? It is because most people only feign these attributes. The point, however, is to inculcate these characteristics.

Try to observe what makes the other people beautiful. We know beauty is always deeper than skin. A healthy life and a kind heart are its real secrets. But our whole effort seems to be concentrated on appearing like a beautiful person. Whereas, any imposed change will only be temporary. The real transformation can only come when the change emanates from within your being. Every human being is born beautiful. The existence does not know ugliness. All bad in us comes from the world. Your success and personality is in your hands. Decide what is right and wrong for you. It is never too late to begin the process of transformation. The moment you shed negativity, positive change happens. Realise your true self. Anything that takes you away from your real nature is like a poison. Do not ignore your potential; it is the biggest injustice that one can inflict on the self. The moment you realise your true path, success kisses your feet.

## THINGS TO REMEMBER

- True success lies in realising your true self.
- Progress means developing your talent every day. Everyone has different capabilities. You need to identify them.
- Material success, big office, expensive cars can be a part of your marketing and branding. These are not the real motives of business.
- True success is to benefit the society.
- You get recognition as you keep learning new skills. Recognition is only the beginning of your success journey.
- Don't fall prey to vanity. It will only hamper your progress.
- You are your best competitor. Keep improving and never compare with others.
- Opportunities come and go. Your confidence and capability matter.
- Develop yourself in a way that you are beneficial to the society and others can emulate you.
- Change is not big or small. Changing even a village can mean a huge success.

# 19

# BEGINNING OF START-UP REVOLUTION IN INDIA

Philosopher Sir Karl Popper said 'No book can ever be finished. While working on it we learn just enough to find it immature the moment we turn away from it.' I get the same feeling every time I read this book. The world of start-ups and innovation is vast enough to merit an entire library of books. The main motive of this book is to share my experiences in this field. Your own life story is no less valuable, many chapters of which are yet unwritten. I endeavour to link those unwritten chapters of your life to the start-up revolution. India is going through an exciting phase. The future belongs to us. We are the 'youngest' nation in the world. All it needs is the right direction to unleash the power of the youth.

One can see a journey from Narendra to Narendra in start-up revolution. One Narendra aka Swami Vivekananda had identified his inner strength and its role in nation-building at an early age. This is the reason he had laid so much emphasis on the awakening of the youth. He knew this is where the real power of India lies. *Awakening India*, a Doordarshan programme that I was a part of, played a pivotal role in introducing me to this great man's ideas. I met many prestigious intellectuals, writers, thinkers and philosophers during this programme. This was a great opportunity to learn about Swamiji's life and message. The great man trotted the world with the message of India's great wealth of knowledge and spirituality. We need it, least of all, from the West. What we do require is to show new direction to the country's youth.

Swami Vivekananda laid great emphasis on hard work. He gave precedence to playing football over reciting Gita because our spiritual traditions are alive anyway through our values. However, we still lack opportunities for our younger lot. The seed for transformation was sown at that time. They remained dormant during slavery of over a century. Many attempts to wipe out our culture couldn't render them impotent. Today, the same seeds have started to sprout. It was the echoing of that Narendra's voice then and incidentally, it is the roar of another Narendra in the same land of Uncle Sam that has caught the world's attention. The Startup India is only a facet of this revolution. These are special times because we are not looking for mere employment opportunities for the youth, we are seeking to make them partners in nation-building. The young entrepreneurs are responding to the call by introducing innovations.

I saw a glimpse of this transformation during my journey to the states of Uttar Pradesh, Madhya Pradesh and Rajasthan as part of an assignment for *Amar Ujala*. I visited several cities and villages of these states. Everywhere, one could sense a fundamental change in the viewpoint of the youngsters. They can see new dawn coming their way. A lot is owed to the current government's efforts but it cannot be expected to change all the mindsets. To look up to the government for everything can cripple the mindset. Today's young Indians are willing to polish their skills to contribute to the country's development.

No government initiative can be judged without giving it due time. The Startup India programme has also been implemented in a phased manner. One must see it along with other similar schemes like Skill India. One must not always look up to the elite class of IITians or IIMians. The ones not privileged enough to get degrees are equally important. As with all revolutions, youngsters across classes are seeking their role in start-up's transformation. If the metropolitan youth is enticed by Startup India, the rural youth is getting empowered through initiatives like Skill Development.

You must have heard the now-clichéd tagline, 'An idea can change your life.' This must come with a rider that only an idea cannot change your life. While the importance of ideas can never be undermined for start-ups, you will need to develop it. Coming up with an idea is just the beginning of an arduous journey. From thinking of an idea to make it happen will test your determination and character. Consistent efforts and thorough knowledge always help. This is where you will find this book useful. There are many things we will need to work hard on. I will give them pointwise.

## EFFECTIVE IMPLEMENTATION OF GOVERNMENT SCHEMES

> *उद्यमेन हि सिध्यन्ति कार्याणि न मनोरथैः।*
> *न हि सुप्तस्य सिंहस्य प्रविशन्ति मुखे मृगाः।।*
> (*Udyamein hi sidhyanti karyani na manorathey, na hi suptasya sinhasya pravishanti mukhe mriga*)

Work gets accomplished by putting in effort, and certainly not by mere wishful thinking. A deer will never enter the mouth of a lion that sleeps.

Only planning will never get you anywhere. Effective implementation is equally important. The government is transforming the methods of implementation from its roots. The use of technology and innovation is one example. The Mahatma Gandhi National Rural Employment Guarantee Act (MGNREGA) is an example of how technology can improve the implementation of social welfare schemes. Following is the excerpt from the government budget referring to this scheme.

'While MGNREGA was made effective from 2006, the streamlining of the programme occurred in 2015 when the government harnessed the benefits of technology. This, inter alia, included the implementation of Direct Benefit Transfer (DBT) and linking it to Aadhar-linked-Payments (ALP). It leveraged the Jan Dhan, Aadhaar and Mobile (JAM) trinity to credit wages directly into MGNREGA workers' bank accounts, thereby reducing the scope for delay in payment. This paragraph highlights the benefit of a careful and effective targeting of the government programmes by demonstrating that DBT-enabled MGNREGA has indeed helped to alleviate the distress of the workers. Post-DBT, delay in payment of wages under MGNREGA, has reduced significantly, thereby providing livelihood security to people in distress. Both demand and supply of work under MGNREGA has increased, especially in districts suffering from distress. The increase in the number of filled muster rolls also implies that distressed workers indeed turn up more frequently for work. The importance of ALP-enabled MGNREGA in alleviating distress is particularly pronounced for the vulnerable sections of society, including women, persons with disability, scheduled castes and scheduled tribes. As the data on demand for work under MGNREGA is available almost real-time, it can be developed into a real-time measure to track distress at the level of a district/panchayat.

This evidence highlights that skilful use of technology, when combined with an unwavering commitment to monitoring effectiveness of government schemes, can make a substantial difference on the ground.

> *योजनानां सहस्रं तु शनैर्गच्छेत पिपीलिका।*
> *आगच्छन वैनतेयोपि पदमेकं न गच्छति।।*
> (*Yojnanam sahasram tu shanerghachet pipeelika, Aagachan vainteyopi padmekam na gachati*)

An ant can walk for a thousand kilometres once it starts walking. But even a Garuda will reach nowhere if it does not move.

The beginning is encouraging and mere ranting on weaknesses won't work. Gladly, our pace is also brisk. We should focus on maintaining it. Indeed, a lot of hard work is still required to bring schemes related to start-ups and skill development to the masses. It was disconcerting to note during my journeys across the states that many youngsters have not even heard of these schemes.

These youths may not have illustrious degrees. However, this should not be a reason to distrust their capabilities. Their vigour can go haywire if not channelised. The increasing penetration of internet and smartphone-related technologies is encouraging. We need to link these schemes to technology.

In addition to the effective implementation of government schemes, we need to focus on certain other areas. India is leading the way in the use of renewable energy. The book discusses many such areas in detail. The government is prioritising investment in science and technology. I am sure that this will ensure a better future for start-ups.

## Renewable Energy

India is in a state of perennial energy shortage with a demand-supply gap of almost 12 per cent of the total energy demand. This trend is significant in the electricity segment that is heavily dependent on coal and other non-renewable sources of energy. To cope with solar energy is the future. Solar energy potential in India is immense due to its convenient location near the Equator. India receives nearly 3,000 hours of sunshine every year, which is equivalent to 5,000 trillion kWh of energy. India can generate over 1,900 billion units of solar power annually, which is enough to service the entire annual power demand even in 2030.

Rajasthan and Gujarat are the regions with maximum solar energy potential. This, coupled with the availability of barren land, increases the feasibility of solar energy system in these regions. Considering India's solar potential, the government has rolled out various policies and subsidy schemes to encourage the growth of Solar Industry, which is expected to experience an exponential growth in the coming years.

## Education and Science

We should be less concerned about big national projects and more about producing high-quality researches. India has some 700 universities of varying quality, from the elite institutions funded by the central government to more than 300 state universities and about 200 private ones. The landscape of scientific education is uneven. We are caught in a vicious circle of mediocrity.

Some of these science students are doing world-class research, publishing in leading journals and boosting global reputation; India is not keeping pace with some of the other emerging nations, which have increased their scientific output more quickly. Fund remains the issue for most of the universities but I think, quality teachers with a world-class pay scale are required in the system. Along with these, Indian textbooks and well-equipped science laboratories are also required. There is a rise in the number of students going for higher education in India, which reflects the rising aspiration of its society. But this rise should be matched with better infrastructure and financial support.

## Research Investments

Quality research work is the key to development. Especially, if we are focusing on innovation and start-ups then we should intensely work on this domain. Investments in science have also dragged. India's research intensity remains lower than those of many other nations, including Brazil and Russia. Twenty years ago, India was ahead of China in research intensity but now, it is less than half. But those numbers do not tell the whole story. The total funding is, perhaps, not as poor as it seems in terms of absolute numbers because the number of full-time scientists doing research is also low. India averages about 4 full-time researchers per 10,000 people in labour force, whereas China boasts of 18 and nations with advanced science and technology sectors have around 80. India spends about $150,000 per scientist per year, which is probably not too far from the optimal levels.

## Encouraging Foreign Technology and Co-operation

The country needs to provide more opportunities to start-ups like H2O Mantra and innovative scientists like Shailesh Kharkwal. We have discussed in detail how technology developed at the National University of Singapore can help solve our country's water crisis. India is also collaborating with countries like Australia and Israel to enhance her technological prowess. I discussed the possibilities of innovation in the Indian context with the globally renowned water scientist of Singapore-origin Professor How Yong. Here are the excerpts.

## PROFESSOR HOW YONG NG, NATIONAL UNIVERSITY OF SINGAPORE

### Innovation as a Global Phenomenon

Approximately over the last two decades, we have observed innovation at a global scale in all fields, particularly in communication technology and electronics. But what merely is innovation? And why do we need it?

Innovation can be defined simply as new solutions or products that solve problems or are better than current solutions. A new solution or product can only be recognised as an innovation when it truly brings tangible benefits to its users, such as ease of doing a task, convenience in life, reduce cost of doing things, etc. Honestly, whether one believes or not but when our ancestors invented fire for the first time, that was innovation.

Humans have been practising innovation since the ancient times; from the innovation of tools to modern smartphones, internet and transportation system.

### Tackling Issue, Inducing Start-ups

NUS Enterprise, the entrepreneurial arm of the National University of Singapore, supports start-ups from all over the world through BLOCK71. It is an initiative by NUS Enterprise in collaboration with the established corporate and government agencies. It is an ecosystem builder and global connector which catalyses and aggregates the start-up community, as well as spearheads new initiatives and provides mentorship and growth opportunities in local and global markets.

Certainly, India should consider having a similar unit, especially in universities, where there is a congregation of great minds. Programmes and platforms to encourage innovation should be initiated.

## Worrisome Future

No doubt, we all are well aware of the fact that with each passing year, our drinking water is turning more toxic. There may not be a single house in the country that will not have the RO system. So majorly, this is why the need of the hour is to innovate in water treatment. I believe the future of drinking water is to provide safe drinking water to every single person in the world and this should be the goal of all leaders and the governments around the world. To meet this challenge, innovation in water treatment and new solutions that are both efficient and cost-effective will be of paramount importance.

## Promoting Start-ups

The National University of Singapore is quite supportive in generating start-ups as many programmes induce skills in the newcomers, for example, the annual summer programme offers a two-week immersive entrepreneurial experience to local and international students. But since ages, start-ups have faced challenges such as understanding the particular subject and understanding the business, both of which is quite different. And many of them are not successful because they might be great in their respective fields but not that good in understanding business and management aspects; but a one-stop solution for all such challenges is diverse skills.

I believe that the chance of success for start-ups will be greatly enhanced if the founders of start-ups include young entrepreneurs with diverse skill sets including relevant technical/ engineering skill, business, marketing, etc. Alternatively, education programme in universities and institutes should include training on these diverse skill sets to well equip young entrepreneurs.

## India Has Immense Possibilities

In India, at this point, it has become a debatable issue that the complete education system must be changed and theoretical subjects must be converted into practical areas of training. Conventional education in terms of providing strong fundamental knowledge is still necessary. On top of this, programmes that encourage innovation and entrepreneurial spirit and teach relevant skills should be provided in schools and universities.

Indians are no less than the citizens of any other developed countries, in fact, it might surprise you that in a government survey it came out that 36 per cent of scientists at NASA are Indians. Certainly, there is no reason why Indian Start-ups cannot enter international market. For example, India has excellent IT training and professionals. To do so, first of all, India must create a conducive environment to encourage and support innovation and start-ups. Efforts made by the government and private entities are necessary to create this environment.

## Water and Future

New technologies and processes of innovation have always helped humans to enjoy services more efficiently in an era of unequalled population and workload growth. No doubt, entrance of technology has eased our work to a great extent, but have we ever realised that technology has harmed the water bodies directly or indirectly. Earlier, the source of drinking water was natural water reservoir, but in today's pollution-prone environment, it's hard to rely on such sources anymore.

Singapore is now an ideal in water treatment techniques all over the world and it's time for India to start taking actions for its continuous deteriorating rivers, that is a non-renewable resource, it won't come back once depleted. It's time that the government must realise that strict actions are the need of the hour. Eventually, hard work gives the right result.

Professor Yong clearly states that a country like Singapore, known for its great start-up ecosystem, is also impressed with India's start-ups and innovation. This is motivating people like Shailesh to return home. According to him, India is better-placed than Singapore in terms of water resources. If Singapore can elevate itself to a developed-country status and become self-reliant in water availability, we can certainly do much better.

It is a crucial phase for India in the energy technology sector. After green and white revolutions, we are now witnessing a start-up revolution. We must all contribute to strengthening it. This book is my contribution as a researcher, writer and a journalist. I am trying to raise awareness among the young entrepreneurs. Faith has great power. You will need to rise above the political ideologies to see the importance of the start-up revolution. Never forget, winners are not the people who never fail, but people who never quit.